The Educated Parent 2

The Educated Parent 2

Child Rearing in the 21st Century

Joseph D. Sclafani, PhD

PRAEGER

AN IMPRINT OF ABC-CLIO, LLC
Santa Barbara, California • Denver, Colorado • Oxford, England

Copyright 2012 by Joseph D. Sclafani, PhD

Library of Congress Cataloging-in-Publication Data

Sclafani, Joseph D.
   The educated parent 2: child rearing in the 21st century / Joseph D. Sclafani.
      p. cm.
   Includes bibliographical references and index.
   ISBN 978-0-313-39776-9 (hbk.: alk. paper) — ISBN 978-0-313-39777-6 (ebook)
   1. Parenting.   2. Parent and child.   3. Parenting, Part-time.
4. Child development.   5. Child psychology.   I. Title.
   HQ755.8.S362   2012
   649.'1—dc23   2011041555

ISBN: 978-0-313-39776-9
EISBN: 978-0-313-39777-6

16 15 14 13 12   1 2 3 4 5

This book is also available on the World Wide Web as an eBook.
Visit www.abc-clio.com for details.

Praeger
An Imprint of ABC-CLIO, LLC

ABC-CLIO, LLC
130 Cremona Drive, P.O. Box 1911
Santa Barbara, California 93116-1911

This book is printed on acid-free paper ∞

Manufactured in the United States of America

Contents

Acknowledgments

Writing a book is always a team effort. I am again grateful to the University of Tampa for awarding my sabbatical leave in 2008 to allow for initial research for this revised and updated edition. It is a privilege to be able to get time to read, reflect, and consider information. It is even more a privilege when that luxury is part of one's career and base salary.

Thanks also are owed to Amy Plewinski, an honors student and graduate of the University of Tampa, for help in researching some of the material in this book.

I am grateful to Dr. Edesa Scarborough, mom to daughter Carly, a friend and colleague, who read book content and gave feedback and helpful comments. I thank Ms. Andrea Cox—mother of daughters Kathryn, Julia, and Caroline—who took time from her busy summer to read near-final drafts of the chapters and contribute valuable observations and remarks.

I want to acknowledge the thorough, professional review of the manuscript by Dr. Anthony R. Dickinson, currently at the Institute for Neuroscience, Chinese Academy of Sciences, in Shanghai. His thoughtful consideration and editorial comments have made this work a better book.

I also thank Debbie Carvalko and the good people of ABC-CLIO for appreciating the merits of my first book and for seeing the need for this revised, more contemporary edition. Our talks allowed me to refine the content and direction of this manuscript, and all of us hope this book will be as well received as *The Educated Parent* was in 2004.

Although there is some review and overlap of content in the chapters that follow, this edition contains much new information. *The Educated*

Parent 2 is a stand-alone read, although what might seem to be missing details may be found in the first edition in most cases. A reader of the first book will quickly notice that this edition has more opinions interspersed with the information provided. These opinions provide more background and a basis for why I chose to share certain information.

This project would never have happened without the loving and complete support of my wife, Linda. She is also a mental health professional, and her experiences as a clinical director of a group home for children have shaped my views of parenting and parenting education. She offered constructive criticism as needed, and ensured that my writer's space and time were productive.

Introduction

Affection without sentiment, authority without cruelty, discipline without aggression, humor without ridicule, sacrifice without obligation, companionship without possessiveness.

~William E. Blatz

Lucky parents who have fine children usually have lucky children who have fine parents.

~James A. Brewer

Seven years have passed since the publication of *The Educated Parent.* Since that time, several new and different issues related to parenting have emerged. The ABC-CLIO folks have agreed that a revised edition with a new emphasis on contemporary parenting is in order. This is that book.

In *The Educated Parent 2,* I again present reviews of research and other published material on issues that educated parents should study. This book is really an extended review of the parenting literature, drawing from a number of sources. I have surveyed the professional literature as well as a number of Internet-based sites for good parenting information. In this edition, I use a more applied theme, so the information should be immediately useful to the reader. I also include much more Internet-based information on purpose, as that is where parents can and will go as they seek facts and data for their education and use.

Throughout *The Educated Parent 2,* I tout the great possibilities of the Internet as a resource for parents. But please be careful to vet or verify what you read online. In the spring of 2011, media outlets warned parents that too much Facebook usage by children could lead to anxiety and depression. Researchers measured a group of 13-year-old girls and followed up a year later, testing them for depressive symptoms. News stories said that Facebook postings allowed the girls to get stuck obsessing over particular emotional issues, unable to move past their teen angst. And so the term "Facebook Depression" was coined.

One big problem remained: the source article the media outlets used stated the study's findings resulted from the teens using Facebook, *but the original never mentioned any particular social network!* Although the study author referred to "texting, instant messaging and social networking" as the means for obsessing over bad news, he named no particular source.

U.S. media, choosing ratings and/or website hits over fact checkers, repeated the error in multiple TV segments and online publications. The moral—double check things or use only sites with experts on board. I would like to add a new caveat emptor-type phrase at this time—*caveat lector* or "let the reader beware."

In line with the first edition, this updated and user-friendly version of the book allows me to give you a background of information that should help you to make good choices about your parenting behavior. As a child psychologist and family therapist since 1984, I have many years of experience, from ten years of private practice after three years of work in a community mental health center, to years of training and educating college students in child development. From my time as a family therapist, I learned that child problems were almost always family problems. For many families, work on improving parenting (from teaching parenting skills to helping out with marital issues) made a significant difference for everyone.

Ann Hulbert has written a superior account of the history of expert advice on parenting. *Raising America* almost made me decide to stop writing this book—no, not really. Covering the last 100 or so years of parenting experts' advice and products, her review discusses not only the experts' messages and tips for child rearing, but also "TMZ" moments regarding their personal and professional lives. Some of her stories about John B. Watson are both jaw-dropping and painfully sad. She covers all the greats—G. Stanley Hall, Arnold Gesell, Benjamin Spock, and others you probably never heard of.

I mention her work because I know many parenting books have come available and I am always humbled to think that you are reading mine. Hulbert's book is recommended reading if you want some context and perspective on parent education, and her last section on what to expect from the experts is priceless. In the final pages of her book, Hulbert quotes Heidi Murkoff's (an author of women and pregnancy books whose comments were in *Newsweek* magazine) instruction regarding all the experts' advice that can leave parents "uncertain how to proceed—paralyzed." Concerning this advice, Murkoff tells parents, "Use it to guide, not dictate," watch out for "parenting pendulum swings," and find what fits who you are. I second that advice.

Whether you are a first-time parent struggling with lots of different advice or a veteran parent of six, the information in this book should make you more effective through more knowledge. Parenting is a job where new challenges arise every week, so the more you know, the better you will be.

ASSUMPTIONS ABOUT GOOD PARENTING

Here are a few starting principles and beliefs about raising children that most experts would agree upon:

- Child development is a *biopsychosocial* phenomenon.
- The best parenting is a two-person job.
- Good parenting requires commitment and sacrifice.
- Despite all of your work, children may not turn out the way you want.
- Parents have to be responsible for and in charge of their children.

First of all, child development is a *biopsychosocial* happening. By this I mean that how a child develops is a complicated, interconnected jumble of many factors and causes. These include the powers of biology and heredity (the *bio*-logical); of language, personality and thinking (the *psycho*-logical); and other social and environmental experiences (the *social*). Parenting behavior shapes the psychological and the social aspects of your child's growth through your behavior, and your genes are a major factor in the biological area. This book will show you how your job as parents can lead to the most positive environment for your children. This book will point out some genetic-based factors that must be addressed, as you need to know this, too.

A second point I believe is that the best parenting is a two-person job. Parenting is best done by two adults unless they are always fighting in front of their children. Having two loving and concerned adults makes for the best parenting situation. But if those adults constantly disagree, fight, and argue, then the quality is gone. This is why it is true that "staying together for the sake of the children" is not the best move if the marital situation has soured.

The research is fairly clear in support of the finding that such constant exposure to conflict and chaos harms children. Having two parents allows both parents a break when needed, and provides for mutual support, which is always needed. I like to make the analogy of tag team wrestling when discussing the importance of a parents-as-team approach. If you know this TV spectacle, you know that in wrestling tag teams, one person from the team is in the ring at a time. When that person gets tired or is getting beat up pretty bad, he can tag his partner. The fresh partner then can enter the ring and pick up where the first partner left off. The new person in the ring has a better chance to succeed in dealing with the opponent. Many days, parenting can feel like being in a wrestling match. Having the security of your "tag partner's" presence always gives hope that even if you are not successful in a particular situation, your partner will be. If your parenting team is on the same page and has discussed its strategy, you will more likely succeed in the long run.

Having said the above, it is also a reality that child rearing is practiced by many single parents and an ever growing force of grandparents. Much of what you will see in this book applies to any caring adult or adult team who has direct responsibility for children. My point is not to judge, but to state the obvious. It is easier to raise children (or take on any life challenge) when two people work together than when one person handles it all alone.

Regarding the third point: Parenting is a responsibility-heavy, commitment-filled role. It is not to be entered into lightly. I do not want to over-dramatize the point, but you sign up for a life sentence when you agree to be a parent. Are you up to this challenge? What if you are not?

In 2011, a bit of controversy ensued when two very opposite stories related to parental commitment were published. One was a book entitled *Battle Hymn of the Tiger Mother* about extreme "Tiger Moms" (written by Amy Chua) and the other was a *Salon* article about a mother (Rahna Reiko Rizzuto) who one day realized, "I never wanted to be a mother. I was afraid of being swallowed up, of being exhausted, of opening my eyes one day, 20 (or 30!) years after they were born, and realizing I had lost myself and my life was over."

Both women made hard choices as to how to best parent and care for their children. Both women's choices were difficult because they both chose a nontraditional path. In the case of Ms. Chua, she chose to be very directive and involved and to plan and monitor her daughters' lives in ways most parents do not. In the case of Ms. Rizzuto, she saw that living the traditional mother role would be inauthentic. So at the risk of being labeled a bad mother who abandoned her sons, she gave up physical custody of them to their father. She writes that she "had to leave my children to find them." She chose to parent from a more distant position, but to remain involved. She says that she defined her own motherhood. Many people disagreed. As mentioned in my fifth point below, a parent has to want to be a parent. So from my perspective, her choice makes sense.

A fourth view I have is that as hard as you try, children may not turn out the way you want. I would be less than truthful if I wrote this book and you believed that the way you raise your child is 100 percent responsible for what and who your child becomes. Put another way, you can't take all of the credit if your child becomes a wonderful adult or all of the blame if she/he fails to live up to your expectations. While I believe that parenting is the single most important factor in determining child outcome, it does not cover every influence that shapes and leads to a child's "final ending" as an adult.

Your parenting influence may be diluted or weakened in cases of divorce, especially if the parents have very different child raising ideas. This leads to confusion in the child. Other out-of-family influences are another cause for consideration. These include certain serious experiences such as child abuse or living in poverty. Genetic or hereditary traits can also trump your best parenting work and can affect who and what your child becomes.

On a positive note, many outside-of-family factors may be good for children. Good teachers and coaches may have long-lasting and deep effects that will endure for your child's whole life. A good neighborhood and concerned neighbors can help in the same way. As parents, you play a major role in determining what environment your children will be raised in. Remember, child development is multidetermined and all of these influences combined will contribute to the "final product."

Finally, parents have to be responsible for and in charge of their children. This means if you don't think you have the time and energy to make sacrifices and place your needs second for 18-plus years, then be very careful about taking on this important role. It may seem strange to find this sentence in a parenting book, but I would be lying if I did not share this belief. It also means that once you have a child, you have to take on the duties of providing guidance and discipline, as well as love, and being quick to respond to your child. These are full-time, no vacation duties—it is *the* 24/7 job. Good parenting means hard work, years of sacrifice and commitments and, if you're fortunate, your child's love and satisfaction on a job well done.

When should parents be *excluded* or removed from a child's life? As noted in the first edition, parents should be excluded in situations involving drug and alcohol abuse, violence and aggression problems, certain personality disorders, and severe untreated mental illness. This book focuses on parents who have the capacity to love, nurture, and guide their children. Active drug- and alcohol-abusing parents, or any persons who lack the psychological abilities we will explore, have no grounds to be allowed an active or unsupervised role in their children's lives. They are takers and destroyers. Until and unless they are "clean" or changed they should be removed from proximity and direct care responsibilities.

CHILD DEVELOPMENT THEMES

In addition to the above, here are some foundational themes I believe, established in the parenting literature, are related to good child rearing:

- Raising children is different in every family, depending on unique experiences and attitudes.
- Parenting, like all social relationships, is a two-way process.
- Families are made of a set of interconnected systems.

Raising children is different in every family because every child is different and special. That is one reason why no one book can tell you specifically how to raise your children. Each family has its own set of values and beliefs about what fathers and mothers do and the role they play in raising their children. After reading this book, I hope you can successfully blend your values and attitudes with what is known from years of research to create a parenting style that is good for your children.

Parenting, like all social relationships, is a two-way (reciprocal) process. You will say and do things which will affect and change your child, and she/he will say and do things that affect and change you over time. As you will see, this interaction starts in infancy with attachment, and continues on into the teen years as the needs of the parent and the child change and develop over time. Parents change their children and children change their parents. Both grow and create new opportunities as the years pass.

The quality of the parent-child interaction also changes over time, with your infant being much more controlled by your actions than your teen will be. This topic was fully explored in detail in the first edition.

A third theme, related to the reciprocity theme, is that of the family as a set of interconnected systems. From my family therapy experiences, I have learned that everyone is shaped by the people around them, and that they shape those people in return. In family systems, your parenting (called the executive subsystem) plays a large role in the development of your child. We will return to this topic in this edition, as I had introduced it in the first book.

The marital/co-parenting relationship is the foundation for how things will turn out. If there is a relatively happy, supportive co-parenting team (called a healthy, functional executive subsystem), children are raised well and parents work together as a team or unit. This efficient parenting team is better equipped to handle the challenges and surprises that arise over time. If the marital/co-parenting team faces stress and conflict, then this negative effect will be seen in bad or ineffective parenting. Children are negatively affected—both directly and indirectly—by parents whose fighting is a source of chaos, instability, and unpredictability.

The other major family subsystem is siblings. Factors such as the number of kids in a family, the years between them, whether they are boys or girls, and birth order all interact to impact how your children will turn out. Being the last-born girl in a family of four boys, or being the fifth born of an all-girl family will have very different results, from very different sibling interactions and toys to whether there is hand-me-down clothing. Brothers and sisters (sibling subsystems) can be a source of comfort and support when problems arise in the parenting subsystem. They can also be a source of bitter rivalry and competition for parental attention and family resources.

ORGANIZATION OF *THE EDUCATED PARENT 2*

What I cover in this book reflects my view of important, current topics for what I call the educated parent. The educated parent wants to be the best caregiver she/he can be. This person seeks out information—facts, figures, data, and evidence—to make the best choices for his or her children. There may be some information you are looking for that I did not cover. If it is important for you, it is important. You will need to look further for that information. There may also be some information that on first look may not seem to apply to you. I suggest you read through it anyway. You never know when you or a friend may need the ideas presented.

This book is divided into nine chapters, with similar themes as in *The Educated Parent*. We begin with what I refer to as Parenting 101—basic parenting skills and obligation topics. Chapter 2 examines wellness and spirituality, two topics that can establish healthy children in well-functioning families. We also cover so-called mommy books and the mommy wars.

In chapter 3, we review the developmental triad—three aspects related to child growth and development that interact to determine your child's final outcome as an adult. In chapter 4, we look at research related to marital quality, parenting techniques, and child discipline. In chapter 5, I discuss your role in your child's education and issues related to setting up your child for success, homeschooling, and your role as an advocate for your child.

In chapters 6 and 7, we review your role in how to detect and protect your child from undue stress and anxiety. One of the negative trends in parenting and child rearing over the past 50 years has been the introduction of children to anxiety-producing circumstances and information at earlier ages. We will review ways to identify and shield your child from some of this. Much of the stress is technology-related, as children are exposed to more adult content and matters that children once knew little of.

In the final chapters, 8 and 9, we will explore the role and importance of fathers and fathering in the lives of children. We will look at the recent research on how daycare placement impacts the development of young children. This chapter will include specific information on how you can choose the best daycare options and placements.

Finally, in the afterword, I will share my current thoughts and opinions on the state of parenting in America. We will examine some challenges, some advances, and some problems as they impact child development in the 21st century.

Always remember that your impact as a parent is permanent. It is also the case, as we shall see, that your life will be forever changed dramatically as a result of this usually wonderful, sometimes exasperating, often joyful, and never boring adventure in child rearing. Please read on, so you may become the best mom or dad you can be—an educated parent.

ONE

Parenting 101

My mom used to say it doesn't matter how many kids you have . . . because one kid'll take up 100% of your time so more kids can't possibly take up more than 100% of your time.

~Karen Brown

Kids spell love T-I-M-E.

~John Crudele

In this opening chapter, we review important topics for educated parents. These include an overview of essential parental behaviors and skills, a discussion of some of the pressures parents face, the concept of good enough parenting, how to handle issues if there is a divorce, and ways in which parents can support and protect their children and teens.

FOUNDATIONAL PARENTING SKILLS

When it comes down to the basics of teaching or explaining, as a faculty member, I always first think about the foundations upon which more advanced learning can be laid. The same is true as I consider parenting. So what better way to start a parenting book than with a discussion of the skills that set the foundation for all parenting and child rearing?

Parenting is one of the few jobs where experience doesn't necessarily make things easier the second (or third) time around. If you have the chance to raise more than one child, you will often find yourself wondering about how different and unique each child is. The up side is that you can enjoy each child for his/her own special blend of strengths and weaknesses, talents and limitations. The down side is that, once you have gone through a period of growth and challenge with one child, what you learned from that experience may not always apply neatly to the next child.

No matter what child you are raising, the following sentence, in my opinion, summarizes what parents should always remember: *The basic parenting skills of consistent discipline, the child's needs for love and nurturance, and the control and guidance functions of parenting always apply.* This is the essential skill set. Good parents will work together to set up and implement a consistent and fair way to establish rules and the consequences that follow when the child obeys or breaks those rules. These consequences will be positive when the child behaves as she/he should; the child achieves or earns rewards for good behavior. This is true no matter what the expectations and discipline plan are. Every family needs a plan that fits the parents' value system and philosophies about raising children. No two are exactly alike. For many families, the parents' plan is the result of some combination of how they were raised in their family-of-origin homes. This is a very important part of what every household should discuss and agree upon before the first child enters the family.

Why is an agreed upon *discipline plan* or program important? Children, to be secure and feel safe in a big, unknown world, need to respect their parents and parental authority. We will cover this topic from different perspectives in later chapters as well. In chapter 4, we will talk about different parenting techniques or programs that you can learn or read about. Some of these even involve training and practice sessions. In chapter 8, we will look at discipline from the father's perspective, and his role in establishing authority.

By establishing a level of authority at home, you will enable your child to be more cooperative and successful when she/he starts school and has to mind the teacher. Your young son or daughter will learn self-control and self-discipline as a result of your setting up limits and rules. Without these external rules, the child does not know how to behave. With this established system, your child learns what is acceptable and what is not. Your child gets your love and appreciation and gratitude when she/he acts the right way. And children will always work for parental acceptance and approval.

Conversely, when your child behaves inappropriately, that will cause you, as the parent, to intervene and correct your child. This is a key step. Good parenting requires you to apply the rule system consistently. Depending on how you communicate to your child your disapproval (e.g., a scolding, a time out, a talking to, a mild spanking), your child will know that they have disappointed you. For most children, your disapproval will lead to feelings of shame and guilt, even in a three-year-old. And you will often hear some crying. Your child will want to regain your approval and do a better job next time. (Your child will also want to avoid your negative consequence.)

Here is where your discipline plan should contain a way for your child to hear from you what the better, more acceptable behavior would be. Do not let the moment pass when you can do some reasoning with your child. "Did you know our rules?" "Why did you do 'X'?" "What will you do differently next time?" "If you do not know what to do, who can you ask for help?" By asking these questions, you teach your child to problem solve and think through their immediate behavior to the consequences. Teaching this lesson in childhood is one of the best ways to prepare your child for their teen and adult years.

Your children will appreciate that you, the adult, are in charge and will safely guide them through their lives. It is important to consider that your child looks to you to organize his or her world. You determine where your family lives, and the neighborhood and friends and school. You decide on what is eaten, what is worn, what is played with, when to go to bed. Establishing this organization and a sense of routine has a calming and secure effect on children, especially the under-10 crowd. Children need to experience loving and positive authority at home as a starting point to live in society as it is now organized.

Fortunately, being a parent does not mean you have to always be perfect, 100 percent consistent, or all-wise in order to raise a healthy, successful child into adulthood. The phrase "good enough parenting" has been coined to refer to the fact that a parent simply must be that—good enough, but not perfect. This revelation is a great guilt reducer. Many parents have a number of specific things they have done or said that they would like to take back. Or they can list things never done that they wish they had made time for. The good news is that your children are generally forgiving and that you usually have to go out of your way to create permanent harm or interfere with normal development.

This means that short of abuse or neglect, you have a lot of leeway in the choices you make in how to raise a mostly happy and healthy child.

If it weren't this way, we would all be worse off than we actually are. Again, I am not saying that you do not have to be consistent. I am saying that no one can be 100 percent consistent all of the time, but you have to aim for it. When you do slip, assuming you make a quick recovery, your child will still be alright. We review the concept of good enough parenting in detail later in this chapter.

Let us turn now to your *child's need for love and nurturance*. One can make an argument that a sure way to show your love is to implement consistent and fair discipline. I will not disagree. But at the same time, children need the comfort of hugs and kisses and play time and tickling and fooling around. The need for physical touch and closeness is a basic human need.

The notion of how a caregiver, usually the mother, first interacts with a newborn and infant is a good analogy for the importance of touch and intimate closeness. Donald W. Winnicott, a mid-20th-century British psychoanalyst and pediatrician, wrote of the importance of "holding." He observed that an important part of the bond that a mother forges with her baby comes from the mother's "attentive holding" of her child. Dr. Winnicott, after years of observing mother–child interactions, described in great detail events such as "the business of picking a baby up" and the "way that the 'mother's technique of holding, of bathing, of feeding, everything she did for the baby, added up to the child's first idea of the mother.'" Although he went on to use this behavioral description as a centerpiece of his explanations of what must go on in therapy sessions—recreating this intimate, care-filled environment—the observations and the importance given to these first acts of tenderness do set the stage for what a newborn and infant experiences.

All children thrive when they know they are loved by their parents. And we know they are harmed and impacted when their home environment undermines their emotional security. In a special monograph sponsored by the Society for Research in Child Development, authors Patrick Davies, Gordon Harold, Marcia Goeke-Morey, and E. Mark Cummings tested several theories which propose that high levels of conflict between parents lead to increased risks in children for a range of later psychological problems. Their goals were "to advance a more refined, updated conceptualization of emotional security in the face of interparental conflict" and to empirically test hypotheses about children's emotional security and what happens when that security is undermined.

The monograph presents a compilation of four extensive studies looking at how children respond emotionally to interparental conflict, how children understand and appraise parent conflict and its impact on emotional security and adjustment, and what, if any, protective factors for children exist in high-conflict families.

It has long been known that marital conflict increases children's vulnerability to psychological difficulties. Researchers have tried to find the processes that lead to those later problems. It appears that a child's emotional insecurity is the link. The research indicates that signs of a child's insecurity in the face of interparental conflict are reflected in three areas: (1) greater levels of fear and distress or anxiety; (2) "prolonged attempts" to become involved in or avoid parental conflicts; and (3) negative evaluations of the consequences parental conflict has for the well-being of the family and self.

Consistent with the hypotheses presented in the monograph, the research linked children's reports of fear, avoidance, and involvement as the major responses to interparental conflict. This resulting insecurity was associated with later and worse levels of mental health difficulties, even when considering the role of a number of other possible causes.

Similarly, the importance of *control and guidance functions* by parents is clear. As part of a discipline plan or as an aspect of attachment, parents need to be in charge. We will discuss these at length in chapters 3 and 4.

Other aspects that I would consider foundational skills or topics include making time for your child and just being there when your child needs interaction with you.

Know Your Child

This seems strange but it is among the most important things a parent can do. By this I mean you need to pay attention to your child from day one. You can only do this by giving your child your undivided attention as you interact. What is his/her temperament? As she/he grows, what are his/her likes and dislikes? How social or shy is she/he?

As your child enters school, does she/he make friends easily? Is she/he a leader or follower? What kinds of music or other arts is she/he interested in? What talents does your daughter/son possess? Does she/he follow some hereditary path in your families? Does a daughter have her father's side of the family's drawing ability or athleticism? Does your son have the sense of humor on his mother's side of the family or a love of reading?

As your child enters the teen years, can you read his/her moods? Can you tell when she/he is troubled? Do you know your teen well enough to know when she/he is telling the truth or not being completely honest? Do you know his/her friends? Do you know their TV, movie, or music preferences?

All of this is important, as you will see. When we get to the chapters covering temperament and attachment, or how certain attitudes and predispositions play out in behaviors that can be positive or negative, or when we see how these leanings impact school performance, you will see how your knowledge of your child will let you be a more effective parent and your child a more adjusted daughter or son.

Knowing your child is also tied into what to expect and when to expect certain behaviors, abilities, or skills from your growing and ever-changing child. Depending upon how much time you have spent with children, you will come to know what children in particular age groups can be expected to do. If you haven't spent much time around children, it will be harder to know what's going on or what's coming next. Professionals call the age range at which a child is expected to be able to do a certain skill or behavior the *developmental norm.* For example, walking usually begins when a child reaches the age range of about 10–16 months. Almost all healthy children start walking after 10 months of age and no later than 16 months.

Not knowing these developmental norms can cause problems for the parent and the child. For example, you would not want to start potty training before your child is physically ready to master this task. If you try to push your child, you will create frustration and failure that would otherwise be avoided if you wait for the child to mature enough to have success.

This book doesn't present these developmental norms, but you can find them in a number of places online. Most infant parenting books have lots of information on all of the things happening in physical, mental, language, and social development in the first two years. Let me make a pitch here for the educated parent to consider a class on child development, either at the college level or through a local community agency.

Finally, if you ever have a question or a doubt about your child and his/her abilities, ask. Ask your pediatrician, ask your mother, ask other more experienced mothers in your neighborhood. All will either help you or send you to someone who can. The question of when or whether a child should be expected to do something is termed *developmental readiness.* Often this term is used specifically to see if a child is prepared physically, mentally, and emotionally for school. We will visit this topic again in chapter 5. For now, let's look at readiness in a more general way.

Before proceeding, let me also give a warning about comparing children. A simple developmental fact of life is that children grow at their own rates. That is why development experts use *normative range data.* Normative range data are basically windows of time in which 90 percent of normal children develop a certain ability or skill. For example, walking alone will happen in most children between 11 months, 1 week through 14 months, 1 week of age, with an average age of walking at about 12 months. This means that you should not expect your child to be walking at 9 months, and that you should not be too worried if your child hasn't started to walk at 13 months. Just because other children with the same birthday are walking first does not mean your child has a major problem. And if your child is walking early, don't rush off to pay the gifted school tuition payment just yet.

Biologically based development occurs at a rate determined by maturation of the nervous and other related systems (a nature factor) *and* the amount of experience and opportunity a child has to display a certain skill or behavior (a nurture factor). Much research has been conducted to show that you can't hurry or accelerate these processes. This same body of research has found that these two key developmental processes—maturation and experience—are interdependent. So, once again, no aspect of child growth is *solely* biological, although in certain areas like motor development, biology may be the more limiting factor.

If you want your child to walk alone as soon as possible, all you can really do is feed him/her a healthy diet and let him/her get on the floor to crawl and climb up on furniture and exercise his/her musculo-skeletal system. Special exercises or specific muscle training are not likely to add any more than a day or two to the time they would have walked anyway, allowing nature to take her course. Research has shown that providing a stimulating environment can add motivation to walk, which will cause the child to grow optimally, but not much faster than she/he would have according to the genetic plan.

We also know that children tend to grow in spurts. So what a child could not do on Sunday, he or she may be able to do two Sundays later *plus* other skills and abilities. Any developmental testing always has to account for this, so a bad performance on one test date is never enough to lead to a diagnosis of a problem.

One other point I want to cover is the issue of *co-regulation.* Co-regulation is defined as the sharing of control in the gradual process of shifting behavioral regulation from parent to child. Knowing that your primary authority occurs early on and that your direct influence will wane is another important developmental factor to keep in mind. It is just as important to note and remember that you will remain the parent and you should maintain and reinforce your expectations for appropriate and proper behavior and choices even with your 18 year old. The difference at age 18 is that your teen will make the final decisions and likely talk back to you.

When your child is an infant, you as the parent will have practically complete control over his/her behavior and options. As your infant enters childhood, efforts at autonomy will appear (the terrible twos and the frequent use of the word "no"), much to your dismay. From when your child reaches two to three years of age and through adolescence, with each passing year, your child's increased competencies will allow for more self-determined behavior and less supervision and direct guidance from you. As your child becomes a teen, even less direct control will be possible, in part because your teen will spend so much time physically away from you, whether at school, at work, or with peers. By this time, you must hope that you have taught your child well, so that she/he may have the ability and will to make proper decisions. Ultimately, your job as a parent will near its formal end, as this teen becomes an independent young adult in the world. Your influence will remain through adulthood, however.

Keys to co-regulation are related to the notion of scaffolding, which we will cover later in this chapter. By providing appropriate supports and resources, you will allow your child the space to learn to make decisions that are healthy and self-directed. By intervening when necessary, or by simply being available, you will make your guidance and strength accessible when your child needs it.

"GOOD ENOUGH" PARENTING

Many parents feel pride and wonder when faced with the responsibility of raising a child. With these obligations and responsibilities come many reasons to question one's abilities and skills related to child rearing. Some of this is very natural. I have referred to the "imposter syndrome"—the feelings parents experience when they can't quite believe that they have been left on their own to raise a child without the preparation needed to be successful. It's as if a parent thinks, "I can hardly take care of myself; how can I be in charge of someone else? Especially a baby or child?"

Other parents feel constant pressure to make all the right moves. *Is my child in the best precollege daycare academy? Am I buying enough educational toys? Are we saving enough money for the eventual elite private school or college tuition costs? Do we need to move in order to be in the best public school district? Should my family homeschool? Should a mother (or father) stay home to ensure proper attachment and allow a child a real "'50's style" childhood full of carefree memories?*

How Does a Parent Know That She/He Is Doing the Right Thing for His/Her Children?

One real fear for some parents is that of being scrutinized, watched, and judged by others as you parent publicly. Most of the time, these others never have the complete picture, so whatever judgment they make is not accurate. So if you spank your child for acting out in a store, people will look at you like you're an abuser, not knowing anything else about what you and your child have gone through previously. Or if you let your child roam and play in a restaurant, others will question why you are not controlling or disciplining your out-of-control child. This will happen even if they do not know you are traveling and your children might need some free time to move about after six hours in a car seat.

Parenting in America is like this. Many people have opinions; few have the information to make sound conclusions. Some people say America is doomed by the neglectful parenting most children receive from their self-absorbed parents who make choices about what is best for the adults and not the children in the family. Others lament for the old days of "spare the rod, spoil the child" and see no hope for the next generation of undisciplined youth.

Unfortunately much of this criticism comes from older people, sometimes your own parents, grandparents, or other family. This generation gap intrigues me. Some of it is based on a "revisionist history" of sorts; these older folks fail to remember their inconsistencies and only recall their best parenting days. Their look back is 20/20 and recalled through a prism of pink lenses. No matter the reality, it is up to you to not give them the ammunition, so to speak, for these critical moments.

And when others do make such comments, rather than become defensive, it might be a good idea to stop and reflect on whether a good point is being made. If someone who cares about you and your children feels the need to say something, I suggest you hear them out—at least the first time—and see if you need to make some changes. My point in all this is that parenting is a tough enough job. You do not need further hardships which call your fitness into question. At the same time, we can all use feedback to make us better. Read on for more.

In a *Guardian* (London, England) newspaper article dated 2001, Joanna Moorhead wrote editorially about parents (with two biological and two adopted children) who faced accusations of neglect. The details of the cause for her article are not what I wish to share, but rather her thoughtful insights on the pressures parents face to be perfect and right and good all the time. Ms. Moorhead wrote:

> Judgment is all around when you are a parent. . . . The judgment of others is an aspect of parenting we are all up against. And something we all indulge in, too, from time to time. He spends too long at work, never sees his kids; she is too pushy, doesn't let them follow their own inclinations. . . . There is a sense in which we are, all of us, guilty of being less than perfect parents.

She goes on to discuss the "good enough" parent concept and how most professionals would agree that perfect parenting is an impossible goal to attain. Ms. Moorhead continues, "[This] is all very well in theory, but in practice our society is riddled with anxiety that what we are doing is far from OK." News stories featuring studies about the harm that can arise from daycare placement or overscheduling or being too busy as parents can cause parents to question their competence and abilities.

Ms. Moorhead adds, "If judgment by our peers is bad enough, judgment by those on the receiving end of our skills (or lack of them) is both inevitable and, sometimes, searingly fierce. Deconstructing our parents' parenting abilities, examining them in minute detail and finding them wanting, is a rite of passage. When we become parents ourselves, we are often more forgiving, perhaps because as well as facing the same problems, we know we will eventually face the same scrutiny."

How do these words impact your opinion of yourself as a parent? Have you felt some of the emotions this account may have stirred? How confident in your parenting and behavior are you?

Good enough parenting means that you are trying your best, but that you have limitations of your own that keep you from being patient, caring, understanding, nurturing, firm, and consistent all the time. What human being could ever be all these things at all times? Again, it is important to value and make every effort to practice important parenting traits. But don't beat yourself up when you fall short.

Good enough parenting means that you are as consistent, fair, and firm as you can be. The more consistent you are, the easier it will be for your child to learn what is expected and how to behave properly. To be a consistent, fair, and firm parent requires planning and effort. You have to know when you are at your best and when you are not, and then plan the challenging aspects of the daily routine around your best times when possible.

British psychiatrist/pediatrician David Winnicott (referenced above) first spoke of the idea of the "good enough" parent. Having treated children and worked with families for many years, Dr. Winnicott noted and observed that children do quite well when their parents do a "good enough" job raising them. In this sense, this means meeting a child's basic needs for love and nurturing and discipline. Striving for personal excellence in parenting is commendable, but flogging yourself for not quite walking the walk all the time is not needed.

At the same time, I am not calling for "phoning in" your parenting. There is much to be said for how parenting choices positively influence your child's outcome. It is good to buy quality toys and provide special opportunities for a child to develop talents and skills. Being an involved parent does usually yield a higher functioning child.

PARENTING AFTER DIVORCE/SEPARATION

This section may seem out of place or surprising, but many families will face this specific challenge. Understanding divorce effects in children is important for families of today, and addressing the best ways to handle postdivorce life has become a basic parenting skill. And as was shown above, ending conflict in families, which is the hopeful outcome of a divorce, is good for children.

As for some numbers, as of October 2010, U.S. Census data were used to derive estimates of the number of children under 18 raised in single-parent families. This number includes single-parent families from all sources (choice, circumstance, divorce, widowhood). The number was 23,808,000.

Here are more numbers of interest, accurate as of 2000:

Families in which the child lived with two parents in 1997: 25.6 million

Single fathers maintaining their own household: 1.786 million
Single mothers maintaining their own household: 7.571 million

Single fathers living in the home of a relative: 240,000
Single mothers living in the home of a relative: 1.633 million

Single fathers who are divorced: 913,000
Single mothers who are divorced: 3.392 million

Single fathers never married: 693,000
Single mothers never married: 4.181 million

Single fathers raising one child: 1,300,000
Single mothers raising one child: 5.239 million

Single fathers raising four or more children: 55,000
Single mothers raising four or more children: 475,000

(*Source:* http://www.usattorneylegalservices.com/divorce-statistics.html)

Much has been written in the area of divorce effects. As detailed in *The Educated Parent,* different research has yielded different answers to the question of how divorce affects or impacts children. Please check the first edition for an entire chapter on these findings. For this edition, allow me to make some updates and spend more time on how your parenting must adapt to the needs of children after a family breakup.

One major emphasis to note here is for parents to resolve their own adult-level issues after a divorce. This is important so that you do not get into "guilty parenting." As used here, *guilty parenting* refers to a child rearing style based upon the need to make up for all the things you believe your child(ren) have lost now that they are from a "broken family." This usually translates to less or inconsistent rule following and a breakdown of routine and structure.

If you fail to remain consistent or decide to give your child repeated "breaks" because she/he is "a poor child of divorce," you scare your child by giving a second message that things really are different and not right. Guilt or other emotions that prevent you from being tough and consistent must be dealt with quickly. If you yelled about keeping a clean bedroom predivorce, you need to yell about keeping a clean bedroom postdivorce.

To a great extent, the way that each parent copes with their separation and divorce is a big predictor of how well their child(ren) will adjust. If a parent is seen as weak, depressed, and out of control, this scares the child(ren), who are looking to parents to maintain the family and take care of them properly. In some cases, a child may take over parenting younger siblings and serve as a source of support for their grieving parent. This is quite harmful for the child and needs to be avoided.

If a parent is seen as coping and adjusting, making progress toward establishing a new family system and schedule, this is a great source of comfort to the child(ren) looking to regain the security and stability that was shaken at the separation.

In any event, *it is your obligation, as the parent, to look out for yourself during the separation and divorce process.* I am reminded as I write this of the warning given on airplanes in the event the oxygen masks appear. Adults (parents) need to put theirs on first before they attend to their child(ren). After divorce, you must attend to getting yourself back so you can then help your offspring.

If you need help, and most people will, get it. Ask family, friends, and others for support and access to resources. If you cannot adjust in a timely manner, you may require the services of individual or group therapy. By all means use these resources for yourself and your family. It is okay to cry in front of your child(ren) as long as you reassure and show them that your sadness does not interfere with your ability to care for them.

HELPING CHILDREN TO ADJUST AND COPE AFTER DIVORCE

A parent who is on the right track to adjustment will more likely identify and respond to their child(ren)'s needs during this often scary and uneasy time. Children are quick to give out signals about their status and what they need; however, these signs may be indirect and need translation. The following steps are usually necessary in helping children adapt more quickly to divorce.

Listening to Your Child's Questions/Comments

A child's questions/comments may be asked or stated to elicit a response on two levels. At the surface, the question can be a simple one. At a deeper level, there can be an expression of concern about an area that the child is unsure of. Some samples and their possible deeper meanings include: questions about not being available (abandonment fears), a child saying they do not want a gift or treat (money worries), or attempts to not go to school (desire to be home to protect a parent).

Staying Open to Your Child's Needs

Once the child's concerns have been identified, see what you can do to reassure or otherwise settle your child's worries. Encourage them to talk with you whenever they have questions or worries. Try to make time to be just with them, without competing activities. Be prepared to seek outside resources such as therapy, support groups for kids, and time with the school guidance counselor.

Making New Traditions and Rituals

One sure way to let children see that you are moving ahead as a new family unit is to introduce new ways of doing family things like celebrations, holidays, birthdays, and so forth. This is often seen with family holidays. Start up new rituals and let these become the new family tradition for that new part of the family. You should encourage your child(ren) to come up with ideas as well and then decide as a family what would be best.

Keeping in Touch with the Ex-in-Laws

The ex-in-laws remain relatives to your child(ren) after the divorce. The amount of contact that was usual prior to the separation/divorce will be a predictor of what level of involvement is expected and needed by your child(ren). Another major variable in this area is the quality of your relationship prior to the marital problems. Some in-laws insist on keeping a relationship, despite their blood relative's disapproval of such continuing contact; others will cut you out of their photos. What is best for your child(ren)? If they are used to regular and frequent contact with their cousins and other relatives, there should be an honest attempt to keep some of that involvement alive. The same holds for aunts, uncles, and especially grandparents who, in many states, have legal rights of access to their grandchildren. This includes some flexibility with respect to changing visit times to accommodate the other family's celebrations. At all times, respect must be shown for these people. Your child(ren) will benefit from this goodness even if it tears you up inside.

VISITATION DO'S AND DON'TS

Visitations may be one of the most troublesome aspects of postdivorce family adjustment. This is often the most contested part of a divorce and the aspect that leads to the most bitterness and rancor. The parent with less contact is impacted more and has to deal with feelings of being second best or less than equal as a parent. The parent with more contact in the living arrangements may seemingly express feelings of superiority. An educated parent should avoid falling into these emotional holes if postdivorce peace is your goal. Consider the following:

Work to Keep Communication Lines Open

One of the keys to successful visits is that parents are flexible and understanding with respect to potential changes in pick-up times or dates. This requires *respectful* communication between exes. There should be a minimum need for such talk, but it is inevitable that there will be a need. Take the high road; keep the conversation limited to the topic and do not rehash old complaints. Better yet—rely on email. It is time- and date-stamped, and there is a neat record.

Make Visits Positive and Natural

How will you spend your limited time together? It is best if the visit has a positive quality, especially at the beginning. It is also important to avoid becoming a "Disney parent" who provides vacations on each visit. This is unrealistic, too expensive, and will alter your image in your child(ren)'s eyes. Similarly, a weekend visit routine that is all work and no play should be avoided.

Children should wherever possible have rules, a schedule, discipline, and a set bedtime routine on visits. Outings such as going to the mall, a park, or other family event are always acceptable. Discipline must be enforced, even if it causes unpleasant moments on the visit.

Prepare Children for Visits

It is the obligation of each parent to have the child(ren) ready for transition times. You must be aware of the time so that you can have your child(ren) clean, dressed, and packed (if necessary). The issue of clothing needs to be worked out. Some families keep separate wardrobes; others send clothes each way. Similarly, toys and games need to be selected for safekeeping at each home. Some families have duplicate favorite games; others have certain games at their house as another way to remind everyone that there are now two separate households. If a child is involved in sports, their uniforms and equipment must be forwarded or duplicated. At first, there will be a need to be patient as some items are likely to be forgotten at one house or the other. Children should not have the additional pressure of being blamed or yelled at for these mistakes.

Maintain Frequency and Predictability of Visits

A fixed, routine schedule is *absolutely necessary* for children under the age of 8 to 10. The predictability of regular contact serves to give a sense of normalcy to postdivorce life. It is most important to keep your work/ life schedule constant as a means of bringing security and stability to your child. When you must make changes, make them with the most amount of warning possible and with a full explanation to your child. Makeup time may or may not be possible. Predictability is important—even if your visit schedule is one day per month.

As a rule, the younger the child the more frequent the visits (although for shorter duration) is best. For teens, it is best to allow them a say in the schedule. You must be flexible to work around their needs for jobs, friends, school, and other teen activities. As a parent, you may feel slighted if your teen chooses to be with friends. This is normal and needs to be respected. Feel free to talk with your teen about how you might spend more time together *and* allow them their teen activities and time with friends.

Although it is essential to keep your agreed upon schedule, there will be times when a change must be made. Work demands, other life events (e.g., illness), and other extraordinary situations can lead to unavailability for keeping the schedule. Flexibility is best accomplished through a history of open communication and with as much notice given as possible.

A LIST OF VISITATION DON'TS

Several visitation issues spark much conflict in families that fight. *Avoiding conflict is the goal of all responsible parents.* Again, act reasonably, and as if you were in the other parent's shoes, and most problems will never happen. Three common issues are reviewed:

Checking on the Other Parent

Visits are not reconnaissance missions for spying children. It is harmful, inappropriate, and wrong to use your child to find out about activities at the other household. If your child brings up some event or activity, polite listening without questions is the best response. If you hear about some unsavory activity or situation, discussion with the other parent must be delicately handled. Avoiding a defensive response will limit conflict and more likely get you information. If you have concerns about a new boy/girlfriend, talk directly with your ex. Expect to be told it's none of your business (because it usually isn't). If you have concerns about other lifestyle issues, discuss these with the other parent without placing the child in the middle, possibly with a trusted third party. These differences may need to be mediated.

Interfering with Visits

Some parents fuel discontent which leads to a disruption in the quality and quantity of visits. It is fairly easy to plant worry or fear of a visit in your child. You can easily cause much grief for the other parent. However this comes at a cost to your child. More hurt will come to the child than to the other parent. Such alienation behavior can backfire and harm your child dearly. Wishing the child well and acting civilly toward the other parent at transitions makes your child feel more secure. There is no need to let the child know about what they will be missing by being with the other parent.

Being on Time

This issue leads to as much sustained conflict as any other. If the visit schedule says pickup at 5:00 P.M., be there within a 15-minute window (allowing for traffic or other likely problems). It is impolite and disrespectful to be too early or late. If you know you will be late, or some event you are attending is too good to leave, use your cell phone to see if the time out can be extended. The other parent is under no obligation to agree—be prepared to leave if necessary. This is not the time or place to fight about it—you should resolve any difficulties afterward and out of earshot of the child(ren). *Requests for changes need to be kept at a minimum—pick your times carefully.*

COPING STRATEGIES FOR CHILDREN

Based on the above, the following are six suggested parental behaviors and attitudes that have been shown to help children cope with the stressors of divorce. The educated parent will understand the importance of these ideas and use them as they fit their situation.

Allow Time to Readjust

Don't expect things to settle down quickly; they won't. You may feel that you have gotten over things, only to be crying for the next two days. This cycle is not unusual—people tend to plateau then move forward again in their adjustment. One old clinical rule of thumb is that it takes about one month per year of marriage (but at least six months) for everyone to settle down emotionally. Each family will have its own timetable based upon how well the parents manage their own grief and can move forward.

Assure Children They are *Not* at Fault

This point cannot be overemphasized. Although children under seven are most likely to feel as if they caused the divorce, a child of any age can harbor these thoughts. Parents must take responsibility for the end of their marriage. Children must be assured and reassured that they played no role in the final decision. This is true even if part of the divorce was over child-related issues.

Assure Children of Their Security and Access to Both Parents

One of the main causes for a child's poor adjustment is the feeling that his/her security has been undermined. There is always the question of abandonment—whether a child can be left by the other parent after one has seemingly left you. Knowing that they still have a bedroom, clothes, toys, and a routine can help to restore security. Each parent needs to reassure the child as needed that they are in charge and that the child does not have to worry about food or shelter. Similarly, children need to know that the other parent is available, even if only by phone or email, should there be a need for contact. Similarly, children need assurance that the other parent is doing okay when separated from them.

Keep a Schedule and Routine

This point, restated here, is related to the security and stability issue. When a child has his/her own routine, with known discipline and rules, she/he senses that although some things have changed (through divorce) the world is still the same. This helps children look ahead.

Continue to Discipline as Always (or Better)

As mentioned above, one sure way to remind a child that there is stability in the postdivorce world is to keep things as they were before—a theme of continuity in his/her life. A set of rules and discipline reminds the child that she/he still has to answer to a parent, that she/he still has to mind, and that the important things have not really changed.

Keep the Children Out of the Middle and Shielded from Conflict

It is sometimes tempting to ask your child to carry a message or make a request of the other parent for you since they will be seeing that person anyway. Avoid this temptation. Children feel burdened when they are messengers. They also feel compromised if the message is negative or leads to a negative response. If you have a message or request, ask yourself—in person, by phone, by email, or by letter. *These messages should also be kept to a minimum* lest you run the risk of being labeled as a harasser or stalker.

Lisa Strohschein of the University of Alberta sought to determine whether it is true that divorced parents show a diminished capacity to parent in the period following divorce. This has long been suspected and documented in different ways in different studies. Using a Canadian-based study, she reviewed national data which followed over 5,000 children. These children, in two-parent families at the study's start, had data isolated and looked at comparing the families who divorced over time to those that remained intact. Strohschein's results showed that divorce was unrelated to changes in parenting behavior, "suggesting that there are more similarities than differences in parenting among recently divorced and continuously married parents."

Bruce Smyth, a faculty member at the Australian National University and former Senior Research Fellow at the Australian Institute of Family Studies, has written on parents' opinions about time spent with their children after divorce. Using data from Australian families (7,682 households and 19,914 individuals), Smyth found that resident mothers and nonresident fathers had very different levels of satisfaction with the amount of father–child contact occurring after divorce. More than half (55%) of the 647 resident mothers in the sample believed that the amount of contact was about right, while a similar proportion (57%) of the 394 nonresident fathers believed that "it was nowhere near enough." (The respondents had not been married to each other.)

Smyth broke the data down further to discover what was behind the level of satisfaction numbers. He found that around half (50–53%) of the resident mothers in the "little or no" father contact or "mid-range" father contact groups believed that the amount of contact "was about right." So 35 percent of resident mothers in these groups reported that "not enough" father–child contact was occurring. Comparatively, three-quarters (75%) of the nonresident fathers who rarely or never saw their children, believed that "they had nowhere near enough contact." Notably, 16 percent of fathers believed that this amount of contact was about right.

When the amount of father–child contact increased, resident mothers and nonresident fathers were less likely to report dissatisfaction—though, "predictably, this pattern was far more pronounced for men than for women," reported Smyth.

When there was shared care, or joint custody in U.S. parlance, resident mothers and nonresident fathers generally agreed that the amount of contact was about right. When fathers with shared care were less likely to believe that the amount of father–child contact was "about right," it was interpreted as a desire for full-time family life with their children.

In order to achieve more parental satisfaction with visit schedules and time spent with children, Smyth suggests that parent–child contact "be structured in ways that encourage the experience of different types of time with children—ways that create the likelihood of "being-in-the-moment" time." He has found, in other research he has conducted, that child contact schedules involve arrangements that "were far more complex than traditional every-other-weekend approaches."

Smyth also argues that, "After separation, time can be a lock—and a key." Some resident mothers never get a break and may feel locked in to parenting while some nonresident fathers believe they are locked out of their children's lives. Instead, parents need to find "new ways of being with [their] children." Ultimately, he says that "what matters is how time is spent and experienced, not just how it is allocated or distributed."

SUPPORTING AND PROTECTING CHILDREN

We now turn our attention to two essential features of parenting—support and protection. Children count on their parents for these basic tasks. By providing these, you give your child an environment where growth and development can be maximized.

Let me present to the educated parent the idea of *scaffolding*. *Scaffolding* is the term given to the emotional and environmental supports that parents make on which their children can experiment, grow, and blossom. Scaffolding grows out of attachment quality, a concept we will cover in chapter 3 in some detail. For now, know that a child in a *secure attachment* with a caregiver will feel confident to explore their environment, knowing that their caregiver "has their back." It is called a secure attachment because the child has the security of knowing that they are protected and watched over as they go about their activities. In the two-to-three-year-old set, you can see such a child playing with an occasional glance back to be sure their caregiver is in visual contact. The child also seemingly knows that if there is some danger, that person will step in to save them.

Scaffolding refers to parenting actions which support and let children develop skills and abilities in a way that is greater than would have happened if they were left on their own. Children respond well and thrive when they have parental encouragement in words and actions. Like the support apparatus built up around a building to allow the structure to be built, added to, or enhanced, parental scaffolding has similar results.

The educated parent is always on the lookout for information that can help as they guide, support, and nurture their children. As this book will repeat, the Internet, for good and for bad, will be the default source for most of the information that is readily available. But one must be careful.

Although sites like WebMD generally have accurate information, some of their content can be misleading. For example, during an April 2011 site visit, I came across a link to information about teens and puberty, specifically girls and their first menstrual cycles. The new web page was entitled "Expert discussions about girls' puberty." In small print under the title were these words: "The following is from our sponsor and includes WebMD user-generated content. The sponsor has sole editorial control."

It turned out that there were some good questions and answers about menstrual cramps and normal blood flows that a young teen might be truly concerned about. These were answered by a registered nurse expert and seemed accurate and thorough. However, this new web page was sponsored by Proctor & Gamble and its Always feminine pads. Always is a feminine hygiene product designed in different sizes to adapt to the user's menstrual flow. So reader beware—the topic was limited specifically to a Q&A directly related to what the sponsor wanted to sell you. You can argue that that was very convenient and helpful or you can argue that a less careful reader might believe that WebMD experts were recommending this specific product.

HOW PARENTS AND CHILDREN INFLUENCE EACH OTHER

Parenting, and all you do as a parent, is a set of interactive processes whereby you and your children react to each other and influence each other from the moment each child is born. It is important to remember that, although you will play a major role in how your child turns out, your child will change you as well. This is referred to as bi-directional influence in psychology circles. You can also refer to them as two-way or reciprocal effects. We will explore some of these influences in more detail in the chapter about temperament and attachment. Along with your parenting style, these factors will cause each family member to evolve and change over time.

In *The Educated Parent,* I reported on research done by Anne-Marie Ambert, who wrote a book detailing the many ways that parents shape their children and how children shape and change their parents. As I wrote then, "parents not only play a great role in influencing their children, but children influence and affect their parents. As you begin raising your children, you will be changed by them and how they react to you. Children affect their parents in multiple ways. Some parents will become stronger and better people as a result of their experiences. Other parents will be torn down and made weaker by the stresses and demands that their children bring to the family."

What do we know about these two-way effects? Let's begin with a review of Ambert's work and then add to what she had learned. One key summary finding of Ambert's research was that the more a child deviates negatively from what would be the expected normal ranges of personal characteristics (these being factors like your child's health status, intelligence level, personality traits and attachment quality, school performance, and general emotional and behavioral adjustment), the more a child's effect on the parents will be negative.

Ambert hypothesized and found data in support of the fact that the child who differs from how most children act violates parental expectations. In other words, *parents have a set of ideas and images of what raising their child will be like,* what their roles and activities will be, and how that child will be in the life of the parent and family. To the extent that a child does not develop or act as was expected, a parent is disappointed and/or disillusioned and/or frustrated. The greater the difference between what was expected, the more that different child affects the parent and his/her feelings of identity as a parent. Such a parent has to change his/her ideas (and possibly their dreams) of what their and their child's roles would and will be. This represents a major identity shift, and this kind of change is very difficult to accept. The result is that a parent takes on a more negative view of his or her self and/or the child.

One important way that children can impact their parents is based upon the child's temperament. This topic is explored fully in chapter 3, but allow me to share some of how this plays out next.

Ariel Knafo and Neta Galansky of Tel Aviv University have looked at "child–parent value transmission." In a 2008 research report focused on ways that children influence their parents' value systems, they proposed five primary processes of how this child influence could impact parents. Given their location and the population of the families in their study, the roles of migration, aging, and parent and child characteristics were important associated variables.

Drawing from developmental psychology theory, they proposed five influences that are typical in two-person relationships and extended these to account for how the children impacted their parents' values. The five ways of child-to-parent influence are:

- Passive child influences, causing change in parental values by the mere presence or development of children;
- Active child influences, due to children directly attempting to influence their parents' opinions or providing parents with relevant information;
- Differentiation, the emergence of a distinction between parents' own personal values and their socialization values;
- Reciprocal influences; in which parents' and children' influences are intertwined; and
- Counterinfluences, in which parental values change in a direction opposite to that of children's values.

On a much lighter note, yet still in a serious way, research by Claus Ebster, in Europe, examines another angle of child influence on parental behavior. Ebster and his team unobtrusively monitored 178 parents shopping with their children in Austrian supermarkets, after which the parents were interviewed. When asked how many products their children had made them buy, on average parents only reported half the number of purchases that had been secretly observed. As was pointed out in Ebster's article, much parent-child shopping is done and the amounts of money spent for unplanned purchases can add up quickly.

The researchers also investigated factors responsible for the number of purchase requests children make. It was found that children primarily request products that are placed at their eye level, such as sweets and toys strategically positioned by retailers on the lower shelves. The best way for parents to reduce the number of purchase requests from their child is to seat the child in the shopping cart (facing the parent) or in a stroller, thereby restricting the child's field of view.

Finally, parents are more likely to yield to a child's request if the product can be used or consumed in the store, such as toys, sweets, and fruit, as it keeps the child busy during the shopping trip and frees the parent from pesky begging and whining behaviors.

The researchers also had advice for children: Being nice and respectful paid off. Parents were much more willing to buy items if asked clearly and politely rather than when a child either got angry or demanded a product or asked for something in a passive way.

Some mothers were better prepared for their shopping trips, anticipating child boredom or later begging. These mothers indicated that they used preventive or preemptive strategies in the stores to control their children. These included giving their children something to hold, eat, or play with while shopping. This led to fewer problems or issues.

And so we have now reviewed a number of topics which form the foundation for good enough parenting behavior. In the next chapters we will build upon this groundwork for educated parents to enhance their skills and information base.

TWO

Parenting Skills for the 21st Century

The greatest wealth is health.

~Virgil

While we try to teach our children all about life, our children teach us what life is all about.

~Angela Schwindt

In this chapter we shall review topics devoted to parenting skills for the 21st century. This discussion will cover information related to wellness and optimal growth and development of your children and family. The subject choices are mine based on my reviews of what some people are writing and talking about, as well as trends that I believe will play out in the next 15–20 years. Some of these are "pendulum" items; that is, areas or topics that were once highlighted but then lost favor, and are now regaining parents' interest.

The ideas of wellness and preventive care should never go out of style. I see wellness—in some form or another—as a cornerstone of how Americans must face the healthcare crisis. If we focus on prevention and good, healthy habits, healthcare issues will be more manageable. If we don't, we will be bankrupt or rationing healthcare in unacceptable ways.

Another topic that is about to reemerge for parents is supervision, monitoring and micromanaging a child's life. In addition, the widespread availability of the Internet will play a role in all families—as a source of information as well as a basis for potential danger or harm. Validated Internet sites, those vetted by true experts, are already making parenting better by providing instantly accessible, accurate information. Sites like WebMD and sites sponsored by legitimate news sources such as *Newsweek* and *Time* magazines and established newspapers, as well as those sponsored/run by federal or state agencies, are typically vetted and responsible in their postings.

Other sections of this chapter will cover spirituality, once a highlight of the 1960s, and now reemerging in some sectors of society. I suspect it will be reemphasized in American families. As I use the term, I refer to a person's sense of purpose and meaning in the world. Although it can include religion-based content, my use of the term is more encompassing to include other intangible, abstract aspects of living related to what was once called a person's essence, soul, or spirit. A fuller definition appears later in this chapter.

My reasons for believing that spirituality will make a comeback include the popularity of the topic on the web and in newly released books. There are references to the link between spirituality and health and the role of our spiritual side in helping with stress management—all related to personal growth and wellness.

Finally, we will visit the topic of the many books on parenting, focusing on the so-called mommy books. In that discussion, we will also comment on the hotly debated topic of stay-at-home versus working moms—the "mommy wars."

HELICOPTER PARENTS AND TIGER MOMS

After a period of time in which parents, with busier adult lives of their own, tended to provide less monitoring for children and teens, other parents have stepped up to reverse that trend. Terms used to describe these parenting types include *helicopter parents* and *tiger moms*. We will explore how these modern parent styles have evolved and where they might go. *Helicopter parenting* is a term that describes parents who hover over their children (like a helicopter) and become too involved in their lives, fostering lack of responsibility and interfering with independence and autonomy. The term *helicopter parent* was coined by Charles Fay and Foster Cline, parenting book authors.

This over-involvement can lead to dependency issues in older children and teens. Later problems might include parental interference in high school or college matters, or parents going on job interviews *with* college graduate offspring. The trend has evolved in part due to parents being told through media portrayals that the world is dangerous and children need increased protection and security. And so, in defense, these parents decided to not let the world hurt or damage their offspring. In a sense this is a co-regulation problem (from chapter 1). Younger children certainly need this parental involvement, but as they enter their teens they need more opportunities to negotiate their world with less and less parental meddling or management.

The problem has expanded to not allowing older children and teens chances to learn independence and responsibility for personal actions. And it has evolved to include safeguarding children's environments to the extreme, or competing for kindergarten placements before a child is born.

Some observers, like social historian Barbara Dafoe Whitehead, make a distinction between over-parenting and helicoptering, the former being worse than the latter. "Over-parenting is not letting our kids take the consequences of their actions, swooping down to rescue them, and the result would be a spoiled brat. But helicopter parenting is entirely different, and I think it is a positive style of child-rearing." The outcome for children of helicopter parents is mixed. Some do turn out dependent and unable to make it in simple life situations without maternal directions and approval. But other studies show these teens grow up to be successful and engaged college students.

I found one study that reviewed results of four national projects in which parent involvement with their college student offspring was measured, followed by surveys with college representatives. In 2010, Patricia Somers identified five different types or styles of helicoptering behavior. Her qualitative work involved interviewing 190 academic and student affairs professionals at public, four-year universities around the country. The five types (with full descriptions to be found in the article) are named as follows:

1. Consumer advocate
2. Equity or fairness advocate
3. Vicarious college student
4. Toxic parents
5. Safety patrol parent

A *New York Times* article by Lisa Belkin nicely framed the issues and discussed one of the real problems with this style—parents becoming exhausted and unhappy trying to control their own life and the lives of their children. As this is written, it seems that helicoptering is near its peak and that parents have gotten the message to allow children some room to make their own decisions and mistakes, and to learn consequences the natural way.

Tiger moms are a different breed (pun intended). A national uproar ensued after the publication of a book—a parenting diary of sorts—by Amy Chua. One really needs to read her book, *Battle Hymn of the Tiger Mother,* to get the full picture, but allow me to summarize some key points. By definition, a tiger mom is a person using an extreme parenting regimen that includes drilled academic learning and demands hours of daily music practice. It involves high levels of control by the parent over the child, not in a helicopter way, but in a relentless, lofty set of expectations for achievement pursued through hard work.

The tiger mom parenting style has been described as both extreme and authoritarian. At the root of the conversation are several themes. Are Asian and Chinese parents better than American parents? Should American parents emulate their levels of expectation and demanding styles? Is American parenting too laid back, under-involved, and over-concerned with children's feelings rather than being results- and achievement-oriented? And does that explain some of the poor test scores our children earn, especially in comparison to Asian students?

Outrage erupted over several excerpted pieces of Chua's book, in which Chua described how she belittled one daughter, even calling her "garbage," and threatened to withhold food and bathroom breaks when her daughter didn't play the piano perfectly. In online commenting, she was labeled an abuser and a tyrant and plenty more names that I cannot print. Others were disturbed at Chua's reaction when her youngest child made her a birthday card which she rejected, telling her child that she expected and "deserved better than this."

Is this parenting style demeaning, rigid, and lacking in nurturing? And will it lead to negative child outcomes? There is no better answer than that which came from Chua's oldest daughter. She wrote the *New York Post* to give her side of the story in an open letter, defending her mom's über-rigid parenting style. She came off as a well-adjusted, capable young woman. And she showed great humor, writing that, "Every other Thursday, you take off our chains and let us play math games in the basement." In the open letter, her daughter listed reasons why she supports her mom's parenting, and concluded that her mother's strict rules made her a more independent adult. Her closing quote spoke volumes: "If I died tomorrow, I would die feeling I've lived my whole life at 110 percent. And for that, Tiger Mom, thank you."

WELLNESS—RAISING A HEALTHY CHILD IN A HEALTHY HOME

We now address several aspects of how parents can adopt wellness and wellness-related topics to provide a structure for raising a healthy child in a healthy home.

Wellness is kind of a catch-all word with multiple meanings. As I use it here, *wellness* refers to a lifestyle that includes parenting practices promoting the healthiest development of members of the household. These parenting practices include the parents serving as role models for appropriate behaviors and choices. The practices also refer to the choices that parents make in regard to how they interact with their children, so that the children learn in positive ways. All you do as a parent has an impact on the wellness of your family, for good or bad.

In *The Educated Parent,* the concept of a *wellness wheel* was used. We will use that model again with updates. One of the new twists on this model will be introducing parenting practices that promote prevention and early intervention.

According to the creator of the wellness wheel, Dr. Bill Hettler, wellness is an "active process through which people become aware of, and make choices toward, a more successful existence." Wellness is a state of total well-being; a lifelong journey, involving time and commitment, toward holistic health. Wellness is about creating a balance, and the wellness wheel allows us to picture how different aspects and features of health and wellness come together. The wheel is a good model—if all of the spokes or dimensions are functioning correctly, the wheel rolls along smoothly. If one of the spokes becomes frail or is no longer able to do its support role, the entire wheel will run off course. This unbalanced wheel can no longer do its job. The more damaged spokes, the more unbalanced and dysfunctional the whole wheel becomes.

So what makes up this wellness wheel and how can an educated parent use this model for a healthier family and family environment? Five spokes—emotional, physical, social, intellectual, and spiritual dimensions.

When one considers what an educated parent should try to accomplish in raising a child, working to shape and mold a well-rounded healthy person makes sense. In looking at wellness models for adults, it was easy to translate this approach to an interesting blueprint or recipe for themes in child development.

These also relate to a new development within the field of U.S. psychology—the positive psychology movement. Positive psychology looks specifically at human strengths and focuses research on ways we can use what we know about people to improve their situations. There is no reason why healthy, functional parenting should not include behaviors and information on playing to the strengths and adaptive abilities of children from the earliest times. Educated parents can apply this information to their own and their children's lives.

For families, the wellness wheel is designed with a hub at its center. The hub is what ties the spokes together and keeps the wheel functional. Let us consider these elements one at a time.

At the hub of the wellness wheel is the self. Specifically, what keeps a person balanced and feeling positive about him/herself are concepts like self-esteem, self-concept, self-efficacy, and body image. These are covered in the first edition of *The Educated Parent,* but I will redefine them briefly.

Self-esteem refers to how a child feels about him/herself. It is a self-judgment about whether an individual believes and feels that she/he is a good person. Self-esteem is an emotional concept, tied to feelings of self-worth.

Self-concept is how a child defines his/her identity. Self-concept would be found in the answer to the question of who one believes she/he is. Generally a child with a positive self-concept likes who she/he is and does, and has positive self-esteem as well.

Self-efficacy is related to the above. Self-efficacy is a belief in oneself that one can be successful and able to do what one needs to in the world. A child with self-efficacy takes responsibility for his/her actions. Self-efficacy allows a child the belief that she/he can achieve and succeed based upon his/her effort. Self-efficacy is the basis for motivation and persistence, especially when placed in a challenging situation.

Finally, *body image* refers to a person's view of his/her physical self. The first three aspects of the hub on our wellness wheel refer to psychological dimensions; body image is about one's physical features. Often body image is tied back to self-esteem.

These four aspects of the hub form the core of a person's sense of well-being. They are the foundation of a healthy, adjusted adult member of society. Let us now review the spokes.

The physical spoke is about keeping healthy and fit. When writing this chapter, I almost chose a quote from Meryl Streep as the opener: "It's bizarre that the produce manager is more important to my children's health than the pediatrician." The sentiment is right on because your child's everyday diet and nutrition will be way more important in the long run than the medical person you will need on the rare occasion of an illness. Your child's (and your) diet and exercise are under your control as parents. These are initiatives emphasized by the first lady, Michelle Obama, who has sponsored the "Let's Move" campaign. Its goal is to end the "challenge of childhood obesity within a generation so that children born today will reach adulthood at a healthy weight." The site (www.letsmove.gov) urges kids and families to get more exercise and to do simple things that make a difference such as cutting out sugary drinks and drinking healthier alternatives.

In the United States, we face real problems related to the amount of exercise children engage in. We live in a sedentary world. Healthy physical development requires exercise on a daily basis. Walking, swimming, running, jumping—just about any large muscle activity is good. This establishes an exercise mentality and is good for preventing later heart disease and other health problems like type 2 diabetes. Too many children do not get their recommended minimum hour per day of physical activity.

The National Football League sponsors PLAY 60, an initiative designed to encourage and inspire children to get 60 minutes of daily exercise and to eat a nutritionally sound diet. There is a website (http://www.nflrush.com/health) that has interactive modules and information for both parents and kids. And it is "way cool."

The physical spoke is also about teaching children hygiene and self-care skills like bathing, brushing teeth, and grooming. Also, safety habits like always using seat belts, helmets and knee pads, and proper skateboard or bicycle behavior are necessary for good physical health and accident prevention. Finally, good nutrition is a must. Parents need to carefully monitor their child's eating habits. Too many children are sugar-guzzling soda addicts or fast food aficionados. While okay in moderation, a constant diet of this food will lead to obesity and poor nutrition. Picky eaters can be changed, but you have to work at it.

The second spoke is the intellectual one. Children need exposure to enrichment activities and general cognitive stimulation. Starting with a colorful crib mobile and toys in infancy, and later reading to children regularly, parents will lay a foundation for their children becoming lifelong learners. The more one structures the home environment to being learning friendly, the more school will be a positive experience. Children should not be left to rot in front of TV sets. Older board games that require thinking and planning like Stratego or Clue, and then more sophisticated mental and creative challenges should be encouraged.

An equally important dimension in the intellectual spoke is allowing for creative expression. Coloring, finger paints, blocks, and Legos are all fun ways for children to exercise their developing brains. Other creative outlets like cooking and baking, gardening, crafts, and whatever you like should also be made available. These exercises are enjoyable, teach important skills, and can provide wonderful parent-child interaction.

We next explore *the mental/emotional spoke.* Mental/emotional activities are about teaching children to stay in control of themselves. These activities cultivate healthy coping skills and teach ways to react to both positive and negative situations. Parents must show children how to adjust emotional responses which can sometimes feel extreme. This process starts with babies who learn to soothe themselves at eight weeks when they are crying in their cribs, and carries on to learning how to deal with school friends who are mean.

Parents can assist their children in this spoke dimension by encouraging and rewarding positive attitudes and ignoring negative ones. Not allowing whining or not tolerating excessive sulking and negativity are important interpersonal-related skills. Children can learn to better handle frustration or delay gratification by how their parents treat them, and in what the parents allow or tolerate. Much recent data on emotional factors, the so-called EQ, suggest that this is a far more important dimension than has been previously recognized.

The fourth spoke is the social one. We are a social species, which requires us to interact with others. Learning how to treat others with respect is an essential lesson. Children should be involved along with their parents in service activities for others. Whether it is a visit to a nursing home, helping out at a religion-related or community facility, or learning to donate to others in need, children need regular exposure to these pro-social habits.

A parents' strong, loving marriage will provide a template for a child's later expectations and behavior in adult intimate relationships (shown in detail in chapters 1 and 3). Parents who respect one another and their children model excellent behaviors for their children. Finally, having humor in a household makes everything go better. The old cliché is true—smiling and laughter are nature's relationship builders. It is great to learn to laugh at oneself and to find humor in all sorts of situations. Certain family inside jokes are a great way of establishing lifelong bonds and memories. Many of these involve gaffes and gas.

The final spoke of the wellness wheel is the spiritual one. Of all the dimensions so far covered, I would guess that this is the least discussed by a great number of parents. The spiritual dimension is not just about organized religion, although that is the primary way most children in U.S. society are introduced to spirituality. In the wellness model, spirituality is also about having a sense of purpose, meaning, and direction in your life. All too often, a criticism of the current young generation (16–24 year olds) is that its members share a lack of direction or life motivation. Some critics are concerned that many in this generation are apparently in search of meaning, often settling for places where it is unlikely to be found—drug use, promiscuity, and risk taking.

The spiritual dimension is an important aspect of any whole and complete person. Parents who can model a spiritual side make it easier for children to acquire their own. Again, this is not just about religion or faith, it is about self-actualizing and becoming the best person you can be. This self-actualized person is in touch with their strengths and weaknesses, striving to become as close as can be to an idealized model of a good, complete person. We will return to this more fully at the end of this chapter.

All of these comments about the wellness wheel apply to both parents and children. A parent on the way to achieving balance and wellness will be a natural role model for his/her children. A parent who puts in the effort to live positively in these five areas will be in a better, healthier position to raise children who can also reach an overall state of health and well-being.

PREVENTION PRACTICES

Prevention refers to practices that can be applied to stop problems before they arise. The notion of prevention in psychology has decades of history. In the 1960s and 1970s, graduate programs were developed which taught future psychologists about the advantages of stopping disorders before they began. In a movement often called community psychology, these programs taught prevention programs divided into three points at which society could address problems—primary, secondary, and tertiary. Most of these practices are now carried out by public health officials. In these days of out of control healthcare costs, prevention can be a very valuable resource saver.

Primary prevention is best described as a psycho-educational outreach approach. Using information about any specific problem or disorder (like drunk driving, smoking, or depression), the program attempts to educate about the costs, risks, and consequences of poor choices. You give evidence and provide a rationale for doing the right thing and why that is good for the person. The receiver of these facts should become motivated to do something to prevent that problem. The next step is to provide alternative choices and other options so that the person can now alter their behavior in a more healthy way. In so doing, the person's new behavior choices should prevent the problem from arising in the first place.

This is the justification for public service announcements (PSAs) that target risky, dangerous behaviors. You should know that the success of these programs is variable. This in part is due to the fact that it is hard to measure how well something was prevented. In other words, how do you prove that you did something specific to make something else *not* happen? Maybe it would not have happened anyway, or maybe it did not happen because of some other reason other than your targeted efforts. This leads to a debate over what approaches really do reduce or eliminate behaviors, if any. And then it leads to questions of whether any funding should be used for such a program.

What we know in terms of establishing good, healthy behavior in children is that modeling is one of the best approaches. Children will act and try to act as the important, influential people in their lives act. So rather than just talk the talk, role models must walk the walk. How this applies to your parenting is by now probably obvious. One of the best ways you can practice primary prevention is to live and demonstrate the good behaviors. You can then follow this up with occasional chats about why you act as you do and why other behaviors are a bad idea.

Secondary and *tertiary prevention* refer to levels of trying to minimize damage and consequences. Secondary prevention focuses one's effort on identifying and treating problems as they first arise in order to limit the damage before it grows worse. In tertiary prevention, interventions or treatments are employed to reduce the negative impact of an already established problem or disorder by restoring abilities and reducing complications to the extent that is possible. Tertiary prevention is really a treatment approach designed to get the best response possible from the person.

For parenting, these levels of prevention would refer to identifying problem areas which have already resulted in undesired child outcomes. So perhaps parents are yelling too much at their child, or resorting to physical discipline, leading to more oppositional behavior or increased anxiety levels. Parents who can see this can then make efforts to change their behavior to a more positive approach. This prevents more serious problems from developing.

Prevention in families can happen on multiple levels. On a more global level, I refer to a family-based philosophy built upon choices for good nutrition, exercise, and other established wellness activities. Parents who exercise, who limit alcohol use, who do not smoke, and who eat sensible foods are living a lifestyle that their children are likely to adopt as well. Similarly, parents need to protect their children from undue levels of stress.

A team of researchers led by Tumaini Coker examined the association of recent family-related stressors with health-related quality of life (QOL) in fifth graders. The team first reported on the rates of stressful life events in their sample, finding that 24 percent of children had no reported recent major stressors. However, 33 percent had 1, 25 percent had 2, 12 percent had 3, and 6 percent had 4 or more major stress events.

The researchers found that quality of life indicators were lower for children with more stressors. As a result, children with more stressors had greater odds of impaired QOL compared with children without any reported family stressors. Psychosocial QOL indicators (e.g., social supports) fully mediated the relationship between stress levels and physical QOL. Parents should try to identify stresses and family-level needs and access community resources for support where available.

On this more specific level, aspects of parenting can determine where certain family members may be at risk. For those individuals, knowing that information allows an educated parent a chance to take specific actions and steps to nurture and guide their child in such a way as to prevent or minimize negative outcomes.

Parents who do not want their children to use tobacco products must be careful about what products they might use and what their expressed attitudes are about users. If you as a parent are concerned about drug abuse, you must be careful about how medications and medicines are stored and used in your house. What are the family attitudes toward illness and reliance on medications? These actions set a foundation for your children's attitudes and views.

If alcoholism or other drug dependence issues run in your family (i.e., you have family members known to your children with drug issues), your children are at risk. This risk has both hereditary and environmental roots. The same is true if obesity or food-related metabolic disorders (such as diabetes) are present in other family members. All of these costly and harmful disorders—tobacco, drug and alcohol addiction, food disorders—are preventable.

As a concrete example of a prevention practice with an at-risk child, let's review some things an educated parent can do if she/he sees that anxiety is an issue. (We will explore aspects of anxiety more fully in chapter 6.) If a family has a young child with an anxious temperament, that child is at risk of developing a far more serious teen- or adult-onset anxiety disorder. We know that many adult anxiety disorders can be traced back to very early ages in those individuals suffering from such disorders. What follows is a description of how psychologists tackle issues such as screening for at-risk children and preventing later disorders.

Clinical psychologist Brian Fisak has developed, with his associates, a promising screening and intervention plan for preschoolers at risk for developing anxiety disorders. His work is an example of how psychology is moving in the direction of wellness through prevention and early intervention.

A parent-based program to try to identify, prevent, and reduce anxiety levels in children would be important based on the evidence just discussed. Dr. Fisak speaks to at least three reasons to make his case: (1) Much pain and discomfort can be avoided if a child can be spared the effects of high levels of anxiety. At the same time, the child will be able to grow and develop in more healthy ways without the anxiety problems which would normally interfere with such development. (2) Identifying children prone to anxiety early in development (before first grade), allows psychologists a chance to give the child more flexibility in their behaviors and outcomes. One problem with anxiety-filled children is that their behavior becomes rigid, inflexible, and less open to change and the possible positive outcomes that therapy and interventions can bring. Dr. Fisak refers to these patterns as "treatment-resistant," meaning that they limit how well a child can benefit if started too late. (3) A parent prevention program, implemented through community-based agencies, can increase the number of children who might be served. One of the terrible realities in our society is that many of the most needy in our population are least connected to the services that could be life-changing for the good. His program has already been tested in typically underserved populations.

So you are now wondering what this program is and what it entails. Fisak calls it the Parent Resilience Program (PRP). Its best feature is that it offers early intervention and a chance to implement prevention practices at the very beginning of development when most needed. He has identified preschool as a good target age, since changes then would prevent many anxiety disorders first diagnosed in elementary school such as social phobias, separation anxiety, and school refusal.

In order to maximize the usefulness of the PRP, Fisak advises that some sort of screening system be employed so that families with at-risk children can be identified. (As the base rates are relatively low, it would be wasteful to apply this program to all parents of preschoolers.) So who is at risk? Children who were infants with shy and inhibited temperaments (covered in chapter 3). Research has shown that these infants are much more likely to develop into children and teens with anxiety disorders.

The PRP consists of eight sessions, with the psychologist working directly with the parents. They discuss and review anxiety-related behaviors and how to teach a child to reduce his/her anxiety and replace those feelings with more positive ones. Fisak's program employs what are called evidence-based interventions. This means that he teaches the parents already proven techniques, methods, and ways to help them to minimize anxiety levels and anxiety responses in their children. This includes changing parenting behavior that may inadvertently create or add to anxiety levels in a child, as well as to recognize and reduce family levels of stress that affect both parents and children.

This last point is an important one as well. Parents themselves must be able to live lives where their stress and anxiety levels do not overflow onto their children, especially those already at risk for anxiety problems. The PRP addresses parental issues and needs and the entire family should experience positive changes that will become self-reinforcing.

PARENT ADVOCACY FOR HEALTH AND WELLNESS

Educated parents must be advocates for their child(ren)'s health at all times. This means that as a parent it is important to keep up to date with health information that could impact your family. It also means that you as a parent have to be assertive at times and need to speak up and ask questions even if your medical provider seems too busy.

In my opinion, although we have a great healthcare system in the United States with many advances and breakthroughs, we also have a medical-industrial complex as part of the healthcare system's weaknesses. What I mean by this is that our healthcare system now has many dollars and much equipment invested, some redundant. These costs must be recouped, and it is the insured patient/family who most often pays the bills.

I assure you that this is a multilayered, complicated situation. When you then throw in defensive medical practices to reduce liability and lawsuits, many medical professionals feel the need to do every test that is insured, or to be sure their patients use the equipment that they own and need to make monthly payments for.

The result of this combination of equipment debt, lawsuit avoidance, and income issues has been that the health of patients is sometimes a seemingly secondary concern. For evidence, I will cite two examples. The first has to do with the number of emergency and other diagnostic scans involving radiation and children.

In a 2011 *Radiology* journal article, it was noted that the most common reasons for CT scans of children were head injuries, headaches, and abdominal pain. Rates of CT imaging have soared according to this report. Although CT scans are a great medical tool, they are also a leading cause of radiation exposure, and thus poisoning, in children. This matters because:

- Children's organs are more sensitive to radiation than those of adults.
- Children have longer life expectancies than adults, giving radiation-caused cancers a longer time to form and therefore future higher rates of cancers.
- Radiation settings often may not be set to match children's body size, leading to an overdose of radiation or certain unneeded overexposure.
- The greater number of CT scans brings higher lifetime doses of medical radiation due to overuse in young populations.

So what can an educated parent do? As cited on WebMD, it is recommended that parents talk with their doctors before they order any pediatric CT scan. You should ask about:

- Whether the scan will result in a clear medical benefit.
- Using the lowest amount of radiation based on the child's size.
- Scanning only the area of the body indicated by the child's symptoms.
- Avoiding multiple scans.
- Using alternative imaging techniques such as ultrasound or MRI.

My second example/"proof" of this problem relates to costs that burden family budgets and/or lead to millions of under- or un-insured children. In October 2009, a national survey by Jackson Healthcare reported on attitudes regarding the practice of medicine within the current healthcare environment. (Three thousand MDs completed an online survey and over 400 physicians completed phone surveys.) In their open-ended responses, "defensive medicine was an issue consistently offered by physicians as the primary problem driving healthcare costs. Survey participants reported that medically unnecessary diagnostic and treatment services were being ordered in an effort to avoid lawsuits."

Although this is a pro-physician website (take note of my fairness comment, attorneys), the data do reflect what many medical professionals believe. Assuming their estimates are accurate, between 650–850 billion dollars are spent each year due to "defensive, or lawsuit-driven, medicine." Such defensive medicine practices extend beyond wasted dollars to other consequences: (1) limiting access to care for high-risk patients; (2) over- and under-treating patients with life-threatening illnesses, and (3) fostering distrust among patients and their physicians, which has resulted in lowered physician morale and manpower." This last point will be a major issue; fewer new medical students want to practice general or family medicine or pediatrics or other lesser paying specialty areas. Although not specific to children's medical issues, the survey numbers also indicated overuse of diagnostic tests and lab tests as well as unneeded hospitalizations and prescription drug use.

I raise the issue because educated parents need to protect their families and play a role in shaping the healthcare debate and reforms that have come front and center for the 2010 decade. I urge that you become informed and involved.

PARENTS' ROLES IN DEVELOPING SPIRITUALITY AND THE SEARCH FOR MEANING IN LIFE

We now address the topic of spirituality, an area I believe will emerge as a premiere parenting topic over the next decade. I believe we will swing back from the excessive bling culture of the 2000s to simpler, less ostentatious ways. (Some of this will be driven by the lingering negative economic fallout.)

If one peruses through a bookstore or an online book site like Amazon. com, you will quickly see that titles covering spirituality are on the increase. Many are New Age-based, others look at the link between spirituality and health (nurses are particularly fond of this area), and even others are repackaged ways to discuss character building or emotional intelligence. There is also a movement toward bringing spirituality into family life and parenting/child rearing.

We must first try our hand at several definitions and distinctions used for this discussion. Most would agree that *religion* is a set of beliefs or doctrines that are divinely inspired. Religions usually have some rules or codes of conduct (like the Ten Commandments), and a number of rituals that provide an identity and keep the community together. Religion is based upon faith. Another tough concept, *faith* has been defined by Dean Borgman as a body of truths combined with an integration of implied values. These values are lived in a way consistent with a belief system. Dictionary.com defines faith as belief in God or in the doctrines or teachings of religion.

Spirituality has been defined by Borgman as a "self-transcendence in which self becomes embedded in something greater than self, including the sacred, leading to connectedness, meaning, purpose, and contribution." The World English Dictionary contains definitions related to the state or quality of being dedicated to God, religion, or spiritual things or values, especially as contrasted with material or temporal ones.

The definition I use in my research is based upon work done by Arthur Chickering, Jon Dalton, and Liesa Stamm. It includes the belief that spirituality is about discovering how to be fully human. They refer to a definition by Teasdale that says, "being spiritual suggests a personal commitment to a process of inner development that engages us in our totality." It is also a "way of life that affects and includes every moment of existence." It reflects a "search for ultimate meaning, direction and belonging." In shorthand, I define it as the search for meaning and purpose (and direction) in one's life. It is tied to our value systems. This implies that we have one. It is tied to character and integrity and authenticity.

We will use spirituality and spiritual development in this latter sense. For parents, it becomes an obligation to purposefully raise a child with a value system and a purpose and a direction. It is not mandating one or telling a child who she/he must be, but providing examples, guidance, and teaching in how to find the child's purpose and meaning in life.

Before returning to the spirituality development topic, I want to first write briefly about faith, organized religion, and religiosity in families. For some, spirituality is tied to faith and religion. James Fowler has proposed a faith development profile in his book *Stages of Faith*. He presents a framework and ideas for a lifespan explanation of a person's understanding of religion that is closely allied with the work of Jean Piaget and Erik Erikson. In his view, faith is a quality of the person, not of a system. It is an orientation of the total person giving purpose and direction to one's hopes, thoughts, and actions.

Fowler proposes six stages (seven if you count the "stage 0," prelanguage stage) which a person progresses through, tied to the person's level of cognitive development and understanding of the world. His theory goes on to track how an understanding and development of faith, linked to Piagetian and Eriksonian mileposts, progresses until one reaches a self-actualizing level. While very popular, this theory has not been validated through research. Rather it is a good guide to understand how a person develops in this area.

Let us now turn to some samples of research that have documented the effect of religious participation on child outcomes. Organized religion is the traditional American way to foster spirituality. Linda J. Waite and Evelyn L. Lehrer reviewed the effects of religion and religious participation on children in the context of families. Waite and Lehrer reviewed studies that have documented associations between religious participation and children's well-being. For example, research on differences in parenting styles by religious affiliation reveals that conservative Protestants display distinctive patterns: They place a greater emphasis on obedience and tend to view corporal punishment as an acceptable form of child discipline; at the same time, they are more likely to avoid yelling at children and are more prone to frequent praising and warm displays of affection. Other religious philosophies also impact parenting emphases in their unique ways.

Waite and Lehrer also reviewed research that found that family religious involvement promotes stronger ties among family members and has a positive impact on mothers' and children's reports of the quality of their relationship. Studies also document the effects of children's own religious participation, showing that young people who grow up having some religious involvement tend to display better outcomes in a number of areas as follows: a lower probability of substance abuse and juvenile delinquency; a lower incidence of depression in some groups; delayed sexual début; more positive attitudes toward marriage and having children; and more negative attitudes toward extramarital sex and premarital childbearing. In addition, Waite and Lehrer reported that "religious participation has also been associated with better educational outcomes" including the probability of obtaining a high school diploma.

In a related work, Jennifer M. Mellor and Beth A. Freeborn of the College of William and Mary used data from the National Longitudinal Study of Adolescent Health (AddHealth) to identify the effect of religious participation on smoking, binge drinking, and marijuana use in teens. Their research looked to these questions: Is it the case that religion directly reduces risky behaviors because churches provide youths with moral guidance or strong social networks that reinforce social norms? Or is it that both religious participation and risky health behaviors are determined by some "common unobserved individual trait?"

Their work replicated past findings to show that adolescents who attend religious services more frequently are less likely to smoke, binge drink, or use marijuana. Teens that lived in areas "where greater proportions of the population adhere to their own faith" had higher church attendance. Using this variable in statistically modified models of smoking, drinking, and drug use, they found evidence that religious participation has a significant negative effect on marijuana and other illicit drug use.

From these studies, it is clear that families with religious involvement can impact child outcomes in positive ways. My point here is to acquaint the educated parent with this work so that you may be informed as you organize your family's lifestyle. I see this as a way to promote spiritual development, but you are free to raise your child in this area through other means.

In their book *10 Principles of Spiritual Parenting: Nurturing Your Child's Soul,* authors Mimi Doe and Marsha F. Walch provide a number of strategies and tips for parents to develop their child's spiritual dimension in a nondenomination-based framework. Their chapter titles are a seeming mix of a religious flavored definition, with a hint of New Age affirmations and self-esteem enhancements. One sees a topic list that includes: Trust and Teach that All Life is Connected; Listen to Your Child; Allow and Encourage Dreams Wishes and Hopes; Add Magic to the Ordinary; and Make Each Day a New Beginning.

On the topic of life's connectedness, they offer specific activities such as involving children in gardening as a rewarding experience that can help them develop a sense of responsibility toward nature. They also suggest promoting quiet moments in order to allow children to listen to sounds of nature. This event is designed to motivate them to find joy in nature rather than technology. Similarly, having a child take care of a pet teaches kids to respect animal life and teaches them responsibilities toward other living beings.

Doe has written a second book, *Nurturing Your Teenager's Soul.* In this book she offers 10 principles for parents, extending her first work to specifically address teen issues. She writes that raising teens with a spiritual focus is "less about doing than being." For her, spiritual parenting involves listening to and honoring teens through coaching rather than controlling, communicating and interacting nonjudgmentally. She writes that a spiritual approach will "orient you to what is most important" and will "guide and ground" you in your child rearing.

Among her 10 principles are themes related to her first book, including support of dreams and understanding the interconnectedness of life. The book has many practical aspects and tips, including conversation starters for each topic, and a parent questionnaire to gauge where you are. At the end, she has provided a detailed list of resources for additional help and guidance.

Doe has developed a website and a system related to spiritual parenting. This site encourages the formation and regular meeting of parent groups, where parents can share and discuss ways to improve and target their parenting toward spiritual development of their children. Started in 2004, the system consists of a step-by-step, weekly set of meeting agendas and goals for the groups to follow. She also offers tips for finding members and different structures that groups can choose to follow. I offer this as an example, not an endorsement, of what is out there for the educated parent looking for ways to promote spiritual development in their children.

In a *Suite 101* online article, Thais Campos offers ways to nurture spirituality and enhance spiritual development in children based upon the Doe and Walch book as well as the work of Robert Coles. In accordance with many writers in this area, her first suggestion is tied to exposure to nature, where children can learn about the connectedness of living things. She offers a specific how-to, which can be comforting when trying to decide how to implement these ideas.

Campos also urges that parents be better listeners. Her recommendation to "take time out of each day to hear about a child's joys, achievements and frustrations" is of value as a general good parenting practice. Her how-to includes question prompts related to talks about things your child is thankful for, feels sorry for, and intends for tomorrow. Campos suggests nurturing and developing spiritual development through another communication exercise—the sharing of dreams and wishes. When parents do this, they help a child set goals and a life direction. These are both basic elements of a spirituality-based life.

While all of this is interesting (to me at least), and I can certainly find no harm in it, there is no research of which I am aware that can show a link between these parenting practices or philosophies and a child's level of spirituality. They appear to have face validity; that is, they look like they should lead to spiritual-based learning. At the least, these tasks and doings can bring a child and parent together to explore and talk.

So let me report on a group that has brought a scientific, research-based perspective to the area of spiritual development. I would like to inform the educated parent about a Minneapolis group called the Search Institute. From their website:

> Search Institute® is an independent, nonprofit, nonsectarian organization committed to helping create healthy communities for every young person. Because we believe that "all kids are our kids," we create books and other materials that welcome and respect people of all races, ethnicities, cultures, genders, religions, economic backgrounds, sexual orientations, and abilities.

The Search Institute is devoted to "positive child and adolescent human development." It is within this context that I discuss its role as an agent of spiritual development. This group's research arm (The Center for Spiritual Development in Childhood and Adolescence) produced a multinational survey report with responses from over 7,000 teens and young adults from 13 countries. Released in 2008, the study was designed to provide "one of the first snapshots of spiritual development across multiple countries and traditions."

The interested reader can access the report online; I have provided the website address at the end of the chapter. Allow me to summarize some central findings relevant to our presentation. (The executive summary presents the eight key findings in a concise way.) From around the world, youths define spirituality using phrases such as "believing there is a purpose to life," "believing in God," or "being true to one's inner self."

According to this study, there are very different levels of belief in personal spirituality that are culture-based. Youth from the United States and Thailand ranked highest; those from Australia the lowest. As the respondents have grown, many ($^2/_3$) report "they have more of a sense that life has meaning or purpose" while also reporting they have had growing doubts or concerns about spiritual and religious issues. The survey respondents knew there was a difference between spirituality and religion, and both were viewed in a positive manner. Other details are also reported.

Dean Feldmeyer and Eugene C. Roehkepartain of the Search Institute have worked for many years in the field of development of spirituality in youth. They are authors of an online resource entitled "The Benefits of an Asset-Building Approach to Parenting," in which they discuss the use of an assessment tool for children and teens. Much of the Search Institute's work is available at little or no cost, and online, as long you register with the group.

I call the educated parent's attention to a checklist that has been developed as a quick and dirty measure of strengths that a child possesses (available online at: http://www.search-institute.org/developmental-assets/ lists). From this strength or asset list, one can build upon where the child has certain skills, attitudes, or abilities, and one can also see where further development may be indicated. By building on existing assets and helping to develop those not present, a parent has a guide for character building and spiritual development in his or her child.

As the authors point out, the asset list "offers some basic goals against which to make decisions and shape family life." Asset building, they argue, "can help parents be intentional about their choices, knowing that what they do can have a tremendously positive impact in shaping their children's lives."

For parents, they list the benefits that can be had in employing this approach. These include helping parents to more easily determine areas in need of child rearing help; it can provide a way for parents to stay involved and engaged with their teens' lives; it focuses on positive aspects of the child and the parenting needed; and in a community committed to their approach, it provides a supportive structure and network for success.

OTHER ISSUES FOR 21st-CENTURY PARENTS

In this final section, I wish to highlight several examples of what seems like hundreds of books for parents that address a key issue for 21st-century parents—working moms. As a group these are called "mommy books," as they address women trying to balance parenting and career responsibilities. There is no apparent shortage of writers who want to weigh in on this topic.

These books are related to the stay-at-home mom versus working/career mom issue—the "mommy wars"—still playing out in the 2010 decade. Read on for a sampling of some current books. I end with two samples of books that address the mommy war questions, and a peace offer.

In her book titled *Mojo Mom: Nurturing Your Self While Raising a Family,* Amy Tiemann writes about the transition to motherhood. She specifically took on the challenge of how to find one's personal identity as a mother and person. She recounts her own transition from college student and new PhD to becoming a mother and redefining her place in the world. These are significant shifts in identity and self-perception. She refers to her new identity as a mojo mom, a person who has her mojo back in the complete feminist sense of being able to have it all. (Tiemann defines *mojo* as energy, the energy that recharges bodies and renews spirits.)

She defines *mommy mojo* as "the feeling you get when you are at the top of your game, juggling the many faces of your life and keeping your own needs in balance with family needs." Her book discusses a number of practical ideas and tips for moms who need encouragement and help in negotiating a rebirth or reinvention of who you are after becoming a parent.

There are chapters dealing with how to get through the first years of parenting, juggling the family-career demands, and dealing with guilt that can arise when choosing between stay-at-home versus working mom pathways. She also discusses ways to keep your marriage strong, including ways that both spouses can learn their new identities as spouses and parents. She refers to fathers as *mojo partners* as they can play important roles in your further personal development. The book is an easy read and is recommended for the educated parent as a good starting point for personal reflection.

Cathy Greenberg and Barrett Avigdor, in their 2009 book *What Happy Working Mothers Know: How New Findings in Positive Psychology Can Lead to a Healthy and Happy Work/Life Balance,* have applied aspects of positive psychology to the needs of working mothers. This book is specifically for working mothers, and the authors try to show ways they can make the work-life balance happen. The authors also emphasize the need to put guilt feelings aside, teaching tips and strategies to help working mothers achieve this goal. (Greenberg has a PhD in behavioral sciences and runs a leadership consulting business based on the premise Happiness = Profit. Avigdor is a certified career coach and Director of Legal Talent Strategy at Accenture, a global management consulting company.)

I have chosen to mention this book because it reads like a business workshop, with many practical tips and case studies, vignettes and short stories told to illustrate the points. Greenberg and Avigdor define what a good mother is by surveying hundreds of working mothers. They choose a definition by Michele Borba, another mommy book author, who says that, " 'Real' mothers are those who are true to their own values and who do the powerful and simple things to raise children who are confident, self-sufficient, and joyful." Such mothers have found their own happiness, which they use to bring happiness and joy into their own families and homes.

The book, ultimately, is about taking a positive view of what your life is about. It emphasizes the need to keep things in perspective using positive psychology principles. Throughout the book, the authors suggest practical ways to tweak your working life and your home life to make everything fit together in a way that you feel less guilty and more fulfilled.

As an example, one chapter is entitled "How to Put the H.A.P.P.Y. in Happy Working Mother." HAPPY is an acronym with tips related to each letter prompt. The chapter then gives life coaching tips on everything from diet, exercise, and sleep, to ways to create happy months and become forgiving of yourself when you fall short of your goals.

Another example is an exercise recommended to be done twice per year with your children. Ask them what they love to do—at school, at home, and with their family and friends. Listen to their answers and look for patterns that allow you to learn your children's strengths. You can then build on these and help them gain happiness and success. In my opinion, this type of exercise should work on many levels as well. It is a time for communication about important topics, it can be a bonding moment for parent and child, and it can start a discussion that can lead to many other areas that need to be talked out.

In another book that uses the word happy, *Happy at Work, Happy at Home,* Caitlin Friedman and Kimberly Yorio provide a different presentation, but a similar message as Greenberg and Avidor. Their book is clearly geared to career/working moms, starting with a chapter about telling your boss you are pregnant and going through the many other challenges that splitting time as a mother and an employee brings about. This book is filled with stories and practical tips for all sorts of scenarios.

There are a number of embedded interviews with working moms that provide questions and answers from women with differing situations and problems. This extends to interviewing a latchkey kid to get his perspective on how his life was affected by having a working mother. There are also handy lists such as "10 things you should do at home to make your life easier." That list suggests items such as planning meals in advance, prepping for the morning at night and for the night in the morning, and using leftovers for snacks and lunches.

Just about every scenario is at least mentioned, from breastfeeding tips to learning to say "no" more often to avoiding the trap of seeking perfection. At the end, Friedman and Yorio warn women to aim for harmony rather than to be a juggler of responsibilities. Ultimately, their book seeks to give "the tools and inspiration" that a working mother needs to be "capable, confident and fulfilled." At the end is a resource section with career and financial advice sections and support and social networking information.

Leslie Bennetts has also entered the mommy book arena and the so-called mommy wars with her book, The Feminine Mistake. In this book, which I mention as a good example of the amount of division and incivility the mommy wars can stir up, her major point is that women need to be careful not to be too dependent on men/fathers. Writing about interviews with women from a wide range of backgrounds, Bennetts tells their stories, always underscoring the point that arguments calling for women to be stay-at-home moms do not consider the adult benefits of work and the price of giving it up. In fact, she argues that working moms may have better physical health, higher self-esteem, and increased emotional health.

Author Susan Faludi wrote of Bennetts' book, "With good sense, hard facts, ample wit, and compelling urgency, Leslie Bennetts delivers an incontrovertible argument for economic self-sufficiency as the fundament of women's well-being. *The Feminine Mistake* should be required reading for all young women, and a lot of older ones, too."

In a March 2007 online post, Bennetts addressed the "avalanche of blistering attacks by women who hadn't read my book but couldn't wait to condemn it." She writes "most stay-at-home wives are likely to face major hardships as a result of divorce, widowhood, a spouse's unemployment or illness, or any number of other challenges." Women who become financially dependent on their husbands "often look back on that decision as the biggest mistake of their lives—even women in stable, enduring marriages."

Miriam Peskowitz has also written about the mommy wars. In her 2005 book *The Truth Behind the Mommy Wars: Who Decides What Makes a Good Mother?*, Peskowitz asserts that the mommy wars are more of a media creation than a reality. Her book recounts two *Dr. Phil* TV episodes where two women were pitted against each other and egged on for most of the show. Before the episodes ended, there was some agreement and shared, common values.

Peskowitz, a trained historian, reports on different types of mothers and choices available to women. From her view, mothers and women have far more in common than media portrayals would suggest. She discusses how nearly a third of women are part-time employees who bridge any divide that a mommy war calls for. She sees this statistic and other data as proof that women really need and want options, not a forced choice to be one type of mother or the other.

Her book is recommended because it asks questions that women need to discuss. How are career choices made, and what flexibility is there for women to transition in and out of the workplace? She wonders why it is often hard for professional women to arrange daycare when attending conferences as an example that she has faced. She covers issues such as the stereotyping of women that goes on and how marketing and political manipulation (e.g., soccer moms or security moms) can pressure mothers.

I was able to find an online post in which Peskowitz made some suggestions for moving beyond the mommy wars and "making life easier for all moms." These include believing in yourself and the choices you make. Do what is authentic for you and your family situation and ignore comments from others. She urges women to be supportive and nonjudgmental of each other. There is much to be learned from each other and through social supports, she says.

Her final tips to end the mommy wars are to ignore media stories—on TV, in magazines, or online. "Don't take the bait," she urges. Finally, she suggests that all moms get together for socializing. Says Peskowitz, "getting to know other women is the number one best antidote to the Mommy Wars."

And so we close with this peace offer. Parenting—for mothers and fathers—requires your commitment to raising your child the best way possible. If you must be a two-career family or you are a working single mother, you have to play the cards dealt to you. Ignore the mommy war debates and focus on a lifestyle and parenting plan that best supports your family.

THREE

Temperament, Attachment, and Parenting Style: The Developmental Triad

Don't worry that children never listen to you; worry that they are always watching you.

~Robert Fulghum

If you want children to keep their feet on the ground, put some responsibility on their shoulders.

~Abigail Van Buren

In this chapter we will review the three major areas that child development and parenting experts know will have the strongest influences on how your child will turn out. While there are hundreds or thousands of variables that come together to fully explain how and why a child becomes the adult she/he becomes, many of those variables are a subset of the three we will now discuss. The threesome of developmental variables in this chapter are among the major influences identified over years of research. The following represents the bottom-line findings for your consideration and review as an educated parent.

Ultimately, the interplay of three factors—each a complex and multipart thing—seems to establish much of how your child will turn out, a grouping called the *child developmental triad.* These are: the child's *temperament, attachment quality,* and the *style of parenting* she/he receives.

Some people, especially college students, find this information dry and technical, or even boring. I see it as the secret to understanding your child. I find this area of research like getting inside information that gives a parent an edge and a direction to do the right thing. No matter your opinion, this stuff is golden and you need to know about it.

WHY TEMPERAMENT IS IMPORTANT AND HOW IT AFFECTS YOUR ABILITY TO PARENT

Let us begin with temperament. For psychologists, *temperament* has a precise definition. It is a rich concept which includes how you react to the outside world, or your constitution, and it serves as a foundation and starting point for your adult personality. A good synonym would be your disposition. Most child psychologists agree that temperament has four qualities:

- It is objectively definable.
- It has a biological basis.
- It is measurable in infancy.
- It remains relatively stable across development.

Your temperament is your inborn predisposition to how you will react and interact with other people, situations in your life, and events. For a parent, a child's temperament will be the "default setting" with which a new son or daughter will enter the world. This means that your child's temperament is like a factory setting for how your baby and then child will behave and act in this world.

The educated parent needs to respect this and should adjust his/her parenting behavior and expectations around what his/her child brings to the family situation. Trying to change these initial settings is not easy, though not impossible. More on this aspect will be presented later.

Temperament has been investigated in different ways. We will review three models—the New York Longitudinal Study (NYLS), the more recent work of behavioral geneticist Robert Plomin and his associates, and contributions from Jerome Kagan.

The NYLS was one of the first systematic research attempts to define and study temperament over the life of individuals. Details of this were presented in *The Educated Parent* and will not be repeated here. For our needs, know that the NYLS group derived three overall temperament classifications (easy, difficult, and slow to warm) based upon assessment in nine categories.

Easy babies are those whose temperament makes them ready to manage, children who seem to quickly adapt to their parents and caregivers. These babies easily handle new experiences and quickly develop eating, sleeping, and elimination schedules which make them predictable. Such a child is predominantly positive in mood and has mild to moderate mood intensity levels. Their frustration tolerance is age appropriate. Roughly *40 percent* of the children followed were classified as easy. As I like to say, a mother and father who are blessed with an easy child are ready to have a dozen more as this is as good as it gets.

Difficult babies have a temperament style that makes raising them more difficult and challenging for their parents. These babies may resist cuddling, may be colicky (negative mood), may not tolerate any deviations from their daily schedules, and are more difficult to predict. These children exhibit behaviors that can make a parent feel inadequate and unprepared since the parents' perception is that the parents cannot soothe or take care of their baby properly. These children have high activity levels (they're squirmy), adjust slowly and with difficulty to change, and are likely to throw tantrums when frustrated. About *10 percent* of children are identified as difficult. If you have a difficult baby first, it may be the case that you will strongly consider the only child family model.

Slow-to-warm babies are a bit in the middle. They have some traits of the easy child and some of the difficult. In general, they have low activity level, mildly negative reactions to new stimuli, display a low intensity of mood, and will eventually like and accept new situations only after repeated opportunities and on their own timetable. Most parents would call their slow-to-warm child "shy." *Fifteen percent* of the NYLS children were classified as slow to warm.

The math doesn't add up since some children exhibited qualities that did not allow them to fall in one category as first defined by the researchers. (A later set of criteria allowed for almost total categorization—60 percent were typed as easy, 15 percent as difficult, and 23 percent as slow to warm.)

The NYLS group was also one of the first to demonstrate that temperament is a *trait variable*; that is, a stable characteristic that tends to hold up over time and across different situations. Many other studies have confirmed this significant finding. This is important to know because it says this is who your child is and how they behave. And it allows you as a parent to begin to make some decisions about how to raise your child and what parenting techniques will work best, or which will lead to problems and clashes. It also allows you to predict possible trouble spots which you can then attempt to change to make your child's life a bit easier.

The NYLS group also discovered the importance of matching parenting behavior to the child's temperament, and revealed that parenting may be one of the few jobs where previous experience may not count for much if you are raising two children who differ in temperament. Simply put, what worked for child number one may not apply to child number two.

Parents need to match how they parent with the temperament of the child they are raising. You have to find a style that works best for who your child is and what she/he brings to the parent-child relationship.

Psychologists use the concept of *goodness of fit* (coined by the NYLS group) to describe the level of match between children's temperaments and their social context, primarily the style of parenting they receive in their early years. A harmonious fit, where the parenting techniques and expectations match up with the child's temperament characteristics, leads to the best outcome. Therefore, parents have to be aware of and sensitive to what the child brings to the family and then coordinate the techniques and ways they raise the child to take advantage of the best way to shape the child as she/he grows. *This is precisely why this information is important—your child's temperament clues you in to how to do the best job of parenting.*

Robert Plomin and A. H. Buss created a second system to classify temperament. Their work is called the EAS model, where E stands for emotionality, A stands for activity level, and S stands for sociability. These variables overlap with the NYLS findings. The *emotionality* variable is a measure of the intensity of emotional reactions, much like the NYLS reaction intensity variable. This can be rated from the low end of little display of emotion (a kind of stoicism) to very intense, overblown reactions far out of measure to what the situation calls for.

Activity level refers to the child's natural level of physical energy. There is a range of natural activity level in people from hyperactivity on one end to hypoactivity (or underactivity) on the other. Five different measures of activity were looked at by Plomin, including one called the reaction to "enforced idleness." This last factor looked at the child's response when forced to sit or be still—how did the child handle restlessness and built up energy? As you know, some children just simply cannot be expected to stay still. Plomin's work helps to show that expecting that from certain children is not only unreasonable but a waste of time.

Finally, *sociability* refers to whether a child is outgoing and people-friendly or more shy and reserved. It has its roots in the personality traits of extraversion and introversion. This refers to whether a person prefers to be with people or to operate alone. Plomin also looked at choice (preference to play alone or with others), direction (moves toward or away from others), and restriction (what did the child do when isolated?) in social settings.

Like the NYLS, Plomin "emphasizes matches and mismatches between the child and its environment, especially between the child and its parents" (Buss and Plomin 1986, p. 156). Plomin's work emphasizes the hereditary bases of temperament, while also inviting looking into the ways environmental factors interact with and impact these inborn predispositions.

A third system proposed by Jerome Kagan and his colleagues relied on direct observations. They characterized infants along a dimension they termed inhibited-uninhibited. Inhibited children exhibited shyness, timidity, and wariness of the unfamiliar, and uninhibited children exhibited less restraint with regard to the unfamiliar and little trepidation. About 15–20 percent of children could be described as inhibited. Their temperament produced a high level of physiological reactivity; when faced with unfamiliar things, these children reacted by showing increased heart rates and a high level of arousal in areas of the brain linked to emotional responses. These same factors are highly correlated with what observers would call shy children by age four or five.

In a study using the inhibited temperament variable, Michele Volbrecht and H. Hill Goldsmith followed 242 twins (135 girls, 107 boys) in a longitudinal design. They looked at variables called "behavioral inhibition" and "inhibitory control" in children three years of age, as well as other family process variables, to see if they were predictors of shyness and anxiety symptoms approximately four years later. Even when controlling for family stress levels, inhibited temperament predicted shyness during middle childhood. Anxiety symptoms in middle childhood were predicted by behavioral inhibition levels, early negative family emotional variables, and family stress. Volbrecht and Goldsmith concluded that their study findings clarified "the relative importance of temperament and family factors in the development of both shyness and anxiety symptoms during childhood."

Evidence from this and other research suggests that these temperament characteristics remain stable over time and may have a genetic base. Current research shows that children who exhibit an inhibited temperament in their second year of life are more likely to develop problems with anxiety during adolescence.

Many studies have now found that how your child behaves in his/her younger years can be a clue as to what you need to teach him/her in order to overcome inborn tendencies that could cause them later trouble.

Inhibited-typed children have been shown to become overcontrolled, cautious, and nonassertive adults. Also, the children with easy type temperament qualities (termed well-adjusted or confident types) continued to express these positive and adaptive traits as they entered adolescence, making their lives a bit easier and a lot more trouble-free. The inhibited-type child could probably benefit from parenting that encourages spontaneity and flexibility while minimizing a child's tendencies toward passivity.

How exactly is temperament, with all of its social implications, biologically influenced? The best, though limited, explanation that science has is related to brain wiring, where each brain is set up to have tendencies in the manner it will respond to both internal and external events. Different brain wirings lead to people who are more or less sensitive to events. Then, no matter the biological predisposition, the child will have a unique environment in which to grow. The combination of the nature and nurture variables determines the outcome.

Let's consider some examples. For one child who is an over-responder, any time something happens she/he will likely have a high emotional response. This could be overjoy at the positive or big crying fits at the negative. Another child may have a high activity response—hyperactivity and great energy in reaction to an event. This child is wired to be this way through a combination of genetic and other biological factors. Certain environmental training can help such a child to gain more control and be more measured in his/her responses. However, the child's *tendency* will always be toward an exaggerated response.

Will a person always be a certain way based upon temperament? Yes, in terms of predisposition and natural inclination. However, such a child is not doomed to a predetermined fate or unable to change. But to change, this child (and eventual adult) will need to work hard at trying to fight nature, so to speak. So an over-responder can learn to temper his/her response so that she/he can stay in the middle more and not be all over the place emotionally or in activity level.

So what does this stuff have to do with parenting? Psychologists Ann Sanson and Mary Rothbart suggest that *at least three important messages for parents have emerged from the body of temperament studies.* First, they believe that each child must have attention and respect paid to his/her individuality. Parents must try their best to be sensitive and flexible in their approach to their child. By sensitivity, it is meant that the parent be a good observer of the signs and signals that the child presents through his/her behavior. As previously mentioned, having parented one child well may not prepare you for the best way to rear the second or third child, even in the same family with the same two parents.

For example, a crying, colicky baby is set up to have less interaction with a parent over time due to his/her irritable behavior. Crying babies inadvertently create a negative experience for their parents' future interactions with them. This leads to less parental contact, which may cause further negative behavior by the infant who wants contact, but is expressing it through crying. The extra crying leads to even less parental contact time.

All of this goes on without being noticed by the people in the middle of it. This is not a criticism of the parent or the infant. I raise the point to illustrate one of the many subtle ways an infant's temperament has a direct effect on parenting behavior and how the parents' changed behavior then influences the child in return. These reciprocal effects then affect other aspects of behavior and development.

A second conclusion reached by Sanson and Rothbart is that parents need to carefully think about how they will structure the child's environment and regulate the events of the child's life as these factors relate to the child's temperament style. For example, a difficult child who is more agitated and bothered by noise and light due to an inborn oversensitivity to stimuli needs a quieter, less busy space than a child of easy temperament. Putting a child in an environment that is overstimulating stresses the child and leads to behavior and responses which you may not want to develop.

A slow-to-warm, shy child may need more time and reassurance when exposed to a new situation like placement into daycare. For example, such a child may need to have a parent with him/her for decreasing amounts of time over several days before being left alone or left for a half or full day of daycare supervision. Making that child's new experience less stressful and more manageable, a transition in increments reflects the educated parent's sensitivity to the child's needs.

The final point raised by Sanson and Rothbart is that parents have much to gain if informed about how temperament shapes their child's behavior and how understanding their child's behavior can make raising the child easier or harder. Books and parenting programs designed to help parents identify their child's type and then tailor their child rearing behavior to maximize a good fit are available in most cities. Most are centered on the challenges of raising difficult-temperamented children. This is a good thing as some research has also shown that these children face a higher chance of being abused. However, if you want to learn more about a slow-to-warm or easy child, ask around or search your bookstore or library.

Even having reviewed all this information, I must caution that no reader walks away with the conclusion that difficult-temperamented children are bad or unworthy or not worth the effort. Nothing could be further from the truth. In fact, any child can be a handful if not raised properly. And even properly raised children don't always turn out as hoped for. If you have a difficult-temperamented child, you can be quite successful as a parent and your child can become an adjusted, competent, functioning adult. Knowing what to expect and how to deal with any temperament makes the educated parent more successful and the child better off.

WHAT ATTACHMENT IS AND WHY IT IS IMPORTANT

In this section, we will review the second part of the child development triad—attachment style. You will learn why some children can form relationships easily and be good friends and peers, and why others may have difficulties. More important, what happens in your child's first years in the area of attachment will have effects that last all through his/her life.

Attachment is defined as the strong affectional ties that bond an infant with his/her caregiver(s). John Bowlby observed, among his many findings, that people, especially young children, take comfort in being with another person (the caregiver) in times of stress, uncertainty, or difficulty. The word *bonding* comes closest to capturing the essence of what Bowlby described. The other major figure in this area of research, Mary Ainsworth, further discussed ways and levels of patterns of attachment and devised a technique to measure these.

Rudolph Schaffer and Peggy Emerson first followed the development of attachment behavior in infants through their first 18 months in research in the 1960s. They found that in the first six weeks, infants are primarily asocial. They are very limited in their ability to discriminate or respond to social versus nonsocial stimuli. Then, from the age of about six weeks though seven months or so (all of these timeframes are approximate), infants will smile at most anyone or thing with a face that approaches them. This could include a loving mother, a Raggedy Ann doll, or a stranger. They will then protest when they are put down or attention is shifted away from them.

Then between seven and nine months, a specific attachment or set of specific attachments forms. Now the child becomes rather picky in whom she/he chooses to be social with and accepting of. The mother is usually the first attachment object, but the child can also attach to the daycare worker whom the child knows and trusts. This child will now exhibit a behavior known as *stranger anxiety* or *stranger wariness* in the presence of unfamiliar faces.

By the first year of life, children make these first genuine attachments and form the foundation for later attachment and future relationships. After this first specific attachment is formed, the child will begin over time to form multiple attachments with other regularly seen people such as fathers, siblings, or a frequently employed babysitter. This development indicates that human infants are born to be social and be in relationships with others. They need and want to be connected to others in their lives. It is important that parents be there to make these attachments real.

Schaffer and Emerson demonstrated that the two key behaviors to set up attachment were the level of maternal responsivity and the total amount of stimulation provided by the mother. A mom who was predictable in her response to the infant's call for attention and interaction, and the mom who was there to play and sing and cuddle with, was the mom who had the closest level of attachment behavior. (Given the time of the research, most of this literature is mother-dominated.)

John Bowlby made the case that attachment makes sense as a way for nature to ensure that mothers (or any caregiver) and infants both get their needs met. For the infant, the needs are obvious—feeding, care, and protection. For the mother, the needs are less physical, but include a psychological well-being in feeling needed and wanted, as well as a feature of the infant that is irresistible to mothers. Bowlby, and others such as Konrad Lorenz (of the famous imprinting studies with ducklings), further believed that human adults had built-in responses to all immature organisms. These perceptions bring about automatic responses of caring and positive approach behaviors. Known by some as the "Kewpie doll effect," it has been shown that normal adults will favorably respond to infant-like features.

This is certainly true about a big-eyed, loveable baby, whose head size is ¼ of its total length, as opposed to the final outcome as an adult when the proportion becomes ⅙. It is equally true when we see a puppy or kitten, which, in their immature physical states, have a larger head to total body length ratio (not to mention big ears and eyes, and fluffy, soft fur). As a result, puppies and kittens also bring out positive, irresistible caregiving responses. This feature invites protection from harm, and it is useful to any immature animal to have adults predisposed to care for it. This is the survival benefit.

Additionally, babies come into the world with cuteness. Their reflexive, inborn smiling behavior, their cooing and gurgling, their sucking and grasping reflexes—all of these give the infant an endearing quality. The perception in the mother is that the baby is happy to be with her and loves her. No one knows for sure what the baby really thinks about all this.

Other features and characteristics help with the attachment process as well. Babies are born with a reflexive smile that occurs when the baby looks at other people. These other people, especially mothers, believe the behavior is purposeful and directed at them. Again, there is no way to know when a newborn's smile is on purpose. But we know that early smiles are reflexes which occur in response to the right stimulus. In any event, the smile captures the mother and the baby is more likely to be taken care of. It is also true that when babies breastfeed, their faces are about nine inches or so from their mothers' faces. Ethologists point out that it is no coincidence that a baby's undeveloped visual system works best when trying to look at objects that are about 8–10 inches away. Evolutionary psychologists see this as a plan to allow babies to immediately focus in and make face recognition memories of their mother. Clearly, this early visual ability sets up a process of interactions that leads to attachment patterns over the next months.

To tie this together, Bowlby's premise was that both infant and mother were biologically (again, read instinctually) prepared to join in an inborn, built-in interactive dance. Their behaviors go both ways, each prompting the other to bring out more behavior to bring them closer together. The cute baby brings about nurturing behaviors and feelings of warmth in the mother. The mother's nurturing behavior in turn cues the baby to smile and coo, which leads to more intense mothering. This is followed by more cute baby responses. In this way, the mom is now hooked—she will not only take good care of this baby, she will lay down her life for him/her.

Bowlby's account also emphasized that the infant plays an active role in the attachment process. This finding suggests that attachment is very important to establish. If one believes that certain behaviors are determined for survival, this all makes sense. And there is a timeframe for this process and consequences for what will happen if you miss the window.

The concept of a specific timeframe for these interactions is called a *sensitive period.* If you miss this window, a secure attachment would not be as likely after that time. With the sensitive period hypothesis, we know that the first three to four years are of prime importance, but there are still opportunities (although more limited as time goes on) for a secure attachment to develop after that. Over time, the cues and responses involved in attachment diminish. The early years are essential for a secure attachment.

Why does this matter? When you were feeling those warm, fuzzy, love emotions with your infant, you probably weren't thinking at all along these biological lines. That's the beauty of this—it just happens. No (or more accurately, very little) thinking is required in this natural process. However, all of this has its purpose, which is to set the stage for further infant-caregiver interactions which lead to healthy growth in the child with the protection and supervision of the adult—your parenting behavior.

Is there a way to measure how much attachment exists between infant and caregiver or between child/teen and parent? Can this even be measured or rated? What would such a thing mean? In fact, there are methods in which attachment can be typed, or assigned a category.

The standard for assessing attachment in infancy was developed by Mary Ainsworth in the 1960s. It is called the Strange Situation. The Strange Situation is a formal systematic protocol to assess type of attachment style in mother-infant pairs. In consecutive three-minute-long episodes, a child is in a room with his/her mother, alone, or with a stranger. Key behaviors are observed and recorded. Upon the mother's return, the critical behavior measured is how the young child interacts with the mother. Does the child approach or ignore her? Does the child seek the mother for comfort? Does the child interact with the stranger, and in what manner?

From these observations of separation and reunion responses, four types of attachment patterns can be determined (originally there were three). They are called *secure, resistant, avoidant, and disorganized.* The most desirable pattern is the secure attachment. Roughly two of three North American children studied fall in this category. Secure attached children have the best outcome in our culture.

These *securely attached* children are at ease and contented when the mother is present, even approaching and interacting with the stranger in the comforting knowledge that Mom is there if anything goes wrong. The mother provides a secure base from which the child is able to explore the environment. When the mother returns, the child is happy to see her and seeks comfort and physical contact.

Ten percent of children are categorized as having a *resistant attachment.* In a resistant attachment (one of three so-called insecure patterns), the child stays close to the mother and does not engage in the desirable exploration behavior. The child is quite visibly distressed when left by the mother and upon the reunion, the child seems ambivalent about her. It is as if the child is angered at the leaving and cannot decide whether to go to the mother for comfort or stay away and resist maternal efforts to comfort or console the child.

Of young children, 20 percent are typed as the insecure attachment pattern termed *avoidant*. Avoidant attached children are not distressed when left by their mothers. They choose to avoid or turn away from their mother in the reunion episodes, even when the mother actively solicits the child's attention.

The final 5 to 10 percent of young children are classified as *disorganized*. In the disorganized attachment pattern, children show the most distress and confusion. These are the least secure of all attachment types. To some observers, the disorganized pattern child is a cross between the resistant and avoidant. The child seemingly acts like a proverbial deer in the headlights. In essence, at the reunion, the child freezes or acts in the approach-avoid behavior of the resistant-type child.

By now, you know more than you may have wanted about the assessment of attachment. I wanted to give you the details so that when (or if) you read about how certain studies were conducted, you can have a feel for whether the methods (and the findings) make sense. As you might imagine, there are challenges to the validity and uses of this method. What kinds of studies use these methods? Of most interest to parents are studies that measure the effects of daycare participation on children. One of the primary reasons to label daycare bad for children is the argument that attachment is disrupted.

Is This True, and So What?

As you might imagine, that is a loaded question. You have also probably guessed that there cannot possibly be a definitive answer. You are correct. We will explore this area of research more fully in chapter 9, so don't forget this section.

Why Is Any of This Important for the Educated Parent?

The secure attachment pattern is the preferred style in North American culture. In most Western cultures, the desired secure attachment occurs when the child feels free to explore his/her environment (while looking over a shoulder to see that Mom is still there) and is allowed to act in an autonomous, self-directed manner. The key is that the child exhibits a sense of security and feels safe in his/her environment as a result of the knowledge that a parent is there for protection and comfort if needed.

Ainsworth believed that attachment quality was based upon the amount and kind of attention received from the parent. Termed the *caregiving hypothesis,* Ainsworth's findings postulated that securely attached children are made (not born) as a result of sensitive, aware, and responsive parental involvement.

Marianne DeWolff and Mariuns van Ijzendoorn reviewed 60 attachment studies. They reported the following key behavior characteristics which promote secure attachments:

- *Sensitivity*—the prompt response level of the parent to the child's signals/needs;
- *Positive attitude*—expressions of positive emotion and affection toward the child;
- *Synchrony*—the structuring of reciprocal interactions with the child, matching parental behavior to the child's mood and activity level;
- *Mutuality*—the coordination of mother and infant to the same activity or event;
- *Support*—watching for the child's signals to provide emotional support for the child's activities and behavior; and
- *Stimulation*—the active direction of behaviors and stimuli to the infant.

These six behaviors are considered the how-to for forming a secure attachment with your child. If as a parent you can tailor your interactions with your infant to include the above, you greatly increase your chances for a secure attachment. You cannot guarantee a secure attachment on the work of parenting alone—remember, this is a two-way (reciprocal) and interactive process which requires input from your infant as well. So parent and child work together to bring this about.

How are the insecure attachments formed? In a phrase, inconsistent parenting responses toward the infant. When a parent's behavior is unpredictable and/or unresponsive, the infant is not receiving the needed stimulation to keep the attachment dance going. There is a breakdown in the stimulus-response-stimulus cycle, which leads the infant to at first increase its attempts to get maternal involvement. If these efforts are not successful, the infant apparently gets frustrated and gives up. This is how

Ainsworth believed that resistant attached relationships are formed. (I say apparently because it's hard to know exactly how an infant might interpret these events.)

Avoidant attached babies seem to emerge as a result of impatient care-giving responses and an ignoring of the baby's signals. This behavior has been interpreted by Ainsworth to indicate that the mothers are, at some level, rejecting their babies. It has also been reported that avoidant at-tached babies may be the result of overzealous parenting where the babies are overstimulated and must retreat (by avoiding the overwhelming input) to protect themselves.

The disorganized attached infant seems to result from unpredictable caregiving which may also involve neglect or abusive behavior. Most abused infants are assessed as having the disorganized type of attachment relationship. Additionally, very depressed mothers who provide incon-sistent care as a result of their psychiatric disability have been found to alternate some level of care with periods of neglect, also leading to the disorganized attachment type.

Any person who is not ready for, or outright does not want, a baby to raise is a candidate for parenting in a way that will lead to an insecure attachment. This might include some single mother situations as well as parents in high levels of marital dysfunction. Having a baby, with all of the attendant responsibilities, is something a parent must want and be pre-pared for.

Jay Belsky, among others (see chapter 1), has reported that emotional difficulties in children can often be traced back to couples with serious marital discord. It is as if the child cannot receive the needed attention and care when parents are fighting. This parental fighting limits their avail-ability for the child. This makes sense, as does the opposite finding regard-ing happily married couples. These couples are found to help and support each other in the duties of parenting, resulting in a securely attached and well-adjusted child. Family therapy theory also supports the finding that a dysfunctional system disrupts the psychologically healthy function of all of its members. This will be reviewed in chapter 4.

ATTACHMENT AS A PREDICTOR OF HOW A CHILD WILL TURN OUT

So why have I devoted pages of words to this topic? One of Ainsworth's original goals was to find out whether these attachment patterns were pre-dictive of later developmental phenomena; that is, outcome measures. She hoped to find a system of classification that could sort out parent-child relationships so that certain types could be changed or improved, if indicated, for the child's betterment.

For parents, a *secure attached* infant grows into a secure attached child and then teen and adult. Secure attached children (one-to-two-year-olds in the original study) are noted for their level of cooperation with parental requests and are much more easily socialized. This leads to a greater likelihood of social competence, which in turn allows for many successful and positive life situations. The apparent internal sense of security is also a foundation for future positive outcomes in self-esteem and self-concept, and another important variable termed *self-efficacy*. Self-efficacy is an internal belief system that one is competent and able to learn new things and to be responsible for one's actions. These are quite desirable traits for any child to have in our culture. In fact, secure attachments become a basis for positive peer relationships and friends.

Nancy McElwain and her University of Illinois research group have shown that preschool children with secure attachments form closer friendships in the early grade school years. Data from 1,071 children from the National Institute of Child Health and Human Development Study of Early Child Care and Youth Development were used. One key finding was that securely attached children develop a more positive, less biased understanding of others, which then promotes more positive friendships during the early school years.

At 4½ years of age, and again in first grade, children were assessed on a measure called a hostile attribution bias. In this assessment, the child, given a series of stories in which a peer did something negative to a child, is asked to say why she/he thought it happened. A hostile attribution bias is found when the child says the hurt was intentional, even though the story leaves that interpretation open.

This study indicated that several processes led from the attachment quality to later friendship quality. In one track, children who were securely attached at age three showed more open emotional communication with their mothers and better language ability at 4½ years. This open communication was related to fewer hostile attributions. The interpretation of this result is that positive family relations may lead to a more positive view of the outside world, and the ability to get along better with friends.

In another data trail, open emotional communication and language ability at age 4½ was related to mother- and teacher-reported friendship quality in first and third grade. Apparently, this communication ability, enhanced by the secure attachment, lets children discuss and better process their emotions—positive and negative. This in turn, is seen in better social competence and quality friendships.

Resistant attached children, as a result of generally more crying time, come to lack the same level of security as the securely attached ones. This leads to less exploratory behavior and fewer opportunities for learning about the world. One consequence for these children is that they generally do more poorly on tests of cognitive ability.

The *avoidant attached* child is at risk for difficulties in future relationships with others. Because of these early negative experiences, they are seemingly avoidant of, and more hesitant in, making close relationships with others. A sad consequence for these children is that they are more likely to have trouble in making and maintaining peer friendships.

Disorganized attached children are much like the avoidant children in terms of long-term consequences. They too seem to have difficulty in forming close relationships with others. They are also more likely to have difficulty in school.

Insecure attachments may be related to a variety of other outcomes. Sarah Anderson and Robert Whitaker recently reported on a study that estimated the association between attachment security in two-year-old children and their risk for obesity at four years of age.

Hypothesizing that "insecure attachment is associated with unhealthy physiologic and behavioral responses to stress," they surmised that poor attachment quality could lead to the later development of obesity. They assessed attachment security at 24 months in the child's home using a standard measure of attachment. Obesity was defined as having a body mass index above the 95th percentile for age.

They found a 23.1 percent obesity rate in children with insecure attachment and a 16.6 percent rate in those with secure attachments. For the children with insecure attachments, the odds of obesity "were 1.3 times higher than for children with secure attachment" after controlling for other variables that could play into the child's size. They concluded that insecure attachments in early childhood may be a risk factor for obesity.

Here is a good point at which to again remind ourselves that less desirable parenting practices alone may lead to insecure attachments. But recall that establishing attachment is a relationship process that also has input from the infant. As you might have guessed, a major factor brought to the table by the infant is his/her temperament. In addition, parenting style is the third dimension with a large influence.

How might attachment style impact adult relationship behavior? Let us review how three such attachment types would be reflected at an adult level. For the securely attached child, she/he will grow up to find it relatively easy to get close to others and be comfortable in depending on other people. She/he will also allow others to get emotionally close, and will have few issues or worries about abandonment or commitment.

For a child who had an avoidant attachment, she/he will grow up to feel uncomfortable with getting close to others. They will have trust issues and feel like they cannot depend on others. When pressed for intimacy, they will become anxious and have difficulties in handling adult demands for closeness and sexual intimacy.

For the anxious/ambivalent child, she/he will become an adult who finds others not getting as close to them as they would like. They will worry about their partner's commitment and have trust issues which can further trouble the relationship. As an adult, these folks may feel a need to get too close, as if to merge completely, with their partner. This often leads to a partner feeling pushed away or scared off by that level of desired intimacy.

Gurit Birnbaum and her associates have reported on how attachment style also appears to be intimately related to people's patterns of sexual interaction. People with secure attachments tend to be more comfortable with their sexuality, more motivated to show love for their partner during sex, more open to sexual exploration, more likely to have sex in the context of committed relationships, and less accepting of casual sex. In contrast, people high in attachment anxieties tend to have sex to reduce their feelings of insecurity and are more likely to consent to unwanted sexual acts and less likely to practice safe sex. People high in avoidant attachment tend to engage in more casual sex in an effort to impress their peers, and they are more likely to use sex to manipulate their partners.

We now turn to the subject of parenting styles.

PARENTING STYLE AND ITS EFFECTS ON YOUR CHILD'S BEHAVIOR

The final feature of the developmental triad is parenting style. *Parenting style* refers to a philosophy and set of standard strategies that parents use in their child rearing. There are many books and systems available for your review. It is best to find one that fits your views of parenting and the kind of role you want to play in your child's life. I would also urge that you consider this information next presented as it also tells of how well children respond to specific parenting styles.

I am a true fan of the work of Diana Baumrind, and still consider her work to be the definitive account of parenting styles and how they impact child outcome. Allow a quick and dirty review here. (You can find full accounts in *The Educated Parent* or on multiple websites.)

Baumrind first identified styles of parenting she termed authoritative, authoritarian, and permissive. (Later work led to a fourth category.) She determined these not by observing parent behavior, but by first observing how well different children behaved. She coined the phrase *instrumental competence,* the term she used to describe a child who was capable and skilled in social settings, and able to relate properly to peers and adults. Instrumentally competent children could control their emotions and their behaviors; they had good frustration tolerance and could delay gratification. They were leaders in their peer group and responsible in their actions. Being instrumentally competent meant that a child was self-directed and self-modulated in his/her behavior and was pretty much a together kid.

Baumrind then made a list of the most important parenting behaviors which led to these instrumentally competent children. The list included behaviors like firm rule enforcement, encouraging of independence and individuality, and acceptance of the child. Joint parenting behaviors were things like expectations that the child would help with chores, parents acting in a directive (teaching) manner, the discouraging of emotional dependency or infantile/regressive behavior, and the provision of an enriched environment.

In Table 3.1, we get these four parenting types:

Table 3.1   Parenting Behavior Styles

	Accepting, responsive	Rejecting, unresponsive
Demanding, controlling	AUTHORITATIVE	AUTHORITARIAN
Undemanding, uncontrolling	PERMISSIVE - INDULGENT	PERMISSIVE - NEGLECTFUL

Acceptance and nurturing levels are on the columns, and expectations, controls, and demands are on the rows. So an *authoritative* parent rates high on both, acting in ways which are accepting and nurturing and demanding and controlled at the same time. *Authoritarian* parents are low on the acceptance/nurturance feature, but high on expectations, controls, and demands. *Permissive-indulgent* parents are high on acceptance and nurturing behaviors, but low on expectations, controls, and demands. And the *permissive-neglectful* parent is low on the acceptance/nurturance element, and low on expectations, controls, and demands.

How do the different parenting styles affect children? Let us look at each of the four styles and how they related to how children behaved and acted. The authoritative parents, by virtue of their warm, involved, and responsive behavior make for a pleasant home environment. These parents create a situation where alternatives and choices are presented to children. The children have input and all appropriate wishes are considered. These parents set standards and limits and communicate these clearly and firmly. They will confront all bad behavior and will not play the never-ending lawyer games of negotiating with children who are never their equals in terms of power and control. Authoritative parents expect and demand independent behavior that is age-appropriate. No babying is allowed. These parents are responsive to their children in every way, and are family-centered in their day-to-day lives.

Children of authoritative parents are well-behaved and self-assured. They have achievement-oriented behavior and their daily activities are goal-oriented. They are good self-managers and know how to cope with stress and handle problems in calm and purposive ways. They are excellent playmates and great peer companions. They are often high-energy, but in a directed, non-hyperactive way. Finally, they have and show respect for adults and authority figures, acting in cooperative and compliant ways rather than in a disobedient or challenging manner.

The authoritarian parent is known best for rule enforcement and order. The rules are there but not necessarily explained in a clear fashion. These parents do not interact in positive ways with their children. They are seen as aloof and detached. They can be emotional when it comes to negative affect, easily showing anger and displeasure. When pushed, they are punitive and harsh in reply. They tend to see their, and all, children as little hellions in need of discipline and control. They do not allow questioning of their rules or authority, and do not care to hear the opinions of their children because they can't know anything important since they're just kids. If there were a motto for authoritarian parents, it would be, "Because I am the parent, that's why."

Children of authoritarian parents are often fearful and anxiety-ridden. They appear as moody and unhappy. They can be deceitful and secretive. They are hostile, but rarely display their hostility in open and direct ways. They can be unpredictable, alternating between aggressive outbursts and pouty, sullen passivity. Due to their anxiety and lack of coping, they are quite vulnerable to stress, making matters worse.

Permissive-indulgent parents are often quite warm and accepting. They view children as free spirits who need lots of room to grow and flower.

They are pleased to see, and encourage, free thinking and unconventional behavior. They are reluctant to set rules or limits for fear of disturbing the natural desires of their offspring. When discipline is applied it is inconsistent. The rules may change as the circumstances do, so children are not sure of what rules may be in place. These parents will cave in to whining and emotional blackmail in an effort to keep the peace and limit conflict and confrontation. For this reason, they also let much unacceptable behavior go without challenge.

Children of permissive-indulgent parents lack any self-control since none was expected. They are quite impulsive and lack self-confidence or self-efficacy. They are generally aimless, living lives with no or unclear directions. They can be unpleasant, alternately acting aggressively or angrily, followed by a sharp reversal into apparent cheerfulness. They are domineering and stubborn and will try most anything to get their way, other than work and effort.

Permissive-neglectful parents barely qualify as parents. They are equally neglectful and self-absorbed. Their narcissism will win out over their children's welfare. They are non-responsive to their children and find ways to avoid interaction, contact, or responsibility. They are often unaware of their child's whereabouts or activities. These parents are psychologically fragile and are somewhat childlike in their interpersonal behavior. These individuals have poor marriages and are likely to be divorced, often multiple times.

The children of permissive-neglectful parents have low self-esteem and are insecure attached. This alienation permeates their lives. They have little self-image or self-confidence. They are aimless and irresponsible. They are often moody, impulsive, and cannot follow rules or answer to authority. As teens they are conduct-disordered, getting involved in truancy, substance abuse, promiscuity, and juvenile delinquency. Having no family support, they are mostly high school dropouts and have few of the skills, aptitudes, and attitudes needed for any kind of conventional success.

Any other book you may read on parenting will really be about the above, even if the terms or names have been changed. In a way, it's a simple philosophy. To raise a socially and instrumentally competent child, the educated parent must be loving, accepting, and responsive to his/her child's needs and signals. A good, effective parent must also not be afraid to control and direct the younger child's life using common sense, enforced discipline, and high expectations. Now, the walk is a lot more difficult than the talk, but the plan is relatively straightforward.

Can parents be expected to act exclusively as authoritative or authoritarian? Probably not. At times even authoritative parents may be having an off day. Based upon a lack of patience or high stress, it may be that the authoritative parent may respond to a child in an authoritarian or permissive-indulgent way. But in general, a parent's style is what suits them, and they are more likely to respond to their child in that fashion. No parent is 100 percent consistent. That's okay as long as your style is generally predictable and your child sees your overall behavior as a pattern of caring. The impacts of a proactive parenting style are found in many child outcomes.

For example, Gustavo Carlo and his team conducted a longitudinal study to observe the ways that parenting style impacts prosocial behavior development. Using families of Spanish children with a mean age of 10.8 years, they looked at parental measures of variables such as fathers' and mothers' warmth and strict control, sympathy, prosocial moral reasoning, and self-and peer-reported prosocial behaviors at each of three-year intervals.

They found that parental warmth, sympathy, and prosocial moral reasoning were all predictive of prosocial behaviors in their children. Further analyses showed "bi-directional effects such that early prosocial behaviors predicted later parenting and adolescents' prosociality."

All three parts of the triad constantly affect and impact each other. Temperament affects attachment quality and parenting style. Parenting style helps to decide attachment quality and the fit with a child's temperament. Attachment quality affects the parent-child interactions and can shape temperament issues. Let's see how some of these details play out.

We do know that temperament and attachment interact. But they are not the only two variables in the mix. Many other factors can impact attachment outcome. Difficult-temperamented infants are not predetermined to a life of problems. One study found that a difficult temperament led to an insecure attachment when the parenting style was highly controlling. So the temperament alone did not determine attachment; it was modified by parental behavior. Similarly, stressed out parents who received support were found more likely to promote a secure attachment with their infants. As Alan Sroufe has pointed out, temperament and attachment are linked, but are also part of a larger social context for emotional development.

There is also the good news that parents of difficult-temperament children ultimately form secure attachments in their children when trained in specific ways to deal with their babies' behavior patterns. Although this takes committed, understanding, and patient parenting, not all difficult children form insecure attachments. Let's look at some parent training efforts designed to maximize the likelihood of a secure attachment pattern.

Sean McDevitt, an Arizona psychologist, has worked for years to develop parent training programs based upon the child's temperament type. His work recognizes that some children are more challenging for parents to rear than others. Mismatching a parenting style and a child's temperament can be a factor in creating children with emotional and behavioral regulation problems. This is in turn makes him/her at risk for developing a variety of problems like depression, oppositional defiant disorder, anxiety, and other behavioral disorders.

Research suggests that effective temperament-based intervention can prevent and/or treat these disorders and problems. The key for the educated parent is to understand the interplay of your child's temperament and self-regulation ability with your parenting style. Once again the use of a goodness of fit approach can determine how parenting techniques will impact the quality of family interactions. When properly done, there is a reduction of stress in the parent-child interactions and a better established attachment relationship.

Remember also that temperament is value neutral—temperament type does not make a child positive or negative, or good or bad. For parents, a child's temperament sets the stage for what can be expected to work or not work as you go about rearing him/her. Some characteristics of a temperament type may be risk factors for future problem behaviors or disorders. Other temperament characteristics may actually give the child a protection from a problem.

Failure to match parenting style and child temperament has been linked to development of behavioral or emotional problems in some children. In part, the experience of stress associated with a bad fit between parenting and the child may set the stage for the development of a behavior disorder. If a parent wants to use plan A and the child is a plan B type, problems will more likely transpire.

Finally, Thomas Wills, James Sandy, Alison Yaeger, and Ori Shinar have continued their work on family factors and teen substance use and abuse as they are shaped by temperament. They have examined the role of temperament interacting with parent-child conflict levels, family life events, and parental substance use as they impact a preteen or teen's decision to be involved with substance use. They found that temperament is an important influence in a teen's use of illicit substances, and related to substance use in different ways. Some temperament factors (based on easy temperament) actually were protective; the teen ultimately was not involved. On the other hand, difficult-temperament teens were more likely to use substances when raised by substance-using parents. If both parents drank and smoked, teens were more likely to follow this example when their temperament was typed as difficult.

One explanation for why this might be is that temperament modifies and alters the impact of the parental and family variables. So a child, based upon temperament features, can make their reaction to family stresses and parental behavior better or worse. A second possible explanation is that parental variables may actually alter the teen's temperament and any attendant changes. So it may be the case that parental discipline styles could impact a child's tendencies based upon the fit or lack of fit between parenting and child responsivity.

PARENTING STYLE AND TEENS

As stated earlier, the sooner you can adopt these good parenting behaviors in your home, the better off your child will be, especially in the all-important teen years. Read on for some of the research findings with teens.

Laura Weiss and Conrad Schwarz used Baumrind's parenting style framework with 178 college students and their families as subjects. They looked at outcomes in four areas—personality, adjustment, academic achievement, and substance use. They reported finding predictable results, as have many studies. This means that they found teens of authoritative parents to have the best outcomes on the four areas measured—good adjustment, good school performance, and low substance use and abuse rates. At the same time, the permissive styles led to the poorer outcomes for their subjects.

Michael Cole, part of the Thinking Learning Communicating (TLC) group, has summarized how teens are impacted by parenting style, finding that:

- Adolescents with authoritative parents are most likely to develop with the best outcomes. They have higher levels of self-esteem, are more socially confident, inquisitive, self-assured, and self-reliant. They also have high respect for their parents.
- Adolescents with authoritarian parents tend to be withdrawn, moody, obedient, fearful of new situations, and have low self-esteem. They also have trouble socializing with others.
- Adolescents with permissive-indulgent parents tend to be more creative, but are behaviorally and verbally impulsive and aggressive, and have

trouble dealing with school-imposed limits. They also believe that their parents do not care about them or how they behave.

- Adolescents with permissive-neglectful parents are in the most danger of engaging in deviant behavior. Drug and alcohol use is extremely high in adolescents who were raised by neglectful parents.

Other summary research has found these characteristics of adolescents raised by permissive parents:

- They have higher rates of dropping out of school.
- They cave and give in to peer pressure in areas like sex, alcohol, and drugs.
- They are less mature in social settings and show more impulsive/rebellious behavior.
- They have lower persistence when completing school tasks.
- They tend toward increased dependence on adults.
- They are unable to commit to an individual identity.
- They have lower self-esteem as adults.
- They are less likely to explore options for personal growth.

What about some specific things that an educated parent can/should do as they raise their children through the teen years? The pro-parenting website of Talk to Them (www.talktothem.org) advises some specific behavior from the framework of the authoritative parent.

In the review of the research, the team at Talk to Them reports that several family factors impact the well-being of children. "Teens who have caring, involved and satisfying relationships with their parents are more likely to be academically successful, socially well-adapted and to avoid risky behaviors." Teens, as was presented in the first chapters, need to experience both physical and emotional connections with their parents. Even if they seemingly ignore their parents, they want them—and their support and guidance—around.

Further, teens whose parents model positive and healthy behaviors are more likely to engage in those behaviors themselves. "Parental awareness and monitoring of their child's behavior has also been shown to positively affect a child's welfare. Parents who know their children's friends and activities, and who set age-appropriate limits have teens with lower rates of risky behaviors." I cannot endorse this sentiment too much.

Toward that end, Talk to Them posted a list of specific parent behaviors for monitoring teens, which I have modified a bit. They include items such as these:

- Monitor what your teens watch on TV.
- Monitor Internet activity, especially social network content and usage.
- Put restrictions on the music teens download or buy; check out the MP-3 player or iPod playlists.
- Know where your teens are, after school and on the weekends—at all times.
- Expect to be told the truth about your teens' plans—trust but verify.
- Be "very aware" of your teens' school world—talk/communicate with teachers.
- Have a curfew—and enforce it.
- Clearly convey your disapproval/disappointment if your teen uses marijuana or alcohol.
- Eat dinner with your teens six or seven times a week or as much as practical.
- Have teens complete regular chores and contribute to the family.
- Have an adult present when the teen comes home from school.

Parenting style does matter—at every age. There is much research to back that claim up. Now let us move ahead to chapter 4 to see about the importance of the triad within a family's organizational and discipline style.

FOUR

The Importance of an Organized Family Life and Discipline

To maintain a joyful family requires much from both the parents and the children. Each member of the family has to become, in a special way, the servant of the others.

~Pope John Paul II

Self-respect is the fruit of discipline. . . .

~Abraham J. Heschel

In this chapter we will examine two broad areas necessary for an educated parent. In the first half, we will address ways in which your family's organization style affects your child. The second half is devoted to discipline issues, especially those related to the use of corporal punishment. In *The Educated Parent,* I also devoted a chapter to these topics. In this revised edition, the material is almost completely different. So if the reader wishes to learn about family systems or how different psychological learning theories can be used to set up discipline, you are asked to read the earlier version.

MARITAL QUALITY AND CHILD OUTCOME

Let us begin with a look at the research which backs up my claims from earlier chapters that a strong family and good, healthy parent-level relationships form the basis for good child rearing. If you type "marital quality and child outcome" into an Internet search engine, you will see that a great many studies have been conducted on this subject. For the educated parent who wants many more details, I recommend several sites.

If you want to do your own exploring, visit this site as a start—www. extension.iastate.edu/marriage/files/bibliography.doc. Here you will find a 25-page compilation of articles on the importance of marital quality as it relates to children's outcomes. Assembled in 2005 by Francesca Adler-Baeder of Auburn University and Jackie Pflieger, her graduate assistant, it summarizes 78 articles on this topic and the related topics of domestic abuse effects, co-parenting, and fathering.

A second interesting source comes from Iowa State University (found online at: www.extension.iastate.edu/marriage/files/SP296.pdf). This resource is a copy of a document called "The Impact of Couple and Marital Relationships on Parenting and Child Outcomes: Going Further." It is actually a leader's guide to workshops on the importance of marital quality and couple relationship quality on parenting. This is part of the Administration for Children and Families' Healthy Marriage Initiative, a federally funded program started under the Bush administration. I present it as an example of the application of research to use by the public, much like I intend this book to be.

So what has been found through these research studies? And what kinds of research are going on now? The answer to the second question is partially found in work underway at the University of Notre Dame and the Me and My Family Project. Sponsored by a federal government grant, this longitudinal (multiyear) project, started in 2000, looks at the specific processes by which marital relations impact families and children. The study will use many different measures of marital, parent-child interaction, and family functioning levels. It will assess how these factors play a role in child outcomes. The goal is to get "substantial increases in knowledge about the effects of marital and family relations on children." Phase Two of data collection began in March 2007. Stay tuned for the results. Let us now turn to a brief summary of research on how good marital relationships lead to positive children's outcomes.

I will begin with studies showing that negative marital/family experiences lead to harmful child outcomes as a reverse sample of evidence. Simply put, more research has been reported on the "bad family—bad child outcome" model than the "good family—good child outcome" ideal.

Allow me to start with some of the research of Paul R. Amato, currently the Arnold and Bette Hoffman Professor of Family Sociology and

Demography faculty member at Penn State. Dr. Amato has been involved in years of research in the areas of marital quality, causes and consequences of divorce, and quality of parent-child relationships.

The grand conclusion from Amato's 2002 study investigating marital quality is that there is such a thing as a good enough marriage. A good enough marriage is just that, pretty good for the husband and wife. Amato says that these good enough marriages are neither passionate, nor deeply fulfilling (at least much of the time), and not marriages in which, "day in and day out, the partners feel happy they found one another." He argues that, in many of these marriages, either partner might wish they had married someone else. At the same time, the adults in these marriages still enjoy the benefits of family stability and social support. And so do their children.

In Amato's view, good enough marriages usually show little obvious conflict, but also little in the way of connection or belongingness. These marriages become weakened, particularly to "attractive alternatives." If a good enough marriage is never tested, by some trial or some other adult, it is likely to continue until one member dies. Amato believes that all family members' lives are better than if they divorced.

Amato, in another study conducted with Alan Booth, found that children of high-conflict parents tend to do better, not worse, if their parents' divorce leads to less conflict. In a 2001 study, parents and their adult children were surveyed about the way in which predivorce marital conflict influenced the impact of divorce on them as children. Amato and Booth used national longitudinal interview data in two separate studies. In the first study, they found that the ending of low-conflict marriages appeared to have negative effects on offspring's lives, whereas the divorces of high-conflict marriages were beneficial.

The low-conflict marriages that ended in divorce were associated with the quality of children's intimate relationships, social support from friends and relatives, and general psychological well-being. All of these were lost or negatively impacted by the life disruption from the divorce.

In the second study, parents in low-conflict marriages that divorced were compared to other parents before divorce in several ways. Low-conflict parents who divorced were less integrated into the community, had fewer obstacles to overcome to be divorced, had more favorable attitudes toward divorce, were more predisposed to engage in risky behavior, and were less likely to have experienced a parental divorce when they were children.

Children of these low-conflict marriages that ended in divorce (including many good enough marriages) clearly did worse because of their parents' divorce. The reason is that the divorce usually comes out of the blue, and they are surprised. This in turn undermines the children's sense of security. These children, when they grow into adults, tend to be more commitment phobic and exit from relationships at the first sign of trouble.

So it is now safe to say that a child's adjustment to divorce depends upon the level of marital conflict before the split. When conflict is high, divorce seems better for children, but when there is little conflict, divorce appears more harmful to children. From the unsuspecting child's perspective, these good enough marriages provide generally positive times. The divorce in these arrangements becomes negative and seemingly unneeded to the child.

In another study, Amato and Booth analyzed a sample of 297 parents, comparing the quality of their marriages in 1980 with those of their children in 1997. They determined that parents with certain characteristics (they were jealous, moody, inclined to fly off the handle, critical, and prone to dominate their spouse) had far worse and lasting effects on their children's marriages than did a parental divorce or poor parent-child relations.

This effect is referred to as an intergenerational transmission. Negative memories and the emotional residue of those aspects of conflict seemed to influence adult children in their marriages far more than any positive experiences. The impact was seen in such behaviors as thinking about divorce or shared activities such as eating main meals together and working on projects around the house.

Notably, parental divorce in and of itself does not substantially negatively influence the happiness of children's married lives. Amato and Booth also were able to show that other variables, such as poor relationships with their parents during the teen years, poorer living conditions, or their levels of education, did not affect marital quality as much as those negative parental attributes.

In a related 2005 study on the security and stability that marriage can bring, Amato and his associate, Claire M. Kamp Dush, examined the association between relationship status, relationship happiness, and a measure of subjective well-being.

Using the Marital Instability Over the Life Course instrument, they found this order of subjective well-being by marital status: married individuals, individuals in cohabiting relationships, steady dating relationships, casual dating relationships, and individuals who dated infrequently or not at all. When in happy relationships, individuals reported higher levels of well-being versus those in unhappy relationships, regardless of the type of arrangement. No surprise here.

Taking their analysis further, when controlling for the happiness variable, Amato and Dush associated relationship status with subjective well-being. Their data revealed that living in more committed relationships was related to increased subjective well-being. Was this because people who are already experiencing high levels of well-being are better positioned to get into more committed relationships? Their data suggest that was not the case.

What about more serious levels of conflict and the damage that conflict can cause in children? Mona el-Sheikh and Lori Elmore-Staton of Auburn University explored the roles of parent-child conflict and attachment quality to parents in older children and teens. How do parent-child conflict levels influence marital discord if at all? In what ways does the quality of parent-child relationships shape child outcomes in the midst of parent conflicts?

El-Sheikh and Elmore-Staton found that parent-child conflict predicted children's externalizing (acting out) problems. The variable types of attachments to parents accounted for both children's externalizing and internalizing problems. Where there was a higher level of parent-child conflict, there was a greater likelihood of negative outcomes. They also found that a secure attachment was a protective factor for behavior problems associated with marital conflict.

They further found that parent-child conflict and attachment to parents are complex factors when determining child outcomes. Many factors determine a child's risk for adjustment problems. This research points out that psychologists must be careful to include multiple data points and measures in assessing how these variables impact children. In their words, this study highlighted "the importance of assessing multiple systems within the family."

In a 2008 study, el-Sheikh and another study group addressed both the long-term consequences of "marital physical violence" and the "more prevalent psychological and emotional marital abuse" and how these variables impact a child's health and welfare. This study used a community sample of 251 families. These two-parent families from Alabama had 123 boys and 128 girls, all in the second or third grade, with a mean age of 8.23 years. A community sample was used (rather than families living in shelters or involved in therapy), as this was thought to be a more realistic observation of the relationship between marital aggression and child outcomes in everyday settings.

This study explored the effects of "physical and psychological aggression" toward the mother and father as they impact children. Previous studies of domestic violence have focused on aggression directed at the mother; in this research, aggression against the father was also examined. This is considered more "real-world," as aggression is often reciprocal in times of escalating conflict.

The el-Sheikh group used emotional security theory (EST) as a way to explain the exact ways that marital conflict harms children. The EST model states that all children want to feel secure in their family, a security based upon the marital relationship quality. When a child's emotional security is threatened from destructive marital conflict, the child makes an internal representation of the marital relationship. This means that children begin to think about their parents' relationship in certain ways, and start to live their lives in accordance with what they think is going on.

This in turn organizes the child's emotional and behavioral responses, which may be helpful in the short term, but leads to disturbed patterns when the child grows older. So, according to EST, children's emotional, behavioral, and cognitive responses mediate, or reconcile, the effects of marital conflict on their adjustment. The el-Sheikh group's findings showed that marital aggression affects children by undermining and threatening their goal of feeling safe and secure in the family.

Children's levels of emotional insecurity were assessed, with distinctions made between spousal aggression against mothers and fathers as well as other variables such as ethnicity, socioeconomic status, and child gender. Of note, no differences were found for African American and European American families, or as a function of socioeconomic status or child gender. Child gender was not a factor in any of the findings; boys and girls were impacted in similar ways.

Aggression against either parent led to similar effects for children. Children's emotional insecurity influenced the relationships between marital aggression and children's internalizing (fear, anxiety, depression), externalizing (acting out, aggressive behavior), and posttraumatic stress disorder (PTSD) symptoms. These findings remained in line with EST model hypotheses by showing that marital aggression against either parent has negative implications for children's emotional security and adjustment outcomes. Further, EST is better considered "a potentially viable process model" for the prediction of PTSD symptoms and internalizing and externalizing problems in children. (PTSD is an unfortunate, but common result for children of domestic violence.)

Let us now turn to other research regarding how families are organized and how that impacts child development. Susan L. Brown of Bowling Green State University, using data from the National Survey of America's

Families (N = 35,938), looked at the relationship between family structure and child well-being. She reviewed several family structures—children in two-biological-parent cohabiting families, two-parent married families, and cohabiting stepfamilies. To measure child well-being, Brown analyzed the "roles of economic and parental resources on behavioral and emotional problems and school engagement."

Brown found that children living in two-biological-parent cohabiting families "experienced worse outcomes, on average, than those residing with two biological married parents." In families with children ages 6–11, economic and parental resources decrease these differences, so they are better off. Among teenagers 12–17, parental cohabitation was found to be negatively associated with well-being, regardless of the levels of parental resources. She also found that "child well-being did not significantly differ among those in cohabiting versus married stepfamilies, two-biological-parent cohabiting families versus cohabiting stepfamilies, or either type of cohabiting family versus single-mother families."

ISSUES RELATED TO DISCIPLINE STYLES

We turn now to some popular parenting discipline methodologies and approaches that an educated parent couple might wish to investigate. Many are available. You will see that they meet the test of promoting child rearing within a sound theoretical grounding. I will not offer any specific information about discipline strategies other than to urge you and your co-parent to choose one that fits your style. Many books and programs exist for your sampling. I urge you to do your own research and see how these models fit in with your views of discipline. And remember, taking an extension (or college-level) course about learning and behavior will help you in many ways and many situations.

Your assignment as a parenting team is to find a program that reflects your values and attitudes as educated, child rearing adults. As long as you both understand how it works and agree to use the system as a team, your children will benefit. Remember that consistency and predictability will help your children.

What about parent training programs that propose specific ways and styles to discipline your children? The "big three"—Parent Effectiveness Training (P.E.T.), Systematic Training for Effective Parenting (STEP), and Confident Parenting—have established programs with many books and training programs available. Let's review a sample and some of the research that evaluates how good and effective such systems really are.

Parent Effectiveness Training (P.E.T.)

Parent Effectiveness Training (P.E.T.) was begun by Thomas Gordon, one of the founders of the humanistic school of psychology, in the 1960s as a parent training class. P.E.T. was made into a book in 1970 and then widely adopted and offered as a training program across the nation. The P.E.T. program is now run from the Gordon International Training website, and benefits of P.E.T. that it offers include:

- "Your children will feel free to discuss their problems and concerns with you instead of withdrawing.
- They will learn self-discipline, self-control and an inner sense of personal responsibility.
- You will learn how to work with each other instead of against each other.
- You'll experience fewer angry outbursts and more problem-solving.
- Everyone can participate in rule-setting so all will feel motivated to comply with the rules.
- Fewer power struggles—less tension, less resentment, more fun, more peace, more love."

And the program promises parents that they will learn these skills:

- How to talk to your children so that they will listen to you.
- How to listen to your children so they feel genuinely understood.
- How to resolve conflicts and problems in your family so that no one loses and problems stay solved.
- A method for troubleshooting family problems and knowing which skills to use to solve them.

P.E.T. is known for four primary techniques—active listening, I-Messages, win-win outcomes, and "behavior windows:"

Active listening describes the ability to restate in your own words the opinions and emotions of your child. An important goal of active listening is to help a child to understand his or her own problems and to figure out solutions independently.

I-Messages are non-blaming, non-judgmental descriptions of the child's behavior, especially where it conflicts with the parent's interests. I-Messages describe how the unacceptable behavior affects the parent and how it makes him/her feel. I-Messages confront the behavior of the child but do not attack him/her. An example of an I-Message would be, "If you play with your food and make a mess, I have to spend time cleaning up and I don't like that."

Win-win conflict resolution tries to find a solution that both parent and child can agree with. It involves all parties in the conflict resolution because children, and people in general, are more likely to agree with and carry out decisions which they helped reach.

The *"behavior window"* teaches a child to determine acceptance and problem ownership. Through a combination of active listening and I-Messages, parent and child learn about how to define problems accurately, who "owns" them, and how to resolve them.

Does P.E.T. work? A 1997 review of several different parent training programs found that behavior-oriented parent-training programs designed to improve behavior problems in children are effective. The results also indicated "that Adlerian and PET type programs are effective, albeit to a lesser extent, and that community-based group programs may produce better changes in children's behavior and be more cost-effective and user-friendly than individual clinic-based programs."

Scott Mooney, in 1995, conducted a meta-analysis comparing Adlerian (STEP), P.E.T., and behavioral parenting approaches. His results indicated that "behavioral approaches have been extremely effective in altering a child's deviant behaviors." Little research was found in his review to support the use of P.E.T. over other behavioral approaches in changing child behavior.

Systematic Training for Effective Parenting (STEP)

Systematic Training for Effective Parenting (STEP) is a parent education program that grew out of a series of books by Don Dinkmeyer, Sr., Gary D. McKay, and Don Dinkmeyer Jr. As with P.E.T., an extensive training program was developed, and the program has been taught to millions of parents since the 1970s. It is based on Alfred Adler's individual psychology and the work of psychiatrist Rudolf Dreikurs, who first spoke about children and attention-seeking behavior.

STEP is designed to help parents understand their young children and gain skills for effective parenting. Parents are trained to look at the long-term goals of parenting; learn about how young children think, feel, and act; and learn skills that can develop their children's self-esteem and confidence. STEP does this by teaching about children's developmental levels and how they change, identifying misbehavior and why a child would act that way, and teaching parents to redirect a child to act in a better way. STEP touts the fact that children will be encouraged to develop positive self-esteem. It also encourages parents to develop skills for effectively communicating with young children and learn how to get cooperation. A final goal is to teach parents how to stimulate children's healthy emotional development and how to help children develop positive social skills.

So, how effective is STEP? As with P.E.T., the research has shown generally positive outcomes. Much of the research on parenting methods finds mixed reviews because of the difficulty in controlling for how well the parents were trained, how consistent the parents were in delivering the program, and the starting point of the children and their behavior problem levels. Read on for more details.

David Gibson conducted a 1999 review (another meta-analysis) of the research on how effective STEP is. He reviewed 61 primary research studies that explored the effectiveness of the STEP program on various populations (different types of children and different ages of parents), in varied contexts (homes, group homes, other facilities), each using different dependent measures to determine the success of the STEP method.

From his summary, Gibson found STEP to be a success with various populations, as measured by a wide array of instruments. He reported that STEP's effectiveness "has been reliably established, although there are several examples within the studies where the changes in knowledge, attitude, behavior, etc. did not reach the desired level of statistical significance." Simply put, most of the research found evidence in support of the program's claims, but there were times when the use of STEP did not reach its goals. Gibson concluded that "there seems to be no population of parents or children that have not benefited from the Adlerian principles developed in the various STEP programs."

In a review of treatment approaches for juvenile offenders, a group using STEP found some success, but these gains lessened with the passage of time. The STEP program was found to be more effective with couples than with mothers or with mixed parent groups. In addition, the program was found to be more effective with younger, less educated parents with younger children.

Confident Parenting

Confident Parenting is a program "based on the belief that society molds the individual's behavior and that there are lawful principles that underlie this social molding process. These principles are derived from experimentally established research findings and understanding these principles provides a basis for a more conscious, self-determined and positive use of the molding process." This definition is found on the program's website (www.ciccparenting.org), along with its history and explanations of its approach and techniques. Dr. Robert Aitchison and his colleagues developed this approach in the 1970s.

Training in this approach is typically done in 10 weeks of two-hour-long sessions. The program teaches five basic methods for managing the consequences of children's behavior and which child behaviors are most likely to be increased or decreased by the use of each method. Confident Parenting is based on social learning theory principles. In the training, parents are shown the effectiveness of each behavioral method and they are taught that success will be determined by the child's unique characteristics and response pattern.

Data on the effectiveness of the Confident Parenting approach are similar to those of P.E.T. and STEP. The 1970s represented a time of great hope in the application of systematic theoretical approaches to parent training. Each system has its strengths and weaknesses and it is up to the educated parent to determine whether any of the approaches fits his/her family.

One might wonder why I chose to discuss these programs in the part of the chapter on discipline rather than the part of the chapter on family structure. The truth is the material could be in either place. However, as a package of information, I consider these parent programs organized around their principles of techniques to consequencing behavior. Let us now review some information on a more contentious consequencing topic—corporal punishment.

CORPORAL PUNISHMENT—TO SPANK OR NOT TO SPANK

The issue of whether it is ever allowable or appropriate to spank or hit a child as a means of discipline remains a controversial topic. There are many matters to consider and this book has only so much space. This topic was covered in *The Educated Parent,* so the reader can look back and reference that material, which looked more at research related to child responses. Allow me to suggest several web resources to give you, as an educated parent; information of use to help you decide how you will resolve this issue as you raise your child.

I begin with a referral to a web resource sponsored by a California group called Parents and Teachers Against Violence in Education. This group has an extensive web page at www.nospank.net. According to their mission statement:

> [T]he defense of children should be more vigorous because they are more vulnerable; because the consequences of their early mistreatment are difficult to reverse; because damaged children tend to grow into damaged adults who are likely to avenge themselves in one way or another. If they will not harm others, then they will likely harm themselves, and they may passively support the mistreatment of children perpetrated by others. Current research in the field of child development overwhelmingly confirms the theory that the earlier and the worse the mistreatment of children, the worse the outcome.

This site contains information about research on corporal punishment, personal accounts of victims of abuse, and a variety of related information. I am not endorsing any of the views expressed, nor can I attest to the validity of every link. However, in my reading, I found this a thorough, well-assembled package of advocacy information. As long as it is all read knowing that the purpose of the information is to stop adults from using corporal punishment, you as an educated parent can sort through the facts and figures to form and inform your decision.

As you may know, corporal punishment—the use of spanking with an open hand or striking a child with an object like a belt, paddle, or switch—is an issue filled with both opinions and emotions. Adults recall whether they were spanked or struck as children with mixed responses. Some say they were hurt and humiliated and would never strike a child. They see any corporal punishment as a form of physical abuse. Others say the physical discipline was all that kept them from bad life choices and they are happy an adult cared enough to make the point physically, as that got the message through.

Although the majority of American parents admit to spanking or agreeing to its use, very few social scientists or behavior specialists today would endorse corporal punishment as a positive discipline choice.

Years of research have clearly demonstrated that spanking children often leads to negative long-term consequences. The more negative outcomes are associated with more frequent and severe spanking. These results include later antisocial behavior and attitudes. Excessive use of physical punishments has been linked to adult social and psychological problems and specific problems like depression and anger/aggression management issues. Other research has shown that children who are spanked learn that it is acceptable to inflict pain on others since it has been done to them. It has also been found that children who are spanked will more likely engage in subsequent aggressive and inappropriate behavior after their punishment. This sets up a negative cycle, as they are then more likely to be spanked again and so on.

If a parent does resort to corporal punishment, how long does it take before a child is negatively affected? And how is spanking related to other forms of family violence? Allow me to share three studies on these points.

Using data from the National Institute of Child Health and Human Development Study of Early Child Care and Youth Development, Matthew Mulvaney and Caroline Mebert examined the impact of corporal punishment on children's behavior problems. They had access to longitudinal data and were able to control for variables (confounds) that have made it harder to address the research question they studied. For example, it is important to try to determine whether the spanking or some aspect of parenting style is the reason for negative child outcomes. It could also be the case that, for some parents, their child's difficult behavior leads to more corporal punishment. But in that case, the difficult child's later problems were not necessarily caused by the spanking but by their general problem behavior.

In their analysis, Mulvancy and Mebert determined that spanking and corporal punishment by parents contributed to "negative behavioral adjustment" in children at both 36 months and at first grade, with the effects at the earlier age more pronounced in children with difficult temperaments. This was true even when differences between families by ethnicity, income, parenting styles, and earlier use of corporal punishment were taken into account.

In a related finding, Mulvaney and Mebert reported that the impact of corporal punishment might worsen as children grow older because those with behavior problems are more likely to deal with peer rejection and victimization. They urged that adults working to change children's problem behavior "be aware of the unique impact that corporal punishment likely plays in triggering and maintaining children's behavior problems." Ultimately, they argue that all children would be better off without spanking.

Catherine Taylor and her team from Tulane University found that children who are spanked frequently at age three years are more likely to be aggressive when they reach five years old. And this finding holds when one accounts for other factors (like parental stress level or depression or family violence) that could have influenced the finding of this behavior.

In this study, about 2,500 mothers were surveyed regarding how often they had spanked their three-year-old child in the past month, their child's level of aggression, and eight areas of other risk factors. Data were part of the Fragile Families and Child Well-being Study, collected from 1998–2005. Forty-five percent of the mothers did not spank in the previous month, while 27.9 percent reported spanking one or two times, and 26.5 percent reported spanking more than twice. Mothers who spanked at the highest rates had more parenting risk factors. When statistically accounting for these likely confounding factors, more spanking received at age three years led to higher levels of aggression in the children at five years old. Taylor's research found that three-year-old children who were spanked frequently (a few times a month) were 50 percent more likely than their peers who were not spanked to be aggressive two years later. The association remained even after accounting for varying levels of natural aggression in children, showing that is it not just the aggressive children who get spanked.

The study suggests that even minor forms of corporal punishment increase the risk for aggressive behavior. Signs of aggression in the children were defined as behaviors such as arguing or screaming; cruelty, bullying, or meanness to others; destroying things; fighting; and frequently threatening others.

In another study looking at how spanking and family violence are associated, Taylor's team found that approximately 65 percent of the children were spanked at least once in the previous month by one or both parents. Among couples reporting any family aggression (87%), 54 percent reported that both spanking and intimate partner aggression or violence (IPAV) occurred. IPAV includes any form of aggressive behavior between family members including "minor, non-physical acts." The highest reported patterns of both spanking and IPAV involved both parents as aggressors either toward each other or toward the child. When bilateral IPAV was present in the home, it doubled the odds that one or both parents would spank, even after controlling for potential confounding variables like parenting stress, depression, and alcohol or other drug use.

In *The Educated Parent,* I wrote this paragraph: "[S]panking younger children (under five years) can be one of a number of effective discipline strategies. Other means can and should be used along with a spanking. With older children there is much less to gain and more to lose through physical forms of discipline. I do not recommend physical punishment for children six years or older. *And if you choose to spank any child, it is your obligation to do it in a manner that is not abusive or damaging.*"

I followed that up with the journal debate between Robert Larzelere and Murray Straus. I also recounted the Diana Baumrind research arguing that parents need a full repertoire of varied discipline strategies and techniques including spanking. Can the use of corporal punishment for any aged child be justified in 2011? Read on.

I searched for a full day in May 2011, trying to find any legitimate research which now allows for or endorses corporal punishment for children. I was unable to find any independent research. I did find several sites that had religious sponsorship or affiliation. I am not about to make any judgments about the biblical or other religious authorities that have been sourced as approvers of corporal punishment. If these values are consistent with your parenting approach, you are urged to evaluate and consider all of what is presented here in order to make the decision that is best for your family and children. But I do ask that you consider in your formulation the social science data.

One well-cited resource was a 2001 article entitled "Spare the Rod? New Research Challenges Spanking Critics" by Den A. Trumbull and S. DuBose Ravenel. It originally appeared on the website of the Family Research Council (www.frc.org); it is no longer available there. At the time of the article's publication, Dr. Den Trumbull was identified as a board-certified pediatrician in private practice in Montgomery, Alabama. Dr. S. DuBose Ravenel was identified as a board-certified pediatrician in private practice in High Point, North Carolina.

This article made 11 counterarguments to the literature that finds that corporal punishment is either ineffective or damaging and harmful to normal child development. It was well researched, citing major figures such as Diana Baumrind and Robert Larzelere. In the article, Trumbull and Ravenel carefully differentiate between "abusive hitting and nonabusive spanking."

They offer guidelines, recommending that verbal corrections, time outs, and logical consequences be the disciplinary methods of first choice, and that spanking be reserved for times when other disciplinary methods have failed. They say, "For very compliant children, milder forms of correction will suffice and spanking may never be necessary."

Trumbull and Ravenel also tell parents that a child should receive "at least as much encouragement and praise for good behavior as correction for problem behavior." They also caution that punishment should be done privately to avoid public humiliation and cite the work of James Dobson, who has said spanking "is inappropriate before 15 months of age and is usually not necessary until after 18 months. It should be less necessary after 6 years, and rarely, if ever, used after 10 years of age."

At present, the Family Research Council has endorsed a Statement on Parental Rights. It says the following; the italics are mine:

> FRC believes that both the responsibility and the authority for raising children rest primarily with their biological or adoptive parents. Government should empower parents to control the upbringing of their children and minimize its interference with the exercise of parental authority, except in cases of demonstrable abuse or neglect. Specifically, public policy should protect the right and maximize the power of parents to choose the form of education they wish for their children, be it public schools, secular or religious private schools, or home schooling. Public schools should avoid undermining parental authority or interfering with transmission of parental values to their children. Medical procedures should not be performed on minors without parental consent, except in cases of medical emergency or public health necessity. *The right of parents to impose necessary discipline, including spanking, upon their children should not be infringed.*

So where do parents in the United States stand on the topic of spanking and corporal punishment? A national survey on spanking, the 1998 General Social Survey, National Opinion Research Center, reported by Michael Miller, found these trends: 79.4 percent of males and 70.7 percent of females supported spanking. By race, 73.6 percent of white and 84.1 percent of black respondents agreed that spanking was okay. And by age, 74.0 percent of respondents under 30, 73.3 percent of 30–49-year-olds, and 76.0 percent of 50 and older responders favored spanking for children.

In 2008, according to a nationally representative survey reported by the Child Trend Data Bank, 77 percent of men and 65 percent of women 18 to 65 years old agreed that a child sometimes needs a "good hard spanking." These proportions have declined a bit since 1986, more so among women than men. In the period from 1986 to 2008, the proportion of women who agreed or strongly agreed that it is sometimes necessary to give a child a "good hard spanking" dropped by 21 percent (from 82% to 65%). Among men for the same period, this proportion fell by 8 percent (from 84% to 77%).

In the same study, college-educated men and women were both less likely than their counterparts with less education to endorse spanking. Black women were more likely to agree or strongly agree that "a good hard spanking" is sometimes necessary. Eighty percent of black women, compared with 61 percent of Hispanic women, 63 percent of white women, and 60 percent of Asian/Pacific Islander women, agreed that a child some-times needs a "good hard spanking."

Spanking/CP is not a controversial issue only in the United States. Manuel Gámez-Guadix, Murray A. Straus, and others looked into issues of corporal punishment in Spain. They looked at the prevalence of corporal punishment (CP) for Spanish children, evaluated the extent to which CP is used in combination with positive parenting or "psychologically aggressive" behaviors, and investigated whether the relation between CP and behavior problems was moderated or changed by a positive parenting context or "by the co-occurrence of psychological aggression." Questions related to psychological aggression included, "How often did you shout or yell at this child?" and "How often did you try to make this child feel ashamed or guilty?" They sampled 1,071 Spanish university students (75% female, 25% male).

CP of children is a widely accepted discipline strategy in Spain, and their findings confirmed a high prevalence of CP of Spanish students, with significantly more mothers than fathers using CP. They also found that more CP was related to greater use of psychological aggression and less of positive parenting. CP was associated with "an increased probability of antisocial traits and behaviors" as the subjects grew into adults, regardless of whether there was positive parenting or psychological aggression. Their results suggest that, though many Spanish parents use CP as a disciplinary strategy, it is related to negative outcomes for children regardless of the parental context in which it is used.

What does other research find about the prevalence of spanking and corporal punishment and trends in its use? In its most recent study, a University of North Carolina–Chapel Hill research group headed by Adam J. Zolotor looked at data on the use of corporal punishment by parents from four cross-sectional population surveys. These surveys were anonymous and by phone; subjects came from across the United States as well as North and South Carolina. The samples were reflective of racial and ethnic profiles in the population.

The Zolotor team found an overall decline in the spanking and slapping of children. Between 1975 and 2002, 18 percent fewer children were slapped or spanked by caregivers. In the U.S. south, the overall trend was unchanged. The team also found somewhat more spanking and slapping in the southeast in 1975 and 1985, and somewhat less in 1995. Researchers asked further about hitting children with an object (like a belt or switch), and found that in 1975, 18.6 percent of parents reported yes. This rate declined to 12.1 percent in 1985, but rose to 28 percent in the 1995 survey. The number rose to 40 percent in the sample of Carolina parents.

Overall, from the four large surveys of self-reported discipline used by parents, there were "promising downward trends in corporal punishment." However, the Zolotor study noted that "spanking remains normative in the US, especially among preschool children, and the rates of hitting with an object remain high."

In another study from 2008, Zolotor's team did phone surveys with 1,435 mothers living in North and South Carolina. They found high rates of spanking and associated physical abuse. In particular, the study found that, while any spanking was associated with increased risk of abuse, spanking with an object was strongly associated with abuse. Among mothers who didn't spank their children, only 2 percent reported physically abusive punishment, compared with 6 percent of mothers who said they spanked their children, and 12 percent of mothers who spanked their children with an object.

In 2008, Elizabeth T. Gershoff and Susan H. Bitensky wrote what I consider the definitive case against corporal punishment of children. With 223 citations, they left no research stone unturned. The first 11 pages of their article are devoted to a literature review of the corporal punishment research body.

Their conclusions from their review are as follows. "[I]f parents' goals are to increase children's moral internalization and to decrease their aggressive and antisocial behavior, there is little evidence that corporal punishment is effective in achieving these goals." Further, their analyses "present strong support for a causal link between parents' use of corporal punishment and children's subsequent behavior problems."

The sum total of the research shows that it "is clearly the case that children with more behavior problems, either for genetic or for other reasons, elicit more corporal punishment from their parents." But after these effects are accounted for, "parental corporal punishment continues to predict levels in and changes in children's behavior problems."

Most countries outside of the United States have concluded "that the evidence points to a connection between corporal punishment and physical abuse." Gershoff and Bitensky cite a UNICEF report that called corporal punishment "the most common form of violence in the industrialized world."

In their paper's conclusion, Gershoff and Bitensky acknowledge that the large level of U.S. parents' support for corporal punishment cannot be dismissed. They cite a 2002 Baumrind quote: "The customs and laws of a society should be given due respect and consideration before banning or stigmatizing a practice, such as physical punishment, that most members practice and consider useful in accomplishing their goals, provided that there is no ethical objection to these goals." For Gershoff and Bitensky, the answer to the question of whether corporal punishment is unethical is a clear yes.

The membership of the American Academy of Pediatrics agrees with Gershoff and Bitensky. The AAP, in an official 1998 policy statement re-affirmed in 2004, stated that: "Corporal punishment is of limited effectiveness and has potentially deleterious side effects." The AAP recommends that parents be taught other, nonphysical methods to manage child behavior problems. In particular, the AAP believes that corporal punishment methods other than open-handed spanking on the buttocks or extremities "are unacceptable" and "should never be used."

The AAP membership believes that corporal punishment interferes with good parent-child relationships and can reduce natural compliance on the part of the child. The AAP policy statement says: "[R]eliance on spanking as a discipline approach makes other discipline strategies less effective to use." In other words, it becomes more automatic and easier to rely on once you get the pattern started.

In a follow-up, the AAP's Committee on School Health issued a second policy statement in 2000, reaffirmed in 2006, on the use of corporal punishment in schools. Says the statement, "The American Academy of Pediatrics urges parents, educators, school administrators, school board members, legislators, and others to seek the legal prohibition by all states of corporal punishment in schools and to encourage the use of alternative methods of managing student behavior." Currently, 31 states and the District of Columbia have school spanking bans. The 19 states still allowing corporal punishment are primarily in the south and southwest regions.

So as I write this, I have been convinced that corporal punishment should be rarely if ever applied to children with behavioral issues. And I chose the word *rarely* with caution. I believe now that I would not strike a child under any circumstance if in authority of that person. I do respect what Baumrind referred to as deferring to the "customs and laws of a society," so I do not believe that I can say to every parent in every parenting situation that corporal punishment must not be practiced.

Rather, I counsel all parents to learn as many behavior modification (used generically, not in the explicit context of operant conditioning) techniques as possible. There are certainly many options for consequencing behavior and controlling children that do not require the use of physical aggression. These should always be used before striking a child.

And for my last word in this chapter, always remember that good child rearing starts with strong, adult parent relationship quality. Moms and dads who take good care of each other provide a basis for taking good care of their children.

FIVE

Parents as Teachers

A child educated only at school is an uneducated child.

~George Santayana

Education's purpose is to replace an empty mind with an open one.

~Malcolm S. Forbes

Of the many responsibilities that parents are concerned with, a child's education always ranks near the top. There has been much dialogue and debate about the state of education in the United States. This mostly refers to public education, the tax-supported system that has become an entitlement in all 50 states.

Among the concerns that an educated parent may have is the desire to be sure that every child can reach his/her true potential and to maximize their learning. In this way each child can truly grow up to be what she/he wants to be as an adult. Most people would still agree that a great education is the best preparation for success in life.

This chapter has a little more how-to in it than the others. One of my goals here is to show you that there is much available online that can make your job a little easier. There is little reason to reinvent the wheel. I have a certain passion for education and parents' role in their children's learning.

I have tried to write in a nonpreachy style, but excuse me if some of this comes across in that way.

SETTING UP YOUR CHILD TO SUCCEED IN SCHOOL

What can educated parents do to enable their students to be as successful and adjusted to school life and work as possible? We will start here with some activities and ways to make school interesting and engaging.

As discussed in *The Educated Parent,* I would present the so-called *Pygmalion Effect,* also known as the *teacher expectancy effect.* This effect means that expectations of teachers have been linked to student performance. That is, if a teacher places high expectations and demands on a child, in part because the teacher believes in that student's ability, then the child will rise to the level of belief in his/her capability. For parents, this means that before school starts, you should talk with your child about their schoolteacher and how she/he will work to get the best out of the students. For too many students, schoolwork and assignments of homework can be the start of a negative relationship. And if the teacher picks up on this resistance and lack of motivation, it is natural that the teacher may place his/her time and effort on a more accepting and willing student. In my opinion, an educated parent should communicate to the teacher high expectations for achievement and sell his/her child's special status from day one.

We will discuss more about parental expectations in the home later, but we must mention right now that your demands and requirements for achievement will be essential for your child's success. When a child grows up with a where-will-I-go-to-college and not a whether-I-will-go-to-college background, the seeds for success are set from infancy.

Let us begin at the beginning. Realistically, this would mean good prenatal care and healthy habits and nutrition from the birth mother. Then, after birth, parents should establish good medical care (wellness checks and vaccinations) and good nutrition and sleep habits for the baby. With those minimal requirements met, the next step to set up your child for academic achievement starts with how well your child is stimulated in infancy and toddlerhood. Research on brain development informs us that the first years are crucial to maximizing a child's potential. The good news is that this can be done without a lot of money or special technology.

Parents can achieve early exposure to literacy with the cost of a few children's books and the investment of your parental time in reading and interacting with your infant/toddler. (Even better, save your money and take some trips to the local library.) An online fact sheet—once entitled "The Importance of Reading to Infants and Young Children, now part of a literacy program called Get Caught Reading (www.getcaughtreading. org/readingtochildren.htm)—shares brain research information findings which I convey with my annotated comments included:

- An infant's brain structure is not predetermined or completed at birth. Early experiences, like being read to, shape the later structure and function of a baby's brain.
- When you read to an infant/toddler, many existing neuronal connections are strengthened, some new brain cells are formed, and other synapses rewire. The experience adds complexity to the brain circuitry and those new changes will remain for the rest of the child's life.
- A number of studies show that development of early literacy skills through early experiences with books and stories is associated with a child's success in learning to read and other later school success.
- Development of literacy is a lifelong, ongoing process that should begin early in life and depends on continued environmental influences and experiences.
- Children who are read to from an early age are more successful at learning to read.
- "[R]eading aloud to children is the single most important intervention for developing their literacy skills," according to a 1985 study by the National Commission on Reading.
- Early reading experiences are recognized by the American Academy of Pediatrics, which recommends that "pediatricians prescribe reading activities along with other instructions given to parents at the time of well-child visits." The Academy strongly recommends daily reading to children from six months of age.

In chapter 8, I also present information on a program called FRED—Fathers Reading Every Day. This four-week program, developed at Texas A&M University, is designed to improve children's reading skills and academic performance through reading and father involvement and to strengthen the emotional bond between fathers and their children. Needless to say, any adult or older child should be encouraged to read to younger children.

For much more information on how one can maximize their child's brain development, I direct the educated parent to the web, specifically two sites I will share next. First is the Better Brains for Babies (BBB) Initiative web page (www.fcs.uga.edu/ext/bbb). From the site:

> BBB is a collaboration of State, local, public, and private organizations in Georgia dedicated to promoting awareness and education about the importance of early brain development in the healthy growth and development of infants and young children. The goal of BBB is to provide families and professionals current, research-based information on brain development and its implications for children throughout the United States. BBB shares research on brain development and information about fact sheets, resources, and additional Web sites through the Resources link on its Web site.

A second site of interest is the ZERO TO THREE: National Center for Infants, Toddlers, and Families website (http://www.zerotothree.org). ZERO TO THREE is a national organization focused exclusively on issues affecting infants and toddlers. Specific information about brain development from this organization is available online at: www.zerotothree.org/child-development.

What else can you do to set up your child for school success? In a phrase, the best thing you can do is to establish a home environment where education and intellectual pursuits matter. I am pretty sure that I am preaching to the choir as I address readers of this book, but a pervasive home environment where books are readily available and read, and where the family members talk about things they have read or learned in school makes a strong impression on children.

When parents are readers, where education is valued, and where lifelong learning is a family philosophy, a child cannot help but grow up motivated and enabled to see school as a positive experience. On the other hand, if parents believe that schools are the only place where children learn and that educators should know all the answers and techniques for student achievement with little family involvement, then we get what we have today—underfunded, failed schools lacking public support.

Educated parents can work to develop three important education-friendly behaviors in their children. These are self-efficacy, self-motivation, and time management skills. Of these, self-efficacy is the most important for school (and life) success. Let us review these in turn.

Great American psychologist Albert Bandura first defined and discussed the importance of *self-efficacy* (mentioned earlier as part of the wellness wheel). Perceived self-efficacy is defined as a person's "beliefs about their capabilities to produce designated levels of performance that exercise influence over events that affect their lives." From this definition, Bandura showed how self-efficacy could influence how a person could feel, think, motivate him/herself, and behave. His work touched on these four avenues for how self-efficacy plays out in life: cognitive, motivational, emotional, and selection processes.

As Bandura noted in many presentations, self-efficacy is tied to achievement and well-being. People with high self-efficacy levels approach difficult tasks as challenges to be mastered rather than as threats to be avoided. This positive outlook helps to create intrinsic interest and deep engagement in activities. Such people easily set challenging goals and stay committed to them. Failure does not deter a person with self-efficacy. Instead such a person sees a lack of success as a challenge to be overcome by extra effort or more learning, both of which can be done under his/her control.

On the flip side, people without a sense of self-efficacy doubt their capabilities and avoid difficult tasks, which they view as personal threats. As a result, they set their personal bars very low and tend to see their failures as personal inadequacies. Since this is all seemingly personal, they give up quickly and are less likely to try again or try harder if given a second chance. And these are the people who become students who barely graduate high school or drop out.

Self-efficacy is developed through several processes. One is working toward mastery. A child cannot only experience success, because she/he will then be easily discouraged by failure. It is best for a child to have some obstacles and frustrations, but to be supported in overcoming them by hard work. Bandura said that a second part of achieving self-efficacy involves observing successful role models. Seeing a person achieving success by constant effort and hard work leads a child to believe that she/he can also master comparable activities and succeed.

A third way to build self-efficacy is through coaching and encouragement, what Bandura referred to as *social persuasion.* A child on the receiving end of encouragement will come to believe she/he can achieve goals, and will work harder and longer to be successful. This is especially true if the encourager helps the child overcome self-doubts. These positive reinforcements and praise will have limited value if they are matched with failed efforts, so it is important to praise only when it is earned.

Finally, what Bandura called *selection* can also lead to self-efficacy. Selection refers to putting a child in a place where she/he is more likely to succeed; that is, one matches the child's abilities with goals and tasks. So it is important to have a child work for higher goals as long as she/he has the tools to succeed. If you put a child in over his/her head, she/he will only learn frustration.

Parents can teach and facilitate self-efficacy. This is an important task related to educational achievement. This starts with the right toys in the infant and toddler stages. In the home, a responsive and interactive parent can create opportunities for a child to learn success through play. Learning how to stack colored donuts or putting differently shaped pieces into shape balls are just two common games that have skill building associated with them. Parental praise can motivate a child to expand efforts and abilities in an upward cascade of successes and more mastery. Along the way, the child gains increased cognitive ability through conversation and problem solving.

From this base, the child can expand into the larger world. Peer and friend interactions lead to social comparisons and modeling. Both of these processes work to reinforce and motivate a child. In the home, a child can only compare him/herself to siblings. Sometimes this works. Sometimes siblings may be much older, or the opposite gender. It is tough for young children to compare themselves to older siblings who have more development-based abilities and freedoms. When they can be with others in the world—at a daycare or classroom or schoolyard—children can learn new ways of thinking and acting.

After age five or six, school is where a child can develop self-efficacy related to academics. In classrooms, students are tested and interact with their teachers. Here they learn information, problem solving, critical thinking, and other valuable skills. And school also offers constant social comparison. As they master cognitive skills, children develop a growing sense of their intellectual abilities. Many social factors interact with the learning environment, such as peer modeling, social comparisons, enhancement of motivation through goals and positive incentives, and teachers giving feedback about successes and failures in ways that reflect favorably or unfavorably on a child's ability.

In a classroom with a teacher who possesses self-efficacy, a child can flourish. Such teachers can be excellent coaches and motivators. They know how to challenge and when to step in to give a boost to a struggling student. This also ties back to the Pygmalion Effect. Teacher attitudes and classroom organization/structure also come into play here. The teacher with self-efficacy sets up a learning environment where success is nurtured and modeled and reinforced, independent of the students' social class or background.

From the site education.com, *self-motivation* refers to the need or desire that arises from within the individual and causes action toward some goal—doing, or not doing, something simply because one wants to, irrespective of external stimuli.

Intrinsic motivation or self-motivation is another important element leading to school success. Self-motivation is the basis for the capability to learn and from that, the idea that learning can be an enjoyable process. Students who are self-motivated have the ability to work on and concentrate on a task for the joy of learning and mastering the needed skill. Children become self-motivated for many reasons. For some, being self-motivated to achieve academic success will help them rise out of poverty, for others it will allow them to get into a specific college or receive an academic scholarship. Students who have a high self-esteem have a strong sense of self-motivation as they believe they are capable of academic success. This of course is all related to self-efficacy.

Time management is another important skill for any student. Devoting dedicated time to schoolwork is essential for learning. Sandra Christenson and Cathryn Peterson, in a 2006 literature review, reported on how students spend their time in and out of school. They found "that 91% of children's time from birth to age 18 is spent outside of school" and once in school, "70% of their waking hours" are spent off school grounds. Christenson and Peterson estimated that 40 percent of students' time awake was uncommitted to anything like school or chores or personal hygiene. Low-income, low-achieving students in Baltimore made considerable gains when they increased their time devoted to "constructive learning activities, activities that involved thinking and supportive guidance from an adult or peer."

Parents need to help their children structure their schedules, taking care to not overschedule and to provide ample time for sleep and exercise. Modeling and assisting children with making time for homework and reading, as well as play and leisure activities, is a good way to teach life balance. Time management and prioritizing are great life skills that can be learned by grade schoolers, and must be practiced by successful high schoolers.

For teens in middle and high school, educated parents need to employ different and more sophisticated strategies to set up school success. The state of Michigan has posted an online e-zine called the *High School EduGuide* in which is published a checklist of "factors for high school success." It is presented as a survey game where you can give your family points for each of the items they recommend. Here are there five areas with key behaviors:

1. *Courses*: Planned a four-year college/career prep schedule. Planned at least one course in those four years where college credit can be earned. Have contact info for a couple sources you can call for tutoring.
2. *Calendars*: Signed up for at least one school-related activity. Kept a student calendar to plan homework projects, deadlines, and events. Scheduled a regular supervised time after school to do homework each day and a way to verify that it's done.
3. *Connections*: Met someone at the school who can help you stay informed and solve any problems. Family has talked with school counselor about their goals and how best to achieve them. Asked an active parent or successful student what to watch out for.
4. *Careers*: Written a career preparation plan signed by the family and school. Spent a couple hours job shadowing and interviewing someone to explore one career. Taken responsibility for a regular paid job, volunteer gig, or family chore.
5. *Colleges*: Spent time on a campus for an event or tour. Parent and student have saved a few dollars for college on a regular schedule. Signed up for a college-based class, summer program, or online activity.

PARENTAL BEHAVIOR AND EDUCATIONAL ACHIEVEMENT

It amazes me that the debate about how to improve education and learning continues to rage even louder. The reason I am astounded is that we already have massive amounts of verified and tested information that gives us direct answers as to what works to make students successful. Why school systems cannot take the information and move from research to practice boggles my mind. My short answer is to inform and empower parents, and then have families take more ownership of their children's learning.

I am quite sure, from my reading and analysis of a sample of the thousands of studies in the area, that parents hold the keys to academic achievement, more than quality teachers, or smaller class sizes, or higher budgets. More on this in the last section of this chapter.

In a now dated, but still accurate literature review of outcomes, the San Diego County Office of Education produced and posted a summary of large-scale studies which showed the impacts of home and family factors on educational achievement. We will use their work as a starting point for our discussion. Their three messages to parents are:

1. Create a home environment that encourages learning;
2. Express high (but not unrealistic) expectations for your children's achievement and future careers; and
3. Become involved in your children's education at school and in the community.

The studies and evidence that support these three common-sense behaviors for success are numerous. For example, in December 2005, William Jeynes reported on a meta-analytic review of 77 published studies to "determine the overall effects of parental involvement on K–12 students' academic achievement and to determine the extent to which certain expressions of parental involvement are beneficial to children." He addressed five overarching questions and his analysis provided good information that all educated parents should consider when helping their children with schoolwork. Let's review some of his statistically-verified conclusions. None of these are surprising at first glance, by the way.

The first conclusion was that parental involvement is directly associated with student achievement. He was able to show this effect with any type of outcome—student grades, teacher ratings, and even standardized test scores. The lesson—be involved and stay involved with your child's schoolwork—be it daily homework, projects, or science fairs. This sends messages to your child on many levels, from direct support to the communication that this work must be important since my parents are involved as well.

A second finding related to specific helpful behaviors that parents can engage in. Jeynes reported that the largest impact came from time-consuming, intense interaction between parent and student. So time spent reading with your child and less direct behaviors such as setting up an education-friendly home environment is valuable. This means talking about schoolwork and parental expressions of expectations were more important than other interventions. In fact, parental expectations trumped all other parental help and got the biggest response in achievement.

Other findings by Jeynes were that the results held true for all children, no matter their minority status, and that programs which encourage and facilitate parental involvement in schools also could result in better child achievement.

Sandra Christenson and Cathryn Peterson, writing for the University of Minnesota Extension online series "Parenting for School Success," completed a 2006 literature review on the effects of family on children's learning (K–12). They identified three key findings related to parent involvement:

1. A partnership orientation where "parents are essential, not merely desirable partners" in ensuring student success;
2. Findings about specific parenting effects on learning outcomes for teens; and
3. The importance of "involving families in a way that directly links to improving students' learning outcomes (i.e., developing students' specific knowledge and skills in academic, social, behavioral, and emotional domains)."

I could provide more redundant information in support of my argument, but I will stop here. There is no longer any debate about the role and importance of parental involvement in their child's success in school. Let us look at some specific behaviors parents can employ to help their children achieve academic success.

The San Diego report (referenced above) showed that student achievement improves when parents are empowered and facilitated to play four key roles in their children's learning. Their set:

- "As *teachers,* parents create a home environment that promotes learning, reinforces what is being taught at school, and develops the life skills children need to become responsible adults.
- As *supporters,* parents contribute their knowledge and skills to the school, enriching the curriculum, and providing extra services and support to students.
- As *advocates,* parents help children negotiate the system and receive fair treatment, and work to make the system more responsive to all families.
- As *decision-makers,* parents serve on advisory councils, curriculum committees, and management teams, participating in joint problem-solving at every level."

For this section of our chapter, the first two roles listed above (teachers and supporters) are relevant. In the last section, we will examine the advocate and decision-maker roles. So what can be your role as an in-home teacher or teacher support system?

The parent as supporter role means that you will spend time and be physically present at your child's school. This happens more naturally and in greater amounts in most private school settings. It is an unspoken truth that private school parents are aware of the price of education and that if they contribute little of their time and talents, they will surely be forced to spend more of their money.

Christenson and Peterson offer these very specific ways for an educated parent to support education in the home. They are:

IN THE AREA OF EXPECTATIONS AND ACCOUNTABILITY

- Parents set high, realistic expectations (e.g., based on present skill level and strengths).
- Parents' expectations for their child's school performance have been discussed (e.g., set goals together).
- Parents hold their child accountable for his/her actions.
- Parents have communicated how they expect their child to behave while in school.
- The child understands the consequences for not meeting the expectations and standards.
- Parents communicate to their child that attendance and participation in school are important.
- Parents are accepting and firm.
- Clear, consistent limits and guidelines about schoolwork and behavior are communicated and reinforced with the child.

IN THE AREA OF VALUES COMMUNICATED

- Parents communicate that effort, not luck, will result in improved school performance.
- Parents and their child discuss the importance and value of education (e.g., set clear academic goals with their child, encourage their child to take tougher courses in school).
- Parents explain to their child why school is important (e.g., talk to the child about how school learning is related to future goals/endeavors).
- Parents help their child set realistic goals and provide their child with regular feedback and support regarding progress (e.g., reviewing homework and tests together).

IN THE AREA OF ENCOURAGEMENT AND SUPPORT

- Parents support their child and encourage him/her to strive for good grades (e.g., have your child teach you one thing he/she learned in school each day).
- Parents' expectations for their child are focused on progress and achievement.
- Parents demonstrate and voice their belief that their child can meet the standards and expectations.
- Parents encourage their child to take more challenging course work.

(*Source:* http://www.extension.umn.edu/distribution/familydevelopment/ components/00079a.html)

These guidelines/recommendation are based upon research and the experience of these educators. They are common sense actions that families can accomplish with little dollar cost, but maximal parental investment.

What do Americans think about who is responsible for the current state of education in America? A poll asking about the quality of public education and who had responsibility for its outcomes was conducted by the Associated Press and Stanford University in fall 2010. The poll was scientific in nature and results were weighted, or adjusted, to ensure that responses accurately reflected America's demographic makeup. Results were reported through the Associated Press by Donna Gordon Blankinship in December 2010.

According to Blankinship, the poll revealed that "68% of adults believe parents deserve heavy blame for what's wrong with the U.S. education system—more than teachers, school administrators, the government or teachers unions." The survey also showed that "only 35%" of the responders agreed "that teachers deserve a great deal or a lot of the blame." Mothers (72%) were more likely than fathers (61%) to blame parents, and conservatives were more likely than moderates or liberals to blame parents. The parent blamers were more likely to cite a lack of student discipline and low expectations for students as serious problems in schools. They were also more likely to see fighting and low test scores as big problems.

Survey responders also noted that student discipline and fighting, violence, and gangs were extreme or very serious problems in schools. Many people reported concern about getting and keeping good teachers. Fifty-eight percent rated education in their local public schools as excellent or good, but 67 percent also believe the United States is falling behind the rest of the world when it comes to education. Of note, a majority of parents sees improvement in the system since they were in school: Fifty-five percent believe their children are getting a better education than they did, and ¾ rated the quality of education at their child's school as excellent or good. Many say their child's school is doing a good job preparing students for college (49%), the work force (39%), and life as an adult (41%). But a variety of research in past years backs up the poll respondents' sense that parenting plays key roles in school performance. Attendance is one such variable to watch. One in 10 kindergarten and first grade students misses a month of school every year, according to Attendance Counts (attendancecounts.org). By ninth grade, missing 20 percent of school is a better predictor of a student dropping out than eighth grade test scores are, according to Attendance Counts data. In the Associated Press poll, 41 percent of responders rated students "not spending enough time in school" as a serious problem.

Attendance Counts notes that the education of all children can be adversely affected when teachers turn their attention to meet the needs of chronically absent children, and available resources may be reduced when funding is tied to attendance. They argue that chronic early absence can be a signal to initiate interventions while problems are smaller and can be corrected.

RELATED ISSUES FOR YOUR CHILD'S EDUCATION

I wish to call attention to three global areas in this section: school placement issues, advanced placement (AP) and dual enrollment matters, and special education issues such as learning disabilities. These three areas can be important in helping your child succeed in school.

School placement issues include when to start your child in school and whether to enroll in a public or private school. When to start school is a question of school readiness. For example, if your child has a September birthday, should she/he start first grade as a six-year-old and be the youngest in class, or is it better to wait for a year of maturation and start first grade at seven, when she/he will be presumably better able to succeed? Most would say wait the year unless the child is exceptionally mature. However, a large-scale study led by psychologist Frederick Morrison found that younger children did not do any worse than their older first grade classmates. In addition, parents who held their kindergartner back a year did not get the result they hoped for. Those children, although oldest in their first grades, did no better than their younger peers.

Morrison's research showed that delaying school does not provide any advantage. The research also showed that it could be harmful in some cases. The true indicator of readiness is not age, but overall developmental level where the needed skills have been attained.

Google "private vs. public school decision" and you will get a wide variety of opinions on how to make this decision for your child. The group EducationBug (www.educationbug.org) has published articles on this comparison topic. Among reasons listed on this site to choose public schools are items such as cost (none), assured teacher certification and curriculum standards, and some school choice with the advent of charter schools. Reasons to select private schools include selective admission which allows for a less troubled student body, greater investment in outcomes by the teachers and families, dedicated teaching of certain religious or philosophical views, and possibly more diverse faculty as those teachers may have different credentialing or certification than those in public schools.

Often this becomes a personal family decision (as is homeschooling, below) which takes into account school district quality and reputation, certain child characteristics, family income level, and possible religious commitment matters. Rather than list many other factors, I urge the educated parent to do the research in reaching this decision.

Advanced placement and dual enrollment coursework are great ways to spur your student to take on self-bettering academic challenges. *AP coursework* refers to a program of courses run by the College Board, a New York-based, nonprofit agency. Students can take the AP courses in high school or as a homeschooled student. There are advantages for students to do the extra work.

Allen Grove of about.com has posted six reasons to consider AP classes. First is to impress college admissions personnel, who will see that you took challenging coursework and are ready for college. Second, AP coursework helps a high school student to develop college-level academic skills. Third, you can save money as AP classes/exams are less costly than college tuition rates. A fourth reason is that many AP classes will fulfill general education requirements and let you get to major courses faster in college. Reasons five and six are about freeing up your schedule to either take electives or to more easily add a second major or a minor.

Dual enrollment refers to a program that allows eligible high school students to simultaneously enroll in a college course, often at a community college. The credits earned must be used toward both their high school graduation requirements and a college degree. Benefits of dual enrollment courses include a better high school level course, the chance to "double dip" and get college credits early, and saving money in later college tuition costs.

Learning disabilities, as broadly used here, refers to a number of conditions which interfere with a child's abilities to be successful in school-related work. Some are neurological disorders that can make it difficult to acquire certain academic and social skills. Others are behavioral or psychiatric-based conditions. Still others may involve physical handicaps.

Federal laws guarantee that all children receive an education, and guarantee that they have access and help if they have a qualifying condition known to interfere with their learning or learning processes. These include the Individuals with Disabilities Education Act of 2004 (IDEA), the Americans with Disabilities Act (ADA), now the Americans with Disabilities Act Amendments Act (ADAAA), and Section 504 of the Rehabilitation Act of 1973 (or Section 504).

If your child shows any signs of difficulty with schoolwork (remember "know your child" from chapter 1), your first step is to consult with his/her teacher. A teacher will have the ability to roughly assess your student's work and progress and determine if it is in the normal range. If the teacher suspects some difficulty after consulting with you, your child will be referred to a diagnostician. This person can be a school psychologist or other trained person. Generally this step involves administration of a test battery and interviews.

Based upon your child's performance and other relevant information, a test report will be issued with findings. At this point your child may receive a diagnosis of a condition requiring remediation or assistance with schoolwork. This is just the beginning.

I refer the educated parent to the Internet and other sources for further information about the specifics of any disability. There are too many to cover in this chapter. Information about the cause, course, and remediation of the disability can be easily found. Or your school can provide this information to you. Of importance to this chapter is your response as a parent.

Research related to parenting children with learning disabilities is limited, and is most concerned with stress management and ways to negotiate the education system and its rules. One recent study to examine the effects of a learning-disabled child on parents and families was done by Lily Dyson. She looked at 11 parents of students aged 8–16 years old who participated in two separate focus group interviews. The study found that children with learning disabilities had family-based effects, including negative reactions from extended family, difficulties in school interactions, and troubles among siblings. Additional specific negative effects included parental guilt, marital discord, and family stress. Dyson's data suggested that both parents and siblings would benefit from support groups.

As a parent of a child with a certified learning disability, you have certain rights. These include the right to help develop your child's individualized education program (IEP), to be kept informed about your child's progress and performance, to have your child placed in the least restrictive environment, and to have a due process hearing if you believe your child is not being properly helped or to settle other disagreements/differences.

HelpGuide, a reliable, vetted online information source, offers these suggestions as things you can do to help your child if she/he has a learning disability. The list includes:

- *Keep things in perspective*—Try not to be intimidated by the news that your child may have a learning disability—all people learn differently. Your most important job is to support your child and to help them keep their self-esteem intact. Challenges can be overcome. Don't let the tests, school bureaucracy, and endless paperwork distract you from what is really important—providing your child with emotional, educational, and moral support.

- *Do your own research and become your own expert*—Learn about new developments in learning disabilities, different programs, and educational techniques that could make an impact with your child. You may instinctively look to others for solutions—schools, teachers, therapists, or doctors—but you need to take charge when it comes to finding the tools your child needs to continue learning.

- *Be an advocate for your child*—You may have to speak up time and time again to get special help for your child. Embrace your role as a proactive parent and work on your communication skills. It may be frustrating at times, but your calm, reasonable, and firm voice may make the difference in achieving what you want for your child.

- *Remember that your influence on your child outweighs all others*—Your child will follow your lead. If you approach the learning challenges with optimism, hard work, and a sense of humor, your child is likely to embrace your perspective or at least see the challenges as a detour rather than a roadblock. Also, remember that the school situation doesn't have to be perfect. Focus your energy on learning what works and implementing it in your child's life the best you can.

(*Source:* www.helpguide.org/mental/learning_disabilities.htm)

HOMESCHOOLING

For some families, homeschooling is the preferred option. What is the current status of homeschooling in the United States? The answer depends upon whom you ask. I found one website (http://homeschooling.gomil pitas.com/weblinks/numbers.htm) with interesting estimates and a well-explained method of how the numbers could be found.

Author Anne Zeise states that there were about 1.5 million homeschooled students in the United States in 2007. Those estimates were based on data from the Parent and Family Involvement in Education Survey (PFI) of the 2007 National Household Education Surveys Program (NHES). The NHES provides descriptive data on the educational activities of the U.S. population and provides a variety of statistics on the condition of education in the United States. Data from the 2007 NHES surveys were conducted with the parents of 10,681 students, including 290 homeschooled students. For 2010–11, Zeise estimated about 1.4 million children were homeschooled, with certain caveats.

She argues that perception of whether or not schools in a certain state are good or bad helps to drive interest in homeschooling. The ease of complying with homeschool regulations and laws in a state also impacts the numbers of children involved. In a number of states, homeschoolers are not registered as such, either because they need not or do not comply with reporting rules. Of the largest states, California and Texas do not have a reporting rule.

Zeise reports that the overall homeschooled numbers' change in rate of growth has been "declining, right along with the birth rates." The numbers increased when the economic turmoil of 2008 to the present happened. She surmises that "many families can no longer afford private schools, and so have turned to homeschooling. Others may have decided to home school when one parent lost their job and could stay home and teach."

Another source, the National Home Education Research Institute (NHERI), claims that the actual number of homeschooled children in the United States, as of 2010, is 2.04 million. NHERI is a nonprofit operation that provides homeschool research and support for those wanting to educate at home.

Is homeschooling right for your child? If you look at who is winning national spelling and geography bees, it might seem so. (In fact, the research comparing homeschooled to traditionally-schooled children shows little, if any, real differences in test scores or other achievement measures.) What are your reasons for wanting to homeschool? If it is to protect your child from exposure to a poor education system, you might want to work to improve that system. Protection from bad kids or bad teachers seems to be a good reason, but I am not so sure. Your child will have to live in a world where she/he cannot choose all of the people with whom she/he will associate. At what point do you let your child have exposure and experiences with all sorts of other people in order to learn how to get along? The longer a child is shielded, the more a child falls behind in the normal socialization process. The future catch up may be harder and more painful than any gain made by having been isolated earlier.

Some of the Homeschooling Research and Scholarship and NHERI page-listed research indicates that some minority families and Muslim Americans are choosing homeschooling to avoid prejudicial or other negative treatment. A number of research reports also suggest that many homeschoolers have chosen religion-based issues and concerns as reasons. Parents of special needs children are also playing a larger role on the homeschool landscape.

A variety of support and other resources for homeschooling are now available, and quite frankly, a rather large business has quickly grown to provide parents with the tools they need to teach at home. When considering the homeschooling option, there is much to bear in mind. What can and will you do differently than could be accomplished by having your child in a public or private school setting? What will you realistically be able to do with your child? How will you structure the days and weeks to be sure that there is the right balance of teaching time without going overboard and having burnout, or going too easy and allowing your child to fall behind? How will your relationship be affected by 24/7 involvement and interaction with your child? Will you act differently when you are Mom or Dad versus when you are the teacher? Or will your interactions with your child be seamless as you act in the roles of both parent and educator with little distinction made, or noticed, by your child?

In *The Educated Parent,* I cited Mary Jo Bratton, who suggests that you first write out your reasons for homeschooling and the educational goals you wish to achieve in each subject area. She suggests, up front, that you consider carefully and answer questions such as these:

• Why do you want to teach your own children?

• Do you want to ensure your child's religious training or academic achievement?

• Do you want to ensure your child's individuality, or assure yourself of a continuance of family and ethnic traditions?

You will need to establish educational goals that focus on some product or outcomes. What do you want your child to be able to do as a result of having been taught the material you will present? How will what you do be different from what could be achieved in a typical school placement?

You need to create a list of specific and measurable educational objectives. You can do this on a subject by subject basis, and relate your goals to those of your local school district. (You will need to contact your local school district to find out about any regulations, grade- or age-specific learning goals, or in-home testing requirements which may be in force.)

You may also want to consider teaching other important values and attitudes needed for success in life. These could include determination and resolve, intellectual curiosity and a commitment to lifelong learning, an appreciation of the aesthetic qualities in the arts and music, and an awareness and tolerance of similarities and differences of peoples of the world. How will you accomplish this? How will you know if you are on the right track?

Homeschooling goals should be sensitive to the needs of the whole child and include physical fitness and good mental health as areas of emphasis as well. A final point involves your knowing your child's strengths and weaknesses. As with the goodness of fit model between parent and child temperament, a parent needs to carefully assess whether the parent-child team will be able to work together well, and whether your child's education needs are best served by homeschooling.

Let us not forget the social dimensions of regular school attendance versus homeschooling. Are there substitute experiences for learning to deal with bullies or how to handle gossip? Who will the child associate and play with on a regular basis? Who will attend your child's birthday parties and how many parties will your child get invited to? What benefits are there to school groups like being part of a marching band or a service club or a school athletic team? Is it important for a child/teen to work on a school yearbook or go to a prom?

Surely, many of the above activities can have alternate adventures provided for by concerned parents, but they will require more planning and effort than when these experiences are naturally acquired in a school setting. And what if your child is shy or has some social phobia? Not having to face this attribute and learning to cope and adjust in more limited settings rather than the world at large will have its price.

There has been very little recent, reputable research on the social consequences of homeschooling. For many, the issue has been settled; there are few significant differences. Mary K. Saunders found that first-year college students who previously homeschooled reported positive social experiences and commitment to their school. Their persistence rates (rates of staying in school) were no different from traditionally-schooled freshmen.

Saunders mailed a social experiences survey to the entire 2004–05 freshman class of Wheaton College after they had finished their first year of college. Based upon 261 responses (43% return rate), she found "no significant effects on the student's integration" into college life based upon previous schooling, and a slightly stronger intent among homeschooled students to remain at Wheaton. In *The Educated Parent,* I reported on work by Larry Shyers, who compared the social adjustment levels between homeschooled and traditionally-schooled students and found no differences.

Homeschooling is a now rather big business, growing bigger each year. One can purchase curricula, textbooks, other learning materials, and even teaching and child management tips. There are many websites and online resources. Some are state-sponsored.

The state of Florida has developed and continues to fund an online curriculum. Called the Florida Virtual School (www.FLVS.net), more than 50,000 students are enrolled in a variety of web-based, technology-based, and traditional courses. FLVS students can be homeschooled or attend public or private schools. They can be enrolled in Advanced Placement or standard on-grade-level courses. Courses are open to students in K–12 all year long. They are considered a "meLearning" community, meaning that you have an individual, student-focused educational experience at your convenience.

For homeschooling families, the site touts the reasons to use the system such as schedule flexibility, access to over 100 accredited online courses for any student resident of Florida at no cost, and access to certified teachers trained in distance education. And the online accredited program is specifically designed to meet Sunshine State Standards and graduation standards.

Ultimately the choice to homeschool is yours. I urge caution and a great deal of parental homework and research in advance of making the decision to homeschool.

PARENTING ADVOCACY IN SUPPORT OF EDUCATION

What role can the educated parent play in support of education? Clearly, parent advocates are essential in the United States given the way that school boards are structured. This is also true because of the level of oversight of elected government officials.

Elected officials will always answer to the electorate. The educated parent thus must become an advocate who votes and gets involved in the debate about how educational systems will be operated and funded.

One country whose education system may be a model for some U.S. school districts is Finland. In a 2011 *Time* magazine article, Joshua Levine reported that Finland's students scored in the top three internationally in reading, math, and sciences. They are second only to South Korean and Singapore students in the Organisation for Economic Co-operation and Development (OECD) assessments. In the latest OECD report (2009), U.S. students, by comparison, finished down in the mid-teens in the same categories.

How do our Finnish counterparts achieve such academic success? Not by adding to a child's workload. According to the *Time* report, there is both a shorter school day than in the United States and a daily homework maximum of an hour. There is a different attitude toward education nationwide. One innovative way the teachers make a difference is to track across grades with their students for multiple years. So a teacher may start with a cohort of first graders and change grades with his/her students for six consecutive years. In this way, the teacher is able to learn individual traits and issues related to each student in the classroom. This continuity would provide great advantages with the right teachers.

Could this work in the United States? Possibly, but several problems might include the shifting residencies of U.S. students, whose families move often in any given six-year stretch of time. Other issues would be related to the federal and state governmental oversight micromanaging that can interfere with what happens in the school district or school level. Other U.S. issues that might interfere with this approach are related to the way U.S. teachers are trained and the role of unions in what may be tried or not tried. According to Levine's report, teachers in Finland are given more respect and the teaching profession is more valued. Finnish schools actually are very selective, so only the best and brightest are trained to teach. And these teachers all earn a master's degree before going into the classroom, making them better prepared as a group.

I mentioned earlier that we know the answer to failed schools. The answer is parental involvement. As Christenson and Peterson have said in their review of variables for school success: "The question, at this point, is not: What are the factors that help increase the probability of student success in school? Rather, the critical question is: How can families, schools, and communities work together to enhance student learning?"

Of note, state legislatures have gotten involved in several ways. On one level, they are concerned about accountability in the way that federal government initiatives have been enacted. I will not spend much time discussing the No Child Left Behind Act of 2002. This was the ultimate accountability law in that it tied school jobs (principals and teachers) to results (all children reading by third grade). By now, we are all aware that the unintended consequence has been an over-reliance on school test scores that focus on some subjects like reading, and pay little attention to social studies or music. This in turn has led to serious school anxiety as discussed more fully in chapter 7.

As an educated parent, you must decide if this is the direction you want for public education. This is a complex issue. Accountability and results are important goals. Why should so many tax dollars and resources be spent when school performance measures continue to decline? But the process has been mired in politics and has many not-so-hidden agendas involving noneducation issues like the role of unions and teacher tenure. I urge the educated parent to become informed and make your opinions known.

State legislatures have sensed the need to include parents in their attempts to fix education. Although many states have initiatives, allow me to present two recent proposals. In Lakeland, Florida, state house member Kelli Stargel proposed a law that would hold parents responsible for their child's performance in class. She believes that school systems need to go beyond just teacher accountability for a complete picture. Florida, like most states, has spent years attempting to reverse declining test scores, raise student standards, and improve overall education quality. Despite a variety of efforts, mainly based upon statewide testing at certain points in the K–12 system (by use of the FCAT), few sustainable gains have been accomplished.

Florida House Bill 255, The Parent Involvement and Accountability in Public Schools Act, was proposed in spring 2011. The bill was designed to get more parental involvement by use of a parent report card distributed four times a year. For parents with children in kindergarten through third grade, the parent card would be included with their child's report card.

In a CNN article by John Couwels, Rep. Stargel was quoted as saying, "We have student accountability, we have teacher accountability, and we have administration accountability. This was the missing link, which was, look at the parent and making sure the parents are held accountable." Couwels also reported that the grading system is based on three criteria that Stargel wrote in the legislation:

- A child should be at school on time, prepared to learn after a good night's sleep, and have eaten a meal.
- A child should have the homework done and be prepared for examinations.
- There should be regular communication between the parent and teacher.

"Those three things are key to a quality education," Stargel said.

As proposed, parents would be given one of three grades: Satisfactory, Needs Improvement, or Unsatisfactory. The grades would be based on the parents' performance in three areas: attendance of the child, preparation of the child for class, and communication level between parent and teacher. (The proposed law would allow for parents to appeal any grade they disagree with.) At this writing, the bill had been referred for committee reviews, at which time the legislative session was adjourned for the year.

What should an educated parent make of this idea? The responses to this proposed law were across the spectrum from acceptance to rejection. Is this a creative way to get parental involvement? Is it a cynical ploy to play teachers against parents? Is it more political grandstanding? Is it another example of a well-intentioned, but woefully inept education fix by a person untrained to deal with the complexities of the problems they attempt to remedy? Is this what we need to force parents to do their part?

Not to be outdone by Florida, Colorado lawmakers proposed and actually passed legislation to increase parental involvement in public education. Elizabeth Stortroen, in an April 2009 *Colorado Statesman* article, reported on Senate Bill 90. (This bill passed and was signed by the governor on May 21, 2009.)

SB 90 requires certain percentages of parental representation on new school accountability committees that are representative of each district's demographics. The bill also creates an advisory council to promote best practices and strategies for parent involvement and a program creating grants for schools to use in implementing parent education.

Ms. Stortroen cited a bill co-sponsor, Representative Debbie Benefield: "What we want to do with this bill is teach parents how to be partners in their child's education and how to be an advocate," she said. "This (bill) has to do with quality parent involvement. It has to do with the fact that a lot of parents truly, until there is an issue in their child's education, have not got a clue on how to effectively advocate for their child's education."

Colorado Senator Evie Hudak, sponsor of SB-90, stated that her bill "seeks to improve parent involvement in education from early childhood through college, with the goal of improving student achievement, closing achievement gaps, decreasing the dropout rate, and improving the enrollment and success in postsecondary education." SB 90 was initiated by the Colorado Parent Involvement Network for Education, whose interest in part is to boost Colorado's ability to comply with the parent involvement provisions of No Child Left Behind.

What do you make of the initiatives in Florida and Colorado or in your home state? It is time for parents to become a force and louder voice in their role in public education. There is at least one national organization, Parents for Public Schools (www.parents4publicschools.com), which can provide some information for the educated parent. (I cannot endorse this particular group due to my lack of information, but my initial response is positive.) If you go online, you will easily find local organizations dedicated to helping parents partner in education.

According to the website, Parents for Public Schools (PPS) "is a national organization of community-based chapters working with public school parents and other supporters to improve and strengthen local public schools. We believe that quality public education is vital to our democracy and to America's future. We value parents as owners of public schools and as peers with all those seeking to improve schools. PPS is invigorated by a diverse membership whose involvement in public schools helps to ensure that quality public education is available equally to all children."

Their description matches my call to action. I urge your consideration and decision to get engaged in this process at whatever level you can. The future is in the hands of the educated parent.

SIX

Childhood Stress, Anxiety, and Behavioral Disorders

A characteristic of the normal child is he doesn't act that way very often.

~Author Unknown

Nothing you do for a child is ever wasted.

~Garrison Keillor

If a child is given love, he becomes loving. . . . If he's helped when he needs help, he becomes helpful. And if he has been truly valued at home . . . he grows up secure enough to look beyond himself to the welfare of others.

~Dr. Joyce Brothers

In this chapter, we will address the issue of children and mental health issues. Increasingly, parents are faced with matters related to stress, anxiety, and even more serious problems. Allow me to provide some information and some research on what to look for and what you can do, as an educated parent, to protect and help your children if one of these difficulties should arise.

In *The Educated Parent,* I addressed several stress- and anxiety-related issues. (I also covered the widely diagnosed attention deficit hyperactivity disorder (chapter 5). The area has grown so much that I now devote this and the next chapter to the subject. In chapters 6 and 7 of this book, you will see an all new presentation with little overlap.

One excellent online resource for the educated parent is sponsored by the National Institute of Mental Health (NIMH; http://www.nimh.nih.gov/science-news/science-news-about-children-and-adolescents.shtml).   This site presents and summarizes a variety of articles and research reports on issues related to mental health problems in children and adolescents. It can be viewed by topic as well as year.

So the educated parent can research quickly some of the latest findings related to ADHD or autism and many other common disorders. These articles are generally brief, to the point, and written in an understandable, nontechnical way. Many of the articles are written with specific findings or results. If you are looking for broad information, there are better sites. But if you have a child with a certain diagnosis, you can keep track of recent research trends in treatment and diagnostic issues. I would caution anyone to be careful about also verifying and collecting information from other sources.

IMPACTS OF STRESS ON YOUR CHILD'S DEVELOPMENT

Stress is defined in different ways. One definition has to do with any circumstances that threaten or are seen as threatening one's well-being, and that thereby tax one's coping ability. Others liken stress to the experience of change. What is agreed upon is that all people encounter stressors, the agents of stress, every day. Psychologists have outlined four principle types of stress:

- *Frustration.* This is experienced in any situation where the pursuit of some goal is thwarted, as when a child is told "no."
- *Conflict.* This occurs when two or more motivations or impulses compete for our action. Three types of conflict have been studied extensively: approach-approach—when a person has a choice between two attractive goals; approach-avoidance—when a choice must be made about whether to pursue a single goal that has both attractive and unattractive aspects, usually resulting in vacillation, or going back and forth; and avoidance-avoidance—when we must make a choice between two undesirable alternatives.

- *Change.* This happens when we have to adapt or adjust to new circumstances. The Holmes and Rahe Social Readjustment Rating Scale life units discussed in *The Educated Parent* measure "change stress."
- *Social Pressure.* These pressures involve expectations or demands that one behave in a certain way; the best examples are pressures to perform, comply, or conform.

Researchers such as Richard S. Lazarus have discovered that minor stresses, called daily hassles, can add up over time to be as stressful as a major traumatic event. So days of problems in school, or fights with siblings, or troubles with friends can become as negative as a parents' divorce or a natural disaster. The child/teen's appraisals of these events, which are very subjective, influence the effect of the event.

Jennifer S. Middlebrooks and Natalie C. Audage, CDC researchers, have reported on the long-term effects of childhood stress. For their work, they define stress as positive, tolerable, or toxic. These are their definitions, verbatim:

Positive stress results from adverse experiences that are short-lived. Children may encounter positive stress when they attend a new daycare, get a shot, meet new people, or have a toy taken away from them. This type of stress causes minor physiological changes including an increase in heart rate and changes in hormone levels. With the support of caring adults, children can learn how to manage and overcome positive stress. This type of stress is considered normal and coping with it is an important part of the development process.

Tolerable stress refers to adverse experiences that are more intense but still relatively short-lived. Examples include the death of a loved one, a natural disaster, a frightening accident, and family disruptions such as separation or divorce. If a child has the support of a caring adult, tolerable stress can usually be overcome. In many cases, tolerable stress can become positive stress and benefit the child developmentally. However, if the child lacks adequate support, tolerable stress can become toxic and lead to long-term negative health effects.

Toxic stress results from intense adverse experiences that may be sustained over a long period of time—weeks, months or even years. An example of toxic stress is child maltreatment, which includes abuse and neglect. Children are unable to effectively manage this type of stress by themselves. As a result, the stress response system gets activated for a prolonged amount of time. This can lead to permanent changes in the development of the brain. The negative effects of toxic stress can be lessened with the support of caring adults. Appropriate support and intervention can help in returning the stress response system back to its normal baseline. (*Source:* CDC Report, 2008)

Based on their review of the research, Middlebrooks and Audage concluded that "prolonged exposure to stress hormones can impact the brain and impair functioning in a variety of ways." These include negative effects on synapses, disruption of brain circuitry, increases in stress hormone releases, and damage to brain areas involved in memory.

Research findings also demonstrate that childhood stress can impact adult health. The Adverse Childhood Experiences (ACE) study has looked at the responses of more than 17,000 adults who reported details of their past histories of stressors and their current health status. Full details can be found in the CDC report cited at the end of this chapter.

Middlebrooks and Audage reported that the more adverse childhood experiences reported, the more adult health problems seen. These health problems include alcohol abuse, depression, and suicide attempts. With a higher number of adverse childhood experiences in their recent past, teens are more likely to engage in risky and harmful behaviors.

The ACE study provides definitive evidence that certain childhood stress experiences can lead to a wide array of negative behaviors and poor health outcomes. The ACE study also found associations between experiencing these stressors and suicide attempts and the risk of perpetrating or experiencing "intimate partner violence" (IPV). In fact, witnessing and/or experiencing IPV acts was linked to other abusive actions, more risky sexual behavior as an adult, more drug/alcohol issues, and more disrupted adult relationships.

The ACE report concludes with important information on screening children for toxic stressors and working to prevent additional exposure and subsequent negative outcomes.

The way to help children deal with stress is to teach coping strategies. These strategies are based upon a child's ability to understand the situation and to identify emotions and thoughts related to the stressor. This does not come naturally and has to be taught. The educated parent can assist a child by first helping him/her to see how she/he reacts and responds under certain circumstances. In this way, the child learns what causes a stress response. The following generic steps are based on a cognitive behavioral model that works well with both children and adults.

Most children from age seven years and higher can learn ways to identify what causes them to feel stressed. They can then learn how to avoid those situations or to recognize them early on. In so doing, children can try to get out of the situation with less harm. If they cannot get away, they can then learn what to do—their coping response. Some of this will involve knowing when to ask for help or support from others.

To get started, parent and child need to communicate about current events or worries that cause stress. Depending on your child's age, she/he can keep a diary of daily events. For a month or so, you can then sit with your child once per week to review what has happened and how your child responded/coped with the events of their last seven days of life.

The American Academy of Pediatrics (AAP) offers several online resources for parents that can help deal with childhood stress. I will summarize two of them here. In the first, a 2010 report, the AAP presents an overview of what stress is and how young children and middle schoolers' lives have daily challenges. The AAP notes that life stress events can impact children if not dealt with appropriately. The AAP also reviews the work on temperament as a mediator, allowing some children better adjustment levels than others.

The AAP report notes that "children are very sensitive to the changes around them, especially to the feelings and reactions of their parents." Family stressors related to job losses or money problems impact parents. That in turn impacts children. Today's "middle years child" raises the concern that this generation faces much more stress and pressure than that experienced by children in earlier times. This is coupled with fewer social supports due to changes in family structures. These include households impacted by divorce as well as two-parent working families. On top of this, often few relatives (like a grandparent or aunt/uncle) live in physical proximity. Add overscheduling and fewer hours of down time, and this age group is stressed out. Parents need to monitor their children for signs of stress and burnout and then act to reduce the stress levels.

All of this ties nicely into the concept of resilience. *Resilience* may be defined as the positive capacity of people to cope with stress and adversity based on internal characteristics. (The classic, original resilience in children work, reviewed in *The Educated Parent,* was done by Emmy Werner and Ruth Smith.) Resilience allows children to overcome negative stress-related consequences.

And this leads us to a second AAP report, named the "7 C's of Resilience." The AAP identifies these characteristics, and urges parents to nurture and help build the seven C's in their children. Kenneth Ginsburg, a pediatrician at The Children's Hospital of Philadelphia, has a website (www.fosteringresilience.com) that also promotes ways to build the seven

C's in children. Ginsburg is the director of health services at Covenant House Pennsylvania, an agency that serves Philadelphia's homeless and marginalized youth.

From a 2006 AAP document, "Helping Your Child Cope With Life," these are the seven C's:

Competence—the ability to handle situations effectively.

Confidence—the solid belief in one's own abilities.

Connection—close ties to family, friends, school, and community give children a sense of security and values that prevent them from seeking destructive alternatives to love and attention.

Character—a fundamental sense of right and wrong that helps children make wise choices, contribute to the world, and become stable adults.

Contribution—when children realize that the world is a better place because they are in it, they will take actions and make choices that improve the world. They will also develop a sense of purpose to carry them through future challenges.

Coping—children who learn to cope effectively with stress are better prepared to overcome life's challenges.

Control—when children realize that they can control their decisions and actions, they're more likely to know that they have what it takes to bounce back.

Another resource in this area is the Center for Effective Collaboration and Practice (CECP; http://cecp.air.org/center.asp). One of the goals of the CECP is "to foster the development and the adjustment of children with or at risk of developing serious emotional disturbance." The CECP has produced a list of family protective factors which can build and foster resilience in your child, and also recommends specific parental activities.

Family protective factors include such things as providing warm, structured, and positive discipline practices, support from extended family, building a stable environment and home, and providing positive experiences for children in the community. Within the home, this would include proper toys and safe places to play and explore, and making time for quality family interaction.

As parents, you can build resilience in your children with such actions as expressing your love physically and verbally, parenting in an authoritative fashion, using praise and punishment as deserved, modeling prosocial behaviors through your empathy and caring, and encouraging your child to persist in the face of adversity. These skills, similar to those related to self-efficacy (as discussed in chapter 5), are important ways to encourage autonomy and problem solving. A parent who tells a child "I know you can do it" helps to build confidence. At the same time, the message of "I'm here" comforts and reminds the child of the trusting relationships that he or she can rely on.

Resilience remains an important topic in the research. The New York Academy of Sciences (www.nyas.org) convened a group of behavioral scientists, psychologists, neurobiologists, pediatricians, social workers, and public policy makers in 2006 to discuss what is known about resilience in children and how to use this information for healthier youth.

The highlights of the conference focused on known aspects of resilience such as temperament and stress tolerance, and expanded some of this work to look at genetic factors underlying them. It is believed that genetics play a large role in making a child more vulnerable (e.g., inhibited temperaments) or more resistant (e.g., positive affect and optimistic outlook) to environmental adversity. Of course, the real mystery is in understanding how genetics and environment interact and lead to a resilient outcome.

The NYAS conference also looked at brain plasticity as a factor related to early intervention and possible harm. Brain processes (as seen with real-time fMRI imaging) that control executive function, including cognition, attention, and impulse control, are most active in children with flexibility and coping skills, indicating that these regions of the brain are important for resilience. The interested reader is encouraged to visit the site for much more information.

IMPACTS OF ANXIETY ON YOUR CHILD'S DEVELOPMENT

We now turn to the topic of anxiety in children. *Anxiety* is a normal reaction experienced by all human beings. It is most commonly associated with stress and worry. An anxiety response can actually be helpful in some situations since it heightens our awareness and lets us be better prepared to act. For example, worrying may help a child work harder at school or prepare more diligently for tests. Anxiety becomes a problem when it interferes with normal, daily living.

There are a number of anxiety disorders, as we will soon see. Collectively, they are among the most common mental disorders experienced by Americans, including children—25.1 percent of all 13–18-year-olds will develop an anxiety disorder. Thirty percent of girls and 20 percent of boys in this age group will be affected. And younger children are also impacted, as we saw in chapter 2.

Allow me to present a brief overview of the most common anxiety disorders in children.

Separation anxiety disorder (SAD) is marked by extreme anxiety and panic when a child is away from home or his/her parents. Such a child is fearful and emotional at the thought of being away from the home base. This disorder affects about four percent of all children (peaking at ages seven to nine years), with girls more likely than boys to show this behavior.

Parents may see a mild form of SAD in the toddler years when leaving a child at a daycare or other place. It is not SAD if the child calms down quickly after realizing that she/he will be okay and will be reunited with parents later in the day. In older children, this may be the root issue if a child does not want to do sleepovers or go to summer camp when all his/her peers are engaging in these activities. One reason for SAD is that a child may fear that some harm will happen to his/her parents while apart. This can also occur with school refusal.

School refusal, also called school phobia, is a condition related to a child's fear of going to school or staying in school for the full day. Sometimes a child will just refuse to go; often she/he will start to complain about not feeling well (headache, stomachache). Soon after being allowed to stay home, your child will feel fine. This needs to happen on a repeated basis to rise to the level of a diagnosis. In more severe cases, one would see tantrums, defiance, and other anxiety symptoms like panic.

School refusal can come about for a number of reasons: from fear of change, stresses at home, marital discord, or bullying threats at school. Often, the affected child is concerned about some harm that may come to his/her parent while she/he is away. Some students will refuse to go to school because of fear of not doing well or trying to avoid a test. (This is different from test anxiety.) School refusal cases are more common at age five or six when school is a new and unknown situation, or again in the preteens as middle school approaches. Sometimes the school refusal is related to social anxieties and peer relations.

The Anxiety Disorders Association of America (ADAA) recommends having your child properly evaluated as a first step. Until a professional can determine why your child is acting this way, little can be done. Once the reason for the behavior is known, a treatment plan can be put together, often involving a combination of behavioral interventions and drug therapy.

The ADAA also cautions parents to be sure the child goes to school. Once you allow your child to stay home, she/he is positively reinforced for the anxiety response, making treatment success more difficult. The

ADAA site offers a number of specific parenting tips to help your child cope. In my practice, I would routinely see two to three cases in the month of September each year. For the most part, school guidance counselors handle these situations with success.

Another possible reason for school refusal is that a child is developing a social anxiety disorder. Also known as a *social phobia,* this disorder occurs when a child is overly fearful in performance situations like reading aloud or giving a speech. It can even be related to fear of answering questions in class or talking to peers. The concern with social phobia is that it will interfere with peer relationships and normal socialization processes in school and other places.

Social phobia can be mistaken for shyness. It is much more intense than that, although its early development can start there. The typical age of onset for social phobia is 13 years old. Of note, as many as 36 percent of people with this disorder live with this condition for more than 10 years before seeking help. By then, many disruptions have occurred in their lives. It is important to treat and overcome this disorder as soon as it is known.

Another anxiety disorder somewhat common in children is called *generalized anxiety disorder* (GAD). With GAD, a child worries about almost everything. Children dealing with GAD are like pessimists in training, always fearing that the worst can and will happen. For a clinical-level diagnosis, the excessive worrying and fretting must last for at least six months. These children lack the coping skills to stop their worry cycles and feel their anxiety is beyond their control. At the same time, they often also realize that they are more worried than they should be and that they are over-responding. Over time, this leads to the onset of a range of physical problems like stomach upset and headaches.

GAD has a more biological basis. It runs in families. It can be related to infants born with inhibited or slow-to-warm temperaments. The good news is that such children can be taught coping strategies and can learn to live with and manage their anxieties if caught early.

Less common anxiety disorders affecting children include obsessive-compulsive disorder; phobias; panic disorders; posttraumatic stress disorder; and elective mutism, a condition where a child refuses to speak except in certain safe places like home. As with GAD, children with certain temperaments are more predisposed to these disorders.

Gail A. Bernstein, Endowed Professor in Child & Adolescent Anxiety Disorders at the University of Minnesota Medical School, has written a status report type summary of progress in the treatment of anxiety disorders in children. As we know, treating anxiety disorders is important because these disorders are associated with negative outcomes in areas such as peer relationship difficulties, academic failure, and later onset of adult disorders including major depression and alcohol abuse.

Bernstein notes the widespread presence of anxiety conditions. She reports that anxiety symptoms "are very common" in child groups. According to her data, "about 70% of grade school children report they worry 'every now and then.'" These worries are most associated with school performance, illness issues, getting teased, making mistakes, or concern about physical appearance.

According to Bernstein, a number of factors play a role in developing anxiety disorders in children. These factors include: genetic issues, temperament type, insecure mother-child attachment patterns, presence of a parent's anxiety disorder, and an overprotective parenting style. Behavioral inhibition in young children, the inhibited temperament we have discussed previously, is also of concern. She defines *behavioral inhibition* as a "persistent, fearful, avoidant behavior in response to new situations and novel stimuli" that increases the likelihood of later developing anxiety disorders.

On the treatment front, there have been many documented successes. Cognitive-behavioral therapy (CBT) for individuals and groups is quite effective in treating youth with separation anxiety disorder, social phobia, and/or GAD. When using drug therapies, selective serotonin reuptake inhibitors (SSRIs) have been shown to "have short-term efficacy and safety" in the treatment of childhood anxiety disorders.

The final frontier has been in the area of early identification and intervention (as discussed in the work of Brian Fisak featured in chapter 2). Bernstein reports on a project from Queensland, Australia in which Mark Dadds and his group evaluated the effectiveness of a cognitive-behavioral and family-based group intervention for preventing the onset and development of anxiety problems in children. The overall results showed that anxiety problems and disorders identified using child and teacher reports could be successfully targeted through an early intervention school-based program. Early intervention programs such as these can prevent the later negative outcomes associated with untreated anxiety.

In a project led by UCLA psychology professor Michelle Craske, work is under way to predict anxiety and depressive disorders before they develop. Her team is currently involved in an eight-year-study, involving 650 young adults, to identify risk factors for anxiety and depression. The team is looking at the personality dimension of neuroticism as a predictive risk factor. By definition, *neuroticism* is the predisposition toward negative emotions such as fear, anxiety, guilt, sadness, or anger.

In this study, subjects were given a task where there was a chance they would receive mild electric shocks. The researchers studied their physiological reactions, such as the "startle reflex," which is measured by eye blinks, heart rate, and sweat gland activity. All participants showed an elevated startle response when the threat of shock was most imminent, a normal reaction. However, those teenagers who scored high in neuroticism showed a stronger startle response under neutral (nonthreatening) conditions—an over-response which leads to higher anxiety levels.

The Craske research suggests that teens/young adults high on the neuroticism scale become unnecessarily anxious, suggesting that their anxiety is out of proportion with the actual threat. Their neurotic response may represent a failure to distinguish between real and potential threats and lead to widespread, higher anxiety levels. This NIMH-funded longitudinal study is the first to examine physiological, cognitive, and personality measures, along with life stressors, all together.

In another study with similar variables, Craske and her colleagues found that 7–12-year-old children with anxious parents were three to five times more at risk for anxiety than those raised by nonanxious parents. So, as with the Fisak data, parents must rein in their anxieties to help their children.

How much of an issue is anxiety for children and families? Anxiety disorders represent one of the top three psychological problems that will affect Americans over the course of their lifetime. Anxiety is also a root issue for other problems such as depression, acting out and defiant behaviors, school performance problems, and relationship difficulties.

School refusal and separation anxiety disorder rates, described above, range from 1.3 percent in individuals aged 14–16 years to 4.1–4.7 percent in children aged 7–11 years. The average prevalence rate is 2–4 percent. As many as ⅓ of children with separation anxiety disorder have other serious problems such as depressive disorder, and a full ¼ have another disruptive behavior disorder, such as attention deficit hyperactivity disorder (ADHD), oppositional defiant disorder, or conduct disorder.

In 1987, a group headed by Allison E. Burke reported that five percent of school-aged children refused to attend school. In 2005, the Centers for Disease Control and Prevention (CDC) looked into reasons for students not graduating high school. As many as 40 percent of the students who did not graduate had a diagnosable mental health disorder. As many as 50 percent of those individuals were thought to have anxiety disorders such as PTSD and school phobia.

In 2003, Helen L. Egger and her associates reported that, among children with anxious school refusal and truancy, as many as 88 percent had a related (co-morbid) psychiatric disorder. Children with truancy histories had high rates of oppositional defiant disorder, depression, and conduct disorders. Anxious school refusal and truancy are different diagnoses and problem sets, but not mutually exclusive disorders, so it is important to know the roles of each.

In 2001, Gerard McShane's team reported that ½ of 192 adolescents with school refusal had a positive family history of psychiatric illness; those admitted for inpatient treatment were more likely to have a diagnosis of co-morbid mood disorder and a maternal history of psychiatric illness.

Separation anxiety disorder is a problem that can appear and reappear over time. Approximately 30–40 percent of individuals with SAD have continued psychiatric symptoms into adulthood; as many as 65 percent in some studies have another co-morbid anxiety disorder.

How does anxiety and the need to escape its negative feelings play out in behavior? A 2010 *Newsweek* article cited a Partnership for a Drug Free America (PDFA) study finding that teen girls are turning to alcohol and drug use in growing numbers. Specifically, the number of teen girls who say they drink alcohol increased 11 percent, from 53 percent to 59 percent of all 13–18-year-olds. Teen boys' rates of alcohol usage stayed level at 52 percent.

The same article also referenced the Monitoring the Future (MTF) study, an ongoing national survey of teens and teen behaviors that focuses on high-school-aged Americans. In this study, the most recent data show that male teen alcohol use rates have declined 25 percent over the past 10 years, but female rates have stayed level. The PDFA survey data indicate that girls tend to see alcohol and drug use as ways to "avoid problems and relieve stress." For boys, alcohol/drug use is seen as a more of a social helper; they make the user more able to socialize and party.

It appears that teen girls are self-medicating away their anxieties. This may be explained by girls' increased levels of sensitivity and emotional reactivity. Other researchers believe that the girls are more honest in admitting why they drink compared to boys. The article cites Leslie Walker, M.D., an adolescent medicine specialist. Said Dr. Walker, "It's a particularly stressful time for kids right now. They're seeing their parents stressed right now about the economy and jobs and thinking, 'What is there going to be for me?' " Walker also explained that girls are trying to work out age-related issues like gender roles and juggling stressors like demands for school success as well as reacting to their families' situations.

This adds up to more stress and anxiety, and more need to escape it. Dr. Walker advised parents to help their teens learn more healthy and appropriate coping mechanisms, as the ones they use in the teen years will carry to their adult years.

How are childhood anxiety disorders treated? As mentioned earlier, interventions from individual and family therapy or anti-anxiety drugs are typical. Dagmar Hannesdottir and Thomas Ollendick examined the role of emotion regulation in the treatment of children with anxiety disorders. They noted that cognitive-behavioral therapy (CBT) has been particularly effective for children with anxiety disorders, but treatment success rates impact about 60–70 percent of children.

What works for the remaining children? Hannesdottir and Ollendick noted that many children with anxiety disorders demonstrate poor emotion regulation skills, yet little attention has been directed toward including emotion regulation strategies with CBT. They argue that it is "possible that CBT programs do not work as well for a portion of children because their emotion regulation deficits" are not addressed. They suggested that adding an emotion regulation component might improve treatment efficacy. This could be done by adding strategies aimed at improving emotion regulation at the individual level and at the family level.

OTHER MENTAL HEALTH ISSUES AND YOUR CHILD'S DEVELOPMENT

We next address two more serious disorders—bipolar disorder and autism/autism spectrum disorders. There has been a dramatic increase in the rates of both of these clinical problems among child and teen populations. In this review, we will try to account for why this growth has occurred and what an educated parent can do to be aware of these conditions in your own child or your child's friends.

Bipolar disorder, previously called manic depression, is a serious mood disorder like clinical depression. In bipolar disorder (BD), feelings, thoughts, and behaviors are impacted by alternating episodes of mania and depression (defined below). According to the National Institute of Mental Health (NIMH), about two million American adults suffer from BD. At least another 750,000 children and teenagers live with the illness, the Child & Adolescent Bipolar Foundation estimates.

Up until the last 25 years, BD was thought to occur rarely in youth. It was estimated that ⅕ of adults with BD exhibited symptoms beginning in their teen years. There is now great controversy over the issue of overdiagnosis of BD in children and teens. In fact, some studies have shown an increase as much as 40-fold of BD diagnosis in youth in outpatient settings, and up to a 4-fold increase in inpatient psychiatric hospitalizations.

In 2007, Carmen Moreno and his team looked at national trends in the diagnosis and management of BD in young people. They had access to the National Ambulatory Medical Care Survey (NAMCS), a national survey collecting data on a sample of visits to nonfederally employed office-based physicians primarily engaged in direct patient care. From this data, they compared rates of growth between 1994–95 and 2002–03 in the number of visits by those under age 20 and those over 20 with a BD diagnosis. For 1999–2003, they also compared demographic, clinical, and treatment characteristics of youth and adult bipolar disorder visits.

The estimated annual number of youth office-based visits with a diagnosis of bipolar disorder increased from 25 (1994–95) to 1,003 (2002–03) visits per 100,000 population, and adult visits with a diagnosis of BD increased from 905 to 1,679 visits per 100,000 population during this period. In 1999–2003, most youth bipolar disorder visits were by males (66.5%), whereas most adult bipolar disorder visits were by females (67.6%); youth were more likely than adults to receive a co-morbid (or simultaneous) diagnosis of attention deficit hyperactivity disorder (32.2% versus 3.0%); and most youth (90.6%) and adults (86.4%) received a psychotropic medication during bipolar disorder visits. These patients were given mood stabilizers, antipsychotics, and antidepressants across both age groups.

Mark Olfson, Stephen Crystal, Tobias Gerhard, Cecilia S. Huang, and Gabrielle A. Carlson have described mental health service use in the year before and after a new clinical diagnosis of bipolar disorder. This offers a unique way to track diagnoses. They reviewed the insurance claims (in 2004–05) for 1,274,726 privately insured youths (17 years and younger) who were eligible for services at least one year before and after a service claim. Of these, 2,907 youths received a new BD diagnosis in that year. Diagnoses of other mental disorders and prescriptions filled for psychotropic drugs were assessed in the year before and after the initial diagnosis of BD.

The one-year rate of a new diagnosis of BD was .23 percent. During the year before the new diagnoses, youths were commonly diagnosed as having depressive disorder (46.5%) or disruptive behavior disorder (36.7%) and had filled prescriptions for antidepressants (48.5%), stimulants (33.0%), mood stabilizers (31.8%), or antipsychotics (29.1%). Most youths with a new diagnosis of bipolar disorder had only one (28.8%) or two to four (28.7%) insurance claims for bipolar disorder in the year starting with the initial diagnosis. The proportion starting mood stabilizers after the index diagnosis was highest for youths with five or more insurance claims for bipolar disorder (42.1%), intermediate for those with two to four claims (24.2%), and lowest for those with one claim (13.8%). What does this mean?

Perhaps as a result of diagnostic intricacies, BD diagnoses are often given as a precaution and are then changed as clearer symptom patterns are observed. Since a diagnosis must be used after each visit, even if uncertain, this may explain some of the clinical diagnosis patterns. Others speculate that some providers may be just treating symptoms with different medications and then justifying their use with a diagnosis. Others may make a diagnosis based on how well the child/teen responds to the medications. Could this explain some of the increase in BD numbers?

No sets of criteria differentiate adult-onset from childhood- or adolescent-onset BD. This presents a major problem for clinicians because of how children and teens behave versus adults. Indeed, the diagnostic criteria for BD are the same regardless of age at onset of symptoms. Everyone knows a moody teen who has emotional swings and irritability and then periods of being down in the dumps, all with acting out in the background. When is this normal and when does this cross over to a clinical diagnosis?

The symptoms of mania include elevated mood lasting for at least seven days without a break. They can include a decreased need for sleep, racing thoughts, rapid and pressured speech, taking on many different activities or projects, hyper-sexuality, reckless and risk-taking behaviors, and delusions of grandeur. So these are issues of severity. On any given day a normal teen can have a subset of these behaviors in a more limited way.

In Bipolar I, the elevated and elated mood of mania may transform into a down period during which agitated and irritable behaviors may develop. In older children and adolescents, BD may be more severe with increased risks of suicide attempts and school-related problems, potentially leading to expulsion or peer rejection. Associated negative behaviors like poor eating habits and a greater chance of substance use and abuse, including smoking, can also lead to health issues.

Stephen Faraone and his group have researched the mania part of BD. They looked at the differences among children with mania, teens with childhood-onset mania, and teens with adolescence-onset mania. In their work, they have tried to determine whether and how mania is different from ADHD symptoms. They found a link with social class; families of children with mania and teens with childhood-onset mania had less money and resources. On further analysis, teens with adolescent-onset mania abused street drugs and had more troubled parent-child relationships than individuals in the other two groups with mania. ADHD symptoms were more common in children and adolescents with childhood-onset mania than in those with adolescent-onset mania. In some youth, it may be that ADHD symptoms may be a marker or predictor for juvenile-onset mania.

Faraone points out concerns that early-onset mania may be misdiagnosed as ADHD or that more children have both ADHD and bipolar disorder. One controversy is whether youths who are later diagnosed with BD may develop symptoms in early life that appear to be ADHD or another behavioral disturbance. For other children, they may just have both bipolar disorder and ADHD. Researchers are still trying to sort this out.

Eric A. Youngstrom and his team have also addressed the question of bipolar disorder (BD) diagnoses in child and teen populations. Specifically, they sought to critically evaluate evidence related to rising rates of this disorder and its validity as a diagnosis. Without getting too clinical or specific, know that a set of criteria must be met in order to get a BD diagnosis. This group looked at a range of questions similar to those raised by Faraone.

Youngstrom's group first looked at the history of BD in youths, including descriptions of the diagnostic sensitivity and specificity of symptoms. They also addressed rates of cycling between manic and depressive episodes. The validity/accuracy of the diagnosis of BD in youths was also evaluated based on traditional criteria including demographics, family environmental features, genetics, and other relevant variables.

The group developed a diagnostic rubric for diagnosing BD in children and teens, including a review of different possible diagnoses. They too noted a set of areas of disagreement in making and using this diagnosis. Problems include: the relative role of elated versus irritable mood in assessment, and also the limits of the extent of the bipolar spectrum—when do definitions become so broad that they no longer describe true bipolar cases?

John M. Grohol, from the website Psych Central, has also questioned the validity of these increased pediatric BD diagnoses. He first reviewed data from Dr. Mark Olfson of the New York State Psychiatric Institute at the Columbia University Medical Center. Olfson offered two possible explanations: either bipolar disorder was historically underdiagnosed in children and adolescents and that problem is corrected, or bipolar disorder is currently being overdiagnosed in this age group.

Grohol has a third explanation. Simply put, it is that unqualified people are making bad diagnoses. He believes that "may help partially explain this result." He continues by saying, "I suspect that such general practitioners are more likely to diagnose a mental disorder, not out of any necessary ignorance or such, but because it is often the easiest thing to do than to try and get a parent a referral to a mental health specialist."

Another problem Grohol cited was one of the issues the research team listed as a study limitation—possible duplication of counted diagnoses. The study's data set used records of visits rather than individual patients, so the number of duplicated data for individual patients is unknown. So the data are of questionable validity.

Another reason the Olfson data are questionable is related to what other research findings show. Other research "shows a far more linear curve for the diagnosis of bipolar disorder in children and teens." One study found population-adjusted rates of hospital discharges of children with a primary diagnosis of BD increased at a much more modest rate than the 40-fold increase noted.

NIMH is now funding a new major research project looking at pediatric bipolar disorder. It is called the Course and Outcome of Bipolar Illness in Youth, or COBY. COBY is the largest and most comprehensive pediatric study of bipolar disorder to date.

In their first report, researchers described their 263 7–17-year-olds with bipolar spectrum disorder. These subjects were followed over a roughly two-year period and asked about mood, behavior, and medical treatment. The group's goal is to determine how bipolar disorder, in all its forms, progresses in children and teens. This includes better diagnostics. They hope to see which and in what ways certain medications may be used in treatment.

To date, the COBY study shows that BD is different in young people compared to adults. For example, study subjects with Bipolar I—the classic form of the illness marked by swings between severe mania and major depression—had symptoms that lasted significantly longer than usually seen in adults. Mood swings were also more frequent in children and teens.

Another significant outcome so far is that researchers have shown that children's and teens' symptoms are variable, causing them to display behaviors that lead to different varieties of BD diagnoses. "Although moodiness and irritability can be common and normal in teenagers, this study helps to clarify that when these symptoms are excessive, persistent and impairing, a bipolar spectrum illness should be considered," said Henrietta

Leonard, one of the COBY team members as quoted in a *Medical News Today* online report.

Other findings from the COBY study:

- More than ⅔ of subjects recovered from their first major manic or depressive episode in the first two years of follow-up.
- Subjects had an average of 1.5 recurrences, particularly of depressive episodes, each year during the two-year follow-up.
- Subjects displayed symptoms about 60 percent of the time during follow-up visits.
- Subjects whose illness started in childhood displayed more symptoms at follow-up visits compared with subjects whose illness began in their teens.

And so we await the final word on this now inexplicable diagnostic situation. Let us turn to another serious disorder, the rates of which have also exponentially exploded in the past 20 years—autism.

A spring 2011 report funded partly by NIMH has shown that the prevalence of autism spectrum disorders (ASD) among children in South Korea is apparently much higher than previously estimated. A group headed by Young Shin Kim of the Yale School of Medicine sampled all children ages 7–12 in a representative South Korean community. The researchers surveyed parents and teachers about the children's social interactions and whether they had communication problems or restricted and repetitive behaviors. The researchers then evaluated 286 children suspected as having ASD based on the answers provided.

Based on careful assessments, the prevalence of ASD among the total study population was found to be 2.64 percent. One hundred and fourteen of the children were already in special school settings. Among the 172 children attending regular schools, the prevalence was 1.89 percent and boys were 2.5 times more likely to have ASD than girls. Among the high-probability group (the 114), the prevalence of ASD was 0.75 percent and boys were 5 times more likely to have ASD than girls.

Of the entire flagged group, 0.94 percent met diagnostic criteria for autism and 1.7 percent met criteria for other types of ASD, including Asperger's Disorder and a catch-all diagnostic category, pervasive developmental disorder not otherwise specified (PDD-NOS).

Why are these results important? This study's method found children that would have gone unnoticed if they had relied solely on record reviews.

As a result of this comprehensive child search, this study's estimate of ASD prevalence was higher than the previously used estimates, which range from 0.6 percent to 1.8 percent.

Interestingly, the rates in the high-probability group were similar to other studies that have focused on the same target populations. The surprise, major finding from this study was that ⅔ of ASD cases were identified from the general population—children not suspected of any problems or referred for any treatment. This particular outcome, if true, gives emphasis to the importance of screening all children as well as clinical populations for future studies. It was also noted "that the highly structured educational system in South Korea may allow children with less severe ASD symptoms to manage in general education settings, despite their impairments."

It should be noted that the authors included Asperger's cases, which resulted in a much higher rate of autism than the one in 110 normally quoted in the United States. The difference between autism and Asperger's Disorder (AD) is that people with AD do not have significant delays in language and cognitive development. Many autism researchers are suggesting that Asperger's *is* autism; thus "autism spectrum disorders" is now used to describe the range of functioning seen in people with autism. This change will become official in 2013 with a new edition of the *American Psychiatric Association's Diagnostic and Statistical Manual.*

Some people are critical of folding AD into the autism grouping. Others believe this will allow for better identification of children who need developmental services and will force insurers and state governments to pay for it.

What is known about the causes of ASD? It is believed, as with all serious neurological-based disorders, that genetics play a role. The mechanism is not known. We know that early intervention is advantageous in immediately improving communication, socialization, and learning skills. Research has shown that the brain is still in major development for five years after birth, and some researchers believe that some trigger mechanism sets off the symptoms of autism in a child. In other disorders, a genetic predisposition coupled with some environmental event (maybe stress, maybe some chemical exposure or other environmental agent) explains the trigger.

One likely reason for the growth in ASD cases is parental awareness and media exposure. These two reasons alone have led to more screenings. It may also be the case that ASD was underdiagnosed; "unusual" children from the past are the ASD children of today.

Three global behavioral abnormalities characterize children with ASD—lack of social interaction, delays and deficits in language development, and repetitive behaviors. Are children with ASD properly diagnosed?

Chris Johnson and Scott Myers, working with the Council on Children with Disabilities, produced a 2007 report for the American Academy of Pediatrics. With a whopping 334 articles cited, this report is the current gold standard regarding assessment techniques. Their work was intended for use by pediatricians, who are considered key to early recognition of autism spectrum disorders, as they are usually the first point of contact for parents. The guide Johnson and Myers produced is for pediatricians to be able to recognize the signs and symptoms of autism spectrum disorders and have a strategy for assessing them systematically.

Johnson and Meyers recommended that all pediatricians be aware of local resources that can assist in making a definitive diagnosis of and managing autism spectrum disorders, including developmental, educational, and community resources as well as medical subspecialty clinics.

In 2011, Karen Pierce and her group reported on the Communication and Symbolic Behavior Scales Developmental Profile Infant-Toddler Checklist. This instrument shows promise as a simple procedure to detect cases of ASD, language delays, and developmental delays at one year. It was tested and distributed at every one-year pediatric checkup completed by 137 pediatricians who screened about 10,500 infants. Screenings were scored immediately, and 184 infants with a risk profile were referred for further evaluation.

Of those, 32 infants received a provisional or final diagnosis of ASD, 56 of language delays, 9 of developmental delays, and 36 of "other." Five infants who initially tested positive for ASD no longer met criteria at follow-up. The remainder of the sample consisted of false positive results. Overall, this screening test is considered valuable and easy to use.

David Kirby, a *Huffington Post* reporter, has mused about these ASD rates. He discusses federal government data from a 2007 telephone survey of parents of nearly 82,000 U.S. children. The National Survey of Children's Health report said that the odds of a parent having a child with ASD are 1 in 63. If it is a boy, the chances climb to 1 in 38, or 2.6 percent, of all male children in America.

By parental report, most of those children later "shed the ASD label as they got older." Parents reported that a rate of 60 per 10,000 children "had autism, Asperger's Disorder etc. at some point, but not currently." Kirby says that this suggests "two rather remarkable things." If real, these results mean that 1 in 63 U.S. children (160 per 10,000) will be labeled with an ASD and out of every 160 children whose parents reported that they had an ASD, 60 of them (37.5%) no longer have the disorders.

Overall, the 2007 NSCH survey revealed a 100 percent increase in parent-reported ASD rates compared to the 2003 NSCH survey (which showed a 50 per 10,000 reported rate). In a survey such as the one used, estimates of rates of a disorder are considered to be accurate.

Kirby goes on to report on a second study, from the CDC's Autism and Developmental Disabilities Monitoring network (ADDM). As he explains, these data "look only at eight-year-old cohorts to allow time for all diagnoses to be made, reported and counted." There are data from cohorts born in 1992, 1994, and 1996. The 1992 cohort had an estimated ASD rate of 1 in 166, or 60 per 10,000 (since revised to 67 per 10,000, or 1 in 150). For the 1994 cohort, the estimate was roughly equivalent at 66 per 10,000. For the 1996 cohort (August 6, 2010 errata report), the revised number increased to a rate of 9 per 1000, or roughly 1 in 100 of the 308,038 children aged eight years residing in the 11 ADDM sites.

In trying to answer why there is an increase, people often refer to the widened diagnostic criteria, expanded media coverage, and greater parental and professional awareness. Here is where I part company with Mr. Kirby, who asserts that some environmental toxin, likely related to vaccinations, is the reason for the increases. Most of the environmental link camp continues to argue that vaccinations (more specifically thimerosal-containing vaccines) can trigger autism.

In fact, more than 20 legitimate studies confirm that there is no link. Further, there is near universal agreement among health professionals that not vaccinating your child is the more risky parental choice.

What about the question of why so many children previously labeled with ASD were no longer diagnosable? Kirby argues that there are three main possible explanations—that "many children never had an ASD to begin with, and were simply 'mislabled,'" that some children "naturally recovered" from ASD, and/or that current treatments actually work remarkably well. None of these three are plausible.

So how can we understand these conflicting data? Studies from the 1980s had rates of autism at about 2 per 10,000 children, nowhere near the current data. This makes little sense. As Kirby notes, "If those studies were wrong, and if the rate was the same then as it is now (as many scientists contend), that would mean that doctors, educators and statisticians are now 7,000 percent more proficient at diagnosing and counting autism than they were before." This would translate to 138 out of every 140 children who had an ASD in the 1980s having an undiagnosed, uncounted, and untreated ASD.

I will close with a summary comment from a story by the *Wall Street Journal* on autism rates in Los Angeles. (The article can be accessed from the reference section.) The conclusion of the research group was that "social influences are the leading cause for the high autism rates." Further, "their findings can be explained solely by parents' educational levels—by adjusting the data for educational levels, the discrepancies in autism rates virtually disappeared."

Whether increased bipolar or ASD rates are a sign of worried parents or bad diagnostics remains to be unequivocally determined. It is clear to me, however, that our children and their developmental behavior patterns have not fundamentally changed. I will let the educated parent make their own determination.

SEVEN

Societal and Cultural Stressors in Your Child's Life

Television! Teacher, mother, secret lover.

~Homer Simpson, *The Simpsons*

I think God's going to come down and pull civilization over for speeding.

~Steven Wright

In this chapter, we will review a range of information about societal and cultural stressors that impact child development. It is my intention to give the educated parent a picture of how school and school policies impact children, the pros and cons of various media exposure, and impacts of technology. With this information, the educated parent can make decisions about their parenting, when and how to shield their child from these stressors, and limit-setting for their children.

SCHOOL AS A SOURCE OF STRESS

Going to school can be a mixed experience for many children. For some children, school is a positive experience they look forward to, even if there is some complaining. Children develop many skills in school, not just academic ones. Schools provide a place for peer relationship skill development, learning to handle frustration and success, and to excel and develop self-efficacy. For other children, school stressors may prove overwhelming, and those children may engage in school refusal or delinquency and dropout behavior.

We will first discuss how the educated parent can support his/her child in a typical public school setting. Some of the issues we will review pertain to all school settings, but private schools can have a different set of worries for children. Please refer back to "Parents as Teachers" (chapter 5) for other details and information and a discussion of homeschooling matters.

In this section, we will address a series of concerns as outlined in an online article by Elizabeth Scott. We will use her list as a launching point for our discussion. The first item to consider will be *social stressors related to peers.* Although schools are often where children make and find friends, children also encounter peer pressures and interpersonal conflicts. These can include not being in the same classes with friends or attending a different school than the neighborhood group. This separation and lack of connection can put a strain on friends when they do get back together. Missing shared experiences becomes another thing to worry about for some children. In transitioning from one school year to the next, certain groups or buddies may be separated. Where ability grouping still exists, friends may be separated by class level (e.g., advance placement (AP) courses or special needs classes).

Issues related to *popularity* are also stressors for some children. Popular children may feel pressure to stay popular and may do things they should not in order to keep their status. In some cases, this may lead to eating-disordered behavior. Less popular children also have much to learn. In difficult cases, when a child may be neglected by peers, social skills training might be necessary. It is important for the educated parent to pay attention to these peer-related issues. Parents can help their child by allowing/inviting friends to the house, facilitating other play by transporting children to playgrounds, or finding other ways to enable positive peer activity.

Encounters with bullies and others who cause conflict is another area of stress. (Cyberbullying is addressed later in this chapter.) Schools can be a place where children learn—and are tested—about interpersonal skills, how to behave, how to make friends, and how to deal with unreasonable peers. One of the reasons why I advocate a traditional school environment over homeschooling is because of the social encounters and social skills building provided by traditional schools. It is most important for children to learn to negotiate the ways that people get together, disagree, fight, argue, make up, and move on. The best way is with other peers. So-called playground justice can be a harsh but meaningful teacher of many lessons.

Teachers can be another source of school-based stress. Teachers have different levels of experience and training and different expectations for their students. Sometimes there are personality conflicts—for whatever reason—that make it hard for child and teacher to relate well. This is another way that some children can learn important people skills. How does one get along with and work with someone they do not like? As a parent you should try to be supportive of a demanding teacher; that person will teach your child to work hard and gain greater achievement.

Of course, parents must pay close attention to teacher-student conflicts in their own diplomatic way if they feel a need to intervene. Parent-teacher conferences may be needed to explore why there is student-teacher conflict. At times these may be mediated by a principal or guidance counselor. It is important for a parent to be an advocate for their child, but not to blindly take the child's side or alienate the teacher. In worst-case scenarios, a child may need a classroom reassignment. This is a last resort option, and not a desired outcome.

In addition to teachers, students face school-based *stressors from standardized testing* or state-level accountability testing. Some of these tests have personal consequences related to whether a child will pass on to higher grades, sit for summer school sessions, or even earn a diploma. These put entire school systems under stress. In these cases, your role is to encourage your children to do their best work and to let them talk out any worries they have from spending a day in a charged or pressured environment. As discussed in chapter 5, your role as a taxpayer and consumer of state-funded education can also help in the long run.

Other in-school stressors might include *improper placements*—your child is in classes that are too difficult or too easy. It is very important for the educated parent to monitor the child's progress and successes/ challenges. Regular discussions or communications with the child's teacher are another way to get feedback in this area. In the case where schoolwork is too easy, the parent must move quickly to be sure the child is challenged academically. Staying in easy classes can breed boredom, apathy, and a disconnect with school and work. It can also lead to behavioral problems as a child seeks other stimulation. When schoolwork is too difficult, a child can get frustrated, develop low self-esteem, and begin to withdraw and develop emotional problems. At older ages, children who cannot do their work or feel incompetent may search out others with similar outlooks and create a group that usually ends up in trouble.

Homework levels can be stressors for some children. In an effort to be tough, some schools or teachers decide that more than an hour of daily homework or required reading of multiple books outside of school time is necessary for student improvement. The level of homework assigned needs to take into account the child's developmental level, skills, and need for practice. On the other hand, having a policy of no homework on weekends or 90-minute minimums is a lazy, one-size-fits-all solution that makes more trouble than it solves. Depending on what is being taught, there is certainly a case for homework on some weekends or on some nights having no work at all.

On the topic of the homework debate, Alfie Kohn has written that "decades of investigation have failed to turn up any evidence that homework is beneficial for students in elementary school." He further adds that, "The only effect that does show up is more negative attitudes on the part of students who get more assignments."

In his *Education Week* article, Kohn cites some interesting data on the efficacy of homework, including:

• There is no support for the idea that homework teaches good work habits or develops positive character traits (such as self-discipline and independence).

• The number of young children who had homework on a specific day jumped to 64 percent, and the amount of time they spent was up 33 percent over a previous survey a few years earlier.

• Any "theoretical benefit" of homework (and he believes there is little to none) must be "weighed against the effect it has on students' *interest* in learning." The "drudgery" of most homework basically sucks any love of learning and school right out of the poor, overburdened student. And this result can have a number of other negative results.

Test anxiety and performance fears raise another area of concern that an educated parent can help a child overcome. Learning style mismatches or learning disabilities can also produce stress in a child. These are areas where you must rely, as an educated parent, on the professional services of your school staff. School psychologists and guidance counselors, among others, need to work with your child to assess and then plan a step-by-step remediation strategy. As an educated parent, you can read about these matters—many good online sources address this—and stay abreast of the school's ideas for your child's improvement.

Family-controlled school stress points are those related to being sure your child has a good diet, plenty of sleep, and a good daily schedule. As they say, breakfast is the most important meal of the day. This is doubly true in preparing a child or teen for a day of school. Busy families and good, healthy breakfasts can co-exist. It takes planning and some creativity. Multiple web sources give ideas for better breakfasts without too much prep time.

Similarly, a good lunch keeps the energy level up for the afternoon. Too many carbs may cause a sleepier student. The educated parent should be aware of the school cafeteria options but also consider packing and sending a lunch. Again, web-based ideas are available for you to discuss menus with your child/teen.

Sleep is another variable that can add to school stress, or, more accurately, a lack of sleep. Although this applies more to middle- and high-school-age students, younger children can also be affected. As a parent, it is most important for you to model and enforce good sleep habits. (For more detail, review chapter 2 materials.) Teens are especially at risk for sleep deprivation.

There can be little question that sleep deprivation has negative effects on adolescents. Early high school start times are part of the problem. Research has shown that teens need more sleep as a side effect of puberty-based changes. Lack of good sleep can also cause difficulties in school, including disciplinary problems, sleepiness in class, and poor concentration. One study of over 3000 high school students found that students who reported that they were getting C's, D's, and F's in school had 25 minutes less sleep and went to bed later than students who reported they were getting A's and B's. Sleep deprivation effects at any age include overall poorer cognitive functioning, lack of physical coordination, moodiness, and other negative effects.

The good daily schedule includes time for homework, for projects, and for other preparations as your teen enters the high school project years. Keeping up with your younger child's school schedule is also important. When is show and tell? When are the special days for wearing certain clothing (e.g., school photo day) or bringing in items? Which cafeteria day has the good pizza?

Finally, we address *overscheduling* as a basis of school stress. Every parent wants to raise a well-rounded child. This is a good goal. But it must be made with attention to how much time your child needs for school success. For younger children, involvement in Scouting, youth sports leagues, or arts activities are wholesome developmental activities. But these must be paced. All children also need down time when they can think, rest, and be imaginative in a spontaneous way.

College admissions standards are known to be increasingly competitive, with the message being that only the most experienced high schoolers with exotic résumés, will be admitted to top-tier colleges. This can make it difficult for college-bound high school students to avoid overscheduling themselves in an effort to stand out and meet the high expectations that have been set up. Parents have to carefully discuss and plan what they are willing to allow.

CULTURAL AND MEDIA-BASED STRESSORS: TELEVISION

Television programming has received a rather mixed reputation in the 60 or so years that its presence has been widespread in homes. The number of hours watched and the impact of the content viewed on developing children and teens has a long history of scholarly debate and disagreement. Clearly, television (TV) has allowed for positive and negative effects in families.

The recent technological advances (HDTV, 3-D TV, 100-inch screens) guarantee that TVs aren't going away. TV viewing offers an inviting aspect that humans are drawn to. And in some families, TVs are used for child care and child entertainment. A 2006 Kaiser Family Foundation report stated that, in a typical day, 83 percent of children under six use "screen media" (DVDs, videos, or TV shows), watching for 1 hour and 57 minutes daily. Media use increases from 61 percent of babies one year or younger who watch screen media for 80 minutes per day, to 90 percent of four-to-six-year-olds watching just over two hours daily. Forty-three percent of four-to-six-year-olds have personal TVs in their bedrooms. The report continues, saying that "the most common reasons parents give for putting a TV in their child's bedroom is to free up other TVs in the house so the parent or other family members can watch their own shows (55%), to keep the child occupied so the parent can do things around the house (39%), to help the child fall asleep (30%), and as a reward for good behavior (26%).

The same report also revealed that 66 percent of parents say "they've seen their child imitate positive behaviors" from TV, while 23 percent say their child imitated aggressive behavior, like hitting or kicking. Forty-five percent of four-to-six-year-old boys were said to imitate aggressive behavior from TV. Fifty-three percent of parents said that TV tends to calm their child down, while 17 percent said that TV got their child "excited."

With this introduction as a backdrop, I shall now present findings from the American Academy of Pediatrics (AAP). The American Academy of Child & Adolescent Psychiatry has also produced a report, part of its series called "Facts for Families." The AAP produced a recent report that summarizes the vast information pool relevant for the educated parent. Read on for some of the findings as they relate to best child rearing practices.

The AAP report opens with usage data of its own, reporting that 8–18-year-olds spend almost four hours per day in front of a TV and almost two additional hours on the computer (outside of schoolwork) and playing video games.

How much is too much TV viewing? The AAP guidelines are that children under two not watch *any* TV and that all other children watch no more than one to two hours a day of "quality programming." The AAP reports that excessive TV viewing has been linked to the following problems:

• Children who consistently spend more than four hours per day watching TV are more likely to be overweight.

• Kids who view violent acts are more likely to show aggressive behavior and fear that the world is frightening and that something bad will happen to them.

• TV characters often depict risky behaviors such as smoking and drinking, and also model gender-role and racial stereotypes.

In support of these findings, Suzy Tomopoulos and her research group followed 259 infants, 249 (96.1%) of whom were exposed to television and videos at age 6 months. The 249 had an average total exposure of about 2.5 hours per day. Using different statistical analyses, they found a relationship between screen time at age 6 months with both lesser cognitive development at age 14 months and poorer language development. Looking further at the type of content viewed, media described as "older child/adult-oriented" was associated with lower cognitive and language development at age 14 months. Of note, "no significant associations were seen with exposure to young child-oriented educational or non-educational content." The Tomopoulos study indicates an association between media exposure in infancy and subsequent poorer developmental outcomes in children from low SES families.

Too much TV time has been shown to interfere with many positive, healthy activities such as physical play, reading, doing homework, playing with friends, and spending time with family. TV time, in moderation, can have positive outcomes. Preschool-aged children can learn many things on educational programming such as *Sesame Street.* Grade schoolers can learn about many wonderful things on channels such as Discovery or the Science Channel. Teens can watch relevant news and sporting events, and parents can keep up with current events on the 24-hour cable news cycle. Everyone can know what is happening in the world as it happens.

Regarding the amount of violent acts seen on TV, the AAP report notes that "the average American child will witness 200,000 violent acts on television by age 18." This matters because children and teens may become desensitized to violence and act more aggressively. TV violence may lead to actual violence due to social learning processes—children act on what they see rewarded and glorified—even if that behavior is only watched and happens to others.

Younger viewers may be especially intimidated by scary and violent images. Expecting them to know better or to understand that TV is not reality is often impossible as the children's level of cognitive development is still too immature. As a result, you may encounter behavior problems, nightmares, and sleep problems as a result of exposure to TV violence.

Even older children can be impacted by violent depictions from fictional shows, the news, or reality-based shows. You can reason with this age group, so parents can provide reassurance and facts to help make sense of the content and make it manageable. Some research has shown that children with emotional, behavioral, learning, or impulse control problems may be more easily influenced by TV violence. The best advice is to not let vulnerable or unprepared children view such programming.

Routine TV content depicts risky behaviors such as sex and substance abuse as "cool, fun, and exciting." Rarely are there real-world depictions of the actual consequences of drinking alcohol, doing drugs, smoking cigarettes, and having unprotected sex. Some studies, reports the AAP summary, have shown that "teens who watch lots of sexual content on TV are more likely to initiate intercourse or participate in other sexual activities earlier than peers who don't watch sexually explicit shows." The same report stated that children "who watch 5 or more hours of TV per day are far more likely to begin smoking cigarettes than those who watch less than the recommended 2 hours a day."

In support of this argument, Jennifer Cullen and her study group looked at how widespread tobacco use was portrayed on popular TV shows in fall 2007. They used Nielsen data to verify popularity in the 12–17-year-old age group. They also tied the tobacco use to type of program by the Parental Guidelines rating system (G, PG, 14, etc.).

A full 40 percent of television shows had at least one depiction of tobacco use. Of these, 89 percent were of cigarettes. Among TV-PG shows, 50 percent showed one or more incidents of cigarette use, in contrast to 26 percent of TV-14 episodes. Episodes with the highest of any tobacco use portrayals were on the FOX network followed closely by the CW. An extrapolation of the data estimated that almost one million 12–17-year-olds were exposed to tobacco depictions through the programming in the time period observed.

According to the 2008 AAP report, American children see 40,000 commercials each year. For those under the age of eight years, there is no connection that commercials are for selling a product. When product placement and show content overlap (as can happen on Saturday morning programs), those children may be brainwashed into begging their parents to buy those products. Ads for fast food restaurants also play into getting children (and teens) to want to eat more unhealthy food, or get prizes, and busy parents quickly cave in.

The AAP recommends that parents teach consumer psychology matters to their children, showing them how to be savvy consumers by talking about what the TV is selling. The AAP advises that parents discuss the product and whether the ad is encouraging healthy or unhealthy choices. I personally know of very few parents (okay, none) who take the time for such teaching.

And finally, I share with my educated parent readers, verbatim, the AAP's practical ways to make TV viewing more positive in your home:

- Limit the number of TV-watching hours.
- Stock the room in which you have your TV with plenty of other nonscreen entertainment (books, kids' magazines, toys, puzzles, board games, etc.) to encourage kids to do something other than watch the tube.
- Keep TVs out of bedrooms.
- Turn the TV off during meals.
- Don't allow kids to watch TV while doing homework.
- Treat TV as a privilege to be earned—not a right. Establish and enforce family TV viewing rules, such as TV is allowed only after chores and homework are completed.
- *Try a weekday ban.* Schoolwork, sports activities, and job responsibilities make it tough to find extra family time during the week. Record

weekday shows or save TV time for weekends and you'll have more family togetherness time to spend on meals, games, physical activity, and reading during the week.

- *Set a good example* by limiting your own TV viewing.
- *Check the TV listings and program reviews ahead of time* for programs your family can watch together (i.e., developmentally appropriate and nonviolent programs that reinforce your family's values). Choose shows that foster interest and learning in hobbies and education (reading, science, etc.).
- *Preview programs* before your kids watch them.
- *Come up with a family TV schedule* that you all agree upon each week. Then, post the schedule in a visible area (e.g., on the refrigerator) so that everyone knows which programs are okay to watch and when. And make sure to turn off the TV when the scheduled program is over instead of channel surfing.
- *Watch TV together.* If you can't sit through the whole program, at least watch the first few minutes to assess the tone and appropriateness, then check in throughout the show.
- *Talk to kids about what they see on TV* and share your own beliefs and values. If something you don't approve of appears on the screen, you can turn off the TV, then use the opportunity to ask thought-provoking questions such as, "Do you think it was okay when those men got in that fight? What else could they have done? What would you have done?" Or, "What do you think about how those teenagers were acting at that party? Do you think what they were doing was wrong?" If certain people or characters are mistreated or discriminated against, talk about why it's important to treat everyone fairly, despite their differences. You can use TV to explain confusing situations and express your feelings about difficult topics (sex, love, drugs, alcohol, smoking, work, behavior, family life).
- *Talk to other parents, your doctor, and teachers* about their TV-watching policies and kid-friendly programs they'd recommend.
- *Offer fun alternatives to television.* If your kids want to watch TV but you want to turn off the tube, suggest that you all play a board game, start a game of hide and seek, play outside, read, work on crafts or hobbies, or listen and dance to music. The possibilities for fun without the tube are endless—so turn off the TV and enjoy the quality time together.

(*Source:* American Academy of Pediatrics, 2008).

CULTURAL AND MEDIA-BASED STRESSORS: THE INTERNET

Computer usage in families is now widespread. According to a 2006 Kaiser Family Foundation report:

- Seventy-eight percent of children six years old and under live in homes with a computer, and 69 percent have Internet access from home. Twenty-nine percent have more than one computer.
- Among all children under six, 43 percent have used a computer and 27 percent use a computer several times a week or more. Among children four to six, 43 percent use a computer several times a week or more.
- There is a large gap in computer ownership by income and parent education. Fifty-four percent of children in lower-income households (less than $20,000 a year) have a computer in the home compared to 95 percent of children in higher-income homes ($75,000 a year or more).

Researchers at the Berkman Center for Internet & Society at Harvard University produced a comprehensive report on Internet safety issues related to children (the Internet Safety Technical Task Force Report, ISTTF) in December 2008. This report formed part of a project commissioned by the states' attorneys general. Of interest for the educated parent are some of the findings related to three areas—unwanted solicitation of children and teens by others; harassment (including cyberbullying); and problematic content, which includes inappropriate sexual imagery, gambling sites, drug information, and hate sites. Let us review each in turn as researched by the ISTTF. (Please note that the research mentioned next was taken from the ISTTF authors' work, and individual citations are not listed in the reference section of this book.)

Unwanted Solicitation

TV shows like *To Catch a Predator* and related stories on the news have many parents concerned about online sexual solicitation and the possibility that these contacts will lead to dangerous real-world encounters between their child and predatory adult strangers. What are the real dangers here and how prevalent is this problem? Some have argued that there is no big problem; that a few sensationalized stories have created a myth of lurking pedophiles and sexual predators that do not exist, or are very small in number.

According to the ISTTF report, actual numbers of children and teens who "receive sexual solicitations online have declined from 19% in 2000 to 13% in 2006 and most recipients (81%) are between 14–17 years of age." When known, the surveyed children identified most sexual solicitors as being "other adolescents (48%–43%) or young adults between the ages of 18 and 21 (20%–30%), with only 4%–9% coming from older adults and the remaining being of unknown age."

Of these contacts, few solicitations resulted in real-world meetings. Contrary to popular opinion, social network sites (like Facebook and MySpace) "do not appear to have increased the overall risk of solicitation." Chat rooms and instant messaging are still the dominant place where solicitations occur, with 77 percent of all such behavior occurring in those methods.

According to this report, *online sexual solicitation* is defined as "an online communication where someone on the Internet tried to get [a minor] to talk about sex when they did not want to," an offender asked a minor to "do something sexual they did not want to," or "other sexual overtures" from online relationships. There are very few studies in this area, but one reported study found that "13%–19% of youth have experienced some form of online sexual solicitation" but that these communications were "not generally disturbing" to the recipients. Further, the report concluded that "close to half of the solicitations were relatively mild events that did not appear to be dangerous or frightening" for the children involved.

So what does happen? How often do children or teens actually physically meet up with an Internet-initiated contact? And what is the nature of these connections? The report states that the "majority of Internet-initiated connections involving youth appear to be friendship related, nonsexual, and formed between similar-aged youth and known to parents." Of note, such Internet-based connections are actually positive for socially isolated children or those with few friends. In fact, in a pleasantly surprising finding, "Parents were generally responsible about their children going to real-world meetings resulting from online contact; 73% of parents were aware of real-world meetings and 75% accompanied the minor to the meeting." So, in reality, many Internet-based connections occur with full parental involvement and approval.

Further, these meetings are often innocuous and rarely harmful. Reports the ISTTF, "Problematic offline sexual encounters resulting from online meetings were found to be extremely rare, and mostly involve older adolescents and younger adults." One national study found that only 4 of 1500 children/teens reported sexual contact—these were 17-year-olds meeting adults in their early 20s. These incidents were "voluntary" and "non-forcible" contacts and could best be characterized as statutory rape cases.

Having discussed all of this information, it is still true that children and teens are victimized and need parental protection and oversight. Of note, the youth who reported online solicitations "tended to be of the age that it is developmentally normal to be curious about sex," and were found to have histories of a troubled home or personal life. The report goes on to conclude that it is this profile of older teens who spend much time online to be more vulnerable than the younger child who is often portrayed as "less safety-conscious," when in fact they are no more careless or unsafe.

One study found 99 percent of Internet-initiated sex crime arrest victims were aged 13–17, with 76 percent being high-school-aged, 14–17, and none younger than 12 years old. In a second study, those solicited tended to be older, with 81 percent of youth aged 14–17 reporting solicitations. The same pattern was found for youth who reported "distressing" or "aggressive" online incidents. By gender, females are victimized more than ¾ of the time, as most perpetrators are male.

Who are the perpetrators? The primary study cited reported that the "adult offenders who were arrested for Internet-initiated relationships online with minors tended to be male (99%), non-Hispanic white (81%), and communicated with the victim for 1 to 6 months (48%). Offenders were of a wide variety of ages, from 18–25 (23%), 26–39 (41%), and over 40 (35%) years of age."

So what is to be concluded from this thorough literature review? The problems of online solicitation are uncommon, but do exist. Parents of teens need to pay special attention to the online activities of their children.

Harassment and Cyberbullying

We now turn to another aspect of media-amplified online stressors for families—the harassment and bullying of children, often social media-based. This is a difficult area from which to get any good data or information. One problem is definitional. Online harassment or *cyberbullying* has been defined as "an overt, intentional act of aggression towards another person online" by Michelle Ybarra and Kimberly Mitchell, or a "willful and repeated harm inflicted through the use of computers, cell phones, and other electronic devices" according to Sameer Hinduja and Justin Patchin. This can include bullying text messages, "sexting," and harmfully-intended postings on Facebook or MySpace or YouTube. It is generally agreed that the sender (perpetrator) is threatening, embarrassing, or humiliating the receiver (victim).

Michelle Ybarra argues that cyberbullying can be worse than bullying because cyberbullying is more pervasive and harder to escape. It is not just at school or in the neighborhood; it is online all the time. Of note, in-person bullying incidents are likely still higher than cyberbullying events. A 2007 report by Amanda Lenhart found that 67 percent of teenagers said that bullying happens more offline than online. Qing Li reported that 54 percent of seventh graders were victims of traditional bullying and less than half that number (25%) were victims of cyberbullying. A 2009 review by Hinduja and Patchin found that 42 percent of cyberbullying victims were also school bullying victims.

Actual numbers are hard to verify. A review of several studies found anywhere from 4 percent to 46 percent of children and teens reporting being cyberbullied. Whatever the number, the research finds that "distress stemming from cyberbullying victimization can lead to negative effects similar to offline bullying such as depression, anxiety, and having negative social views of themselves." All of us have heard of teen suicides linked to these cyberbullying incidents.

What else is known about cyberbullying victims? There appears to be a strong correlation between age and likelihood of victimization. Four studies found that "victimization rates were found to be generally lower in early adolescence," and other research shows that the rates are "higher in mid-adolescence (around ages 14–15). Other studies have concluded that there is a peak period for online harassment—between eighth grade and 15 years of age.

People who commit cyberbullying acts are hard to identify, but the general consensus is that minors are almost exclusively harassed by other minors. Often the cyberbullies are known to the victim through school. Different bullying types are done by gender. Girls use shunning, embarrassment, relational aggression, rumor spreading, and social sabotage as they would in traditional bullying. Boys tend to use online harassment methods.

Does cyberbullying overlap with in-school bullying? It would seem that there is some of this behavior going on but the data are too uncertain for any conclusions. Do cyberbullied teens cyberbully in retaliation? Yes they do. Some studies have shown ¼ to ⅓ of victims resort to cyberbullying to retaliate.

Problematic Content

Most parents have concerns about "problematic content" on the Internet. This often involves violent media (movies, music, and images) and pornographic content that is otherwise legal for adults. Other problematic content reviewed in the research includes hate speech and content discussing/depicting self-harm, such as sites discussing suicide or how to engage in anorexic behaviors ("pro-ana" sites). Access to online gambling and drugs is another area of worry.

The Internet Safety Technical Task Force (ISTTF) review we have been presenting identifies three "core concerns" regarding problematic content: (1) youth are unwittingly exposed to unwanted problematic content during otherwise innocuous activities; (2) minors are able to seek out and access content to which they are forbidden, either by parents or law; (3) the intentional or unintentional exposure to content may have negative psychological or behavioral effects on children.

Janis Wolak and her team, in a recent national study, found that 42 percent of youth reported either unwanted or wanted exposure to pornography; of these, 66 percent reported only unwanted exposure, and 9 percent of those indicated being "very or extremely upset."

Some children (roughly 20% of all teen Internet users) specifically use the Internet for pornographic access. These sites are visited for sexual excitement, curiosity, or even informational purposes. One case study by Leneigh White and her team indicated that "most unwanted exposure comes from 'spam' emails, mistyping of URLs into a web browser, and keyword searches that 'produce unexpected results.'" Before widespread Internet access, such incidental or unwanted exposure to pornographic content was rare. One national survey found that 25 percent of minors aged 10–17 viewed unwanted pornography in the past year. Six percent of this group reported being "very or extremely upset" by the unwanted online exposure. In a follow-up survey five years later, 34 percent of minors aged 10–17 reported being exposed to unwanted pornography, and 9 percent of them indicated being "very or extremely upset."

As menacing as these figures are, it should be noted that more children are exposed to sexual content and nudity on cable TV than on the Internet. The majority of researchers in this area, as summarized by Ybarra and Mitchell, believe that "concerns about a large group of young children exposing themselves to pornography on the Internet may be overstated."

Parents are also concerned about violent content and exposure to gruesome images and story lines. These can be accessed from online sources or through video game consoles that are connected online. More worrisome, much online violent content can be accessed through traditional news reports. We will speak to video game effects later in this chapter.

We now turn to the topic of hate speech sites, defined as those with online content designed to threaten others and act as propaganda and recruiting vehicles for offline organizations. The content may be racist, anti-Semitic, anti-homosexual, sexist, or otherwise discriminatory. (Some may even be religion-based, like the Westboro Baptist Church site.)

Laura Leets reports that teen viewers generally find these types of websites threatening, but teens are more likely to be influenced or persuaded by these sites. The producers of this hate content are often technically savvy and know how to use social media, blogs, and texting.

Fortunately the number of these hate sites is very small. The Southern Poverty Law Center, which tracks these sites and organizations, reported 497 hate sites in 2003. The number grew to over 1,000 as of February 2011, still a fraction of the whole Internet. More worrisome are some data that suggest that minors also produce content, so they are not just consumers, but can be active producers and propagators of hate speech.

We now turn to websites that have information related to self-harming behaviors. These sites promote self-injury and suicide or encourage anorexic and bulimic lifestyles (otherwise known as "pro-ana" and "pro-mia" sites). Unfortunately, very little is known about teens that participate in self-harm websites and even less about how these sites may translate into actual behavior. It seems, from work done by researchers like Ybarra and Mitchell, that teens who visit these sites are already psychologically troubled, have been abused, or live in chaotic, conflicted families.

The sites themselves often look like they are designed to help others. But if you examine their content, one sees that they are really about teaching and enabling self-harm. For example, pro-ana sites show how to rearrange food on a plate so you seem to be eating a meal. They also have photos of extremely obese women in bathing suits as a way to play into the eating disordered fear-of-fat thinking and serve as a motivator to keep thin.

Other online dangers considered by the Internet Safety Technical Task Force report include child pornography and risky behavior such as posting personal information online. As for the child pornography issue, there are situations involving grooming of young people as well as the solicitation dangers we discussed earlier. Other risky behavior includes children/teens posting full names, addresses, birth dates, and school locations. Males tend to post more of this demographic information than females. Females tend to post more personal images and videos.

Children and teens with psychological and family troubles are clearly an at-risk group. Wolak's team reports that children/teens with histories of depression, physical abuse, and substance abuse are more likely to make poor choices online. For example, depressed youth were more likely to report increased unwanted exposure to online pornography, online harassment, and solicitation, and were eight times more likely to be victimized.

Most parents simply do not know the actual numbers just described. Some believe that filters and other technology can protect their children. A positive home environment (with involved parents, rules and discipline, monitoring and supervision) protects youth against these dangers. Parents who discuss Internet threats had more safety-conscious children according to Michele Fleming. More family rules regarding the Internet were correlated with less risk of a face-to-face meeting with someone met online. The ISTTF report concludes that "family cohesion and shared activities were found to lead to less exposure to negative content such as pornography."

CULTURAL AND MEDIA-BASED STRESSORS: VIDEO GAMES

Computers and high-tech game console equipment have opened the door to offline tech-based worries. Video game effects on children and teens will be addressed next. There is a system of ratings designed to help parents understand the nature of game content and whether it is suitable for exposure to children and/or teens. The Entertainment Software Ratings Board (ESRB) has a six-tier system. The ratings are: EC (Early Childhood) for age 3 and up; E (Everyone) for age 6 and older; E10+ (Everyone 10 and older); T (Teen) for age 13 and up; M (Mature) for age 17 and older; and finally AO (Adults Only) for ages 18 and older.

Retailers of video games have only voluntary buy-in to enforcing the ratings' age suggestions. Different states are enacting legislation to make the ratings more binding. For example, in California selling M-rated games to minors can be penalized with a $1000 fine for the seller. According to the Federal Trade Commission, it is estimated that 80 percent of retailers follow these ratings when selling to children. A pending U.S. Supreme Court ruling will try to settle some of these matters. They are expected to rule on whether selling M-rated games to minors can be regulated.

The scope of this issue is highlighted with some quick numbers:

- $10 billion in sales of video games annually;
- $1 billion in revenue for the game *Call of Duty: Black Ops* in the first five months after the game's release;
- 82 percent of games are rated for teens and younger.

Video games are now an established universal play activity for children and teens. This section is not discouraging the activity at all. Many positive uses and hours of fun can be had. For example, the Cub Scouts now have a video game "belt loop" and "pin" award. The award and activity acknowledge the popularity of video games for boys and teach responsibility in their use. The requirements (Boy Scout Trail, 2011) are as follows:

For the video game belt loop award:

1. Explain why it is important to have a rating system for video games. Check your video games to be sure they are right for your age.
2. With an adult, create a schedule for you to do things that includes your chores, homework, and video gaming. Do your best to follow this schedule.
3. Learn to play a new video game that is approved by your parent, guardian, or teacher.

For the video games pin award, the Scout must first earn the video games belt loop, and then complete five of the following requirements:

1. With your parents, create a plan to buy a video game that is right for your age group.
2. Compare two game systems (for example, Microsoft Xbox, Sony PlayStation, Nintendo Wii, and so on). Explain some of the differences between the two. List good reasons to purchase or use a game system.
3. Play a video game with family members in a family tournament.
4. Teach an adult or a friend how to play a video game.
5. List at least five tips that would help someone who was learning how to play your favorite video game.
6. Play an appropriate video game with a friend for one hour.
7. Play a video game that will help you practice your math, spelling, or another skill that helps you in your schoolwork.

8. Choose a game you might like to purchase. Compare the price for this game at three different stores. Decide which store has the best deal. In your decision, be sure to consider things like the store return policy and manufacturer's warranty.

9. With an adult's supervision, install a gaming system.

I reprint these requirements as they are a good set of guidelines for all parents to follow with their children.

Are there positive effects to playing video games? Certain games can teach problem-solving, goal-setting, and decision-making strategies. They can also teach cooperation, sharing, and teamwork. In this way, there is a cognitive development component related to planning and complex problem-solving. Video games also teach children that it takes hours of practice in order to be successful. Repeated play with higher scores gives them a sense of achievement and can be a self-esteem booster. Video game play may also help in the development of the player's perceptual, cognitive, and motor skills.

Douglas Gentile and his international research group have presented findings of three separate studies, conducted in different countries with different age groups. The research team used different scientific methods and statistics. (The research used both experimental and correlations designs.) All the studies, each with a different angle on the problem, found that playing games with *prosocial content* caused players to be more helpful to others after the game was over. Prosocial video games involve characters who help and support each other in nonviolent ways.

In Study One, using over 700 Singapore teens (average age about 13), the team looked at the association between video game habits and prosocial behavior. The subjects reported their favorite games and gave ratings of how often game characters helped, hurt, or killed other characters. They were also asked questions about how they would spend time and money helping people in need, to cooperate with others and share their belongings, or to react aggressively in different scenarios. In line with other studies, the researchers found a strong correlation between playing violent video games and hurting others. But the study also found a strong correlation between playing prosocial games and helping others.

Study Two considered the long-term relationship between video game habits and prosocial behavior in Japanese children aged 10 to 16. These 2,000 subjects completed a survey about their prosocial video game play time, and rated how often they had helped other people in the last month. After a four-month wait, they were surveyed again. The researchers found a significant relationship between exposure to prosocial games and helpful behavior months later.

The authors concluded that there may be an upward spiral of beneficial effects with positive, prosocial game play as there is a negative downward spiral with violent game play and aggression.

In Study Three, the research group carried out an experiment with American college students with a mean age of 19. After playing either a prosocial, violent, or neutral game, participants were asked to assign puzzles of different levels of difficulty to a randomly selected partner. This partner could win $10 if they solved all the puzzles. Those who played a prosocial game were more likely to assign the easier puzzles to their partners. Conversely, those who had played violent games were more likely to assign the hardest puzzles, as if to purposefully penalize their teammate.

Although positive video games have advantages, many studies detail the negative effects of video games on children. Various studies have shown a relation between aggressive behavior and playing video games that have violence in them. Playing games that have a lot of shooting and killing increases anger levels in children, leading to aggressive behavior in real life. Further, as violent behavior is rewarded in the game world, they may become motivated to repeat it in real life. Children may start feeling that shooting and killing are normal and feel no guilt about beating or clobbering siblings or peers. There are also results showing a direct correlation between poor academic performance and playing video games. Studies have shown that some children spend too much time playing video games and ignoring their studies, resulting in poor scores at school. Video games can also have negative effects on the physical health of children. Sitting for hours before the video game consoles can increase the risk of obesity, carpal tunnel syndrome, muscular diseases, and skeletal and postural disorders in kids. Other more documented, severe chronic health effects of video games can include increased heart rate and high blood pressure! To decrease the negative effects of gaming on children, parental control is essential. Parents should keep a close eye on the sort of games their children play. When buying games for kids, parents should check the age limit mentioned on the cover. They should avoid buying games that have excessive violence in them. The most important thing that parents must observe is the amount of time their children spend in front of the video game consoles. They should not allow their kids to spend more than two hours per day playing video games. Video games are definitely fun and entertaining and are also good for relieving tension. However, overindulgence can lead to addictive behavior with video games. In this case, there can be physical (obesity and motor development problems) as well as psychological effects (withdrawal from the constant excitement and arousal) on children.

In a 2008 study published in *Pediatrics,* C. A. Anderson and his international team "tested whether high exposure to violent video games increases physical aggression over time in both high-(United States) and low-(Japan) violence cultures." They hypothesized that the amount of exposure to violent video games early in a school year would predict changes in physical aggressiveness assessed later in the school year. This longitudinal approach had two data recording times—time 1 and time 2. To make the study more rigorous, they adjusted their data to statistically control for gender and previous physical aggressiveness.

The consensus of findings regarding violent video game play is that playing violent video games causes a short-term increase in aggressive thoughts, feelings, and behavior. When using cross-sectional studies, research typically shows positive correlations between routine violent video game play and both mild and severe forms of physical aggression.

In the Anderson study, "despite the differences between samples in measures of high levels of video game violence exposure, physical aggression, country, and age, each sample yielded statistically reliable positive correlations between time 1 game exposure and time 2 physical aggression." These were "of a magnitude that falls in the medium to large range for longitudinal predictors of physical aggression and violence."

This study is important because it was one of the first to show longer time effects of video game-related exposure on aggressive behavior in two distinct and different cultures. In fact, the effect was similar even though Japanese and U.S. cultures have different violence and aggression levels in everyday life. Of additional interest is the fact that this finding occurred in all the children studied. Other research has maintained that "only highly aggressive children (either by nature, culture, or other socialization factors) will become more aggressive if repeatedly exposed to violent video games." Finally, this study showed that violent video game play is a causal factor in later aggression.

In fact, violent video game playing has long been suspected to increase aggression. In a study conducted by Brad Bushman and Bryan Gibson, they showed that, at least for men, "ruminating about the game" can increase the effect of the game's influence to lead to aggression long after the game is over.

Their study randomly assigned college students to play one of six different video games for 20 minutes. Half the games were violent (e.g., *Mortal*

Kombat) and half were not (e.g., *Guitar Hero*). Half of the players from each group (violent or nonviolent) were told to over "the next 24 hours, think about your play of the game, and try to identify ways your game play could improve when you play again."

Bushman and Gibson tested their subject's aggressiveness the next day. For men in the nonruminating group, the violent video game subjects tested the same as the men who had played nonviolent games. But in the violent video game ruminating group, they were more aggressive than the other groups. Of interest, women who played the violent video games and thought about the games did not experience increased aggression the next day.

This study is the first lab-based experiment to show that violent video games can fuel aggression for an extended period of time. The authors noted that it is "reasonable to assume that our lab results will generalize to the 'real world.' Violent gamers usually play longer than 20 minutes, and probably ruminate about their game play in a habitual manner."

DO VIDEO GAMES OR INTERNET TIME CHANGE BRAIN ORGANIZATION?

There is still controversy and disagreement over how exposure to video games impacts developing brains. Douglas Gentile, a leading researcher in the area of video game effects, recommends that scientists might stay out of the public debates by sticking to their findings and staying away from the politics and money issues. Gentile says that five aspects of video games can affect players: amount of time played, content (educational, prosocial, violent), on-screen structure (features of what must be watched on the monitor), mechanics (motor skill improvements or deteriorations), and context, defined as how social the game playing is. Through his personal research and in reviewing the work of others, he believes that these variables can actually explain the different research results obtained so far. These differences may not be contradictory so much as revealing of different perspectives or aspects of the game experience.

For Gentile, researching these five dimensions of video games should produce multiple benefits. It would allow for people "to get beyond the dichotomous thinking of games as simply good or bad." He has concluded that, "Video games are neither good nor bad. Rather, they are a powerful form of entertainment that does what good entertainment is supposed to do—it influences us."

What about actual brain function changes or rewiring effects? Can we explain the behavior changes from a biological/brain perspective?

Helen Phillips, writing for the *New Scientist,* reported results of a 2005 study that examined the P300 brain wave response. Researchers have looked at the P300 wave for several decades. It is easily measured via EEGs. The P300 response is thought to reflect processes involved in how we evaluate a new, low probability, or rare stimulus. (It is a measurable brain reaction that occurs about 300 milliseconds after we notice a new stimulus in our environment. The size of the wave is related to reports of surprise or other emotions.)

Thirty-nine experienced gamers were assessed as to the amount of violent games they played. They were then shown real-life images, mostly of neutral scenes, but interspersed with violent or negative (but nonviolent) scenes, while recording P300 responses. Subjects with the most violent games histories had P300 responses to the violent images that were smaller and delayed. This meant that they were somewhat desensitized to the violent imagery. This was also correlated with those subjects giving harsher punishments when they played later games where this was an option.

The study's first author, psychologist Bruce Bartholow, was quoted as saying that this was "the first study to show that exposure to violent games has effects on the brain that predict aggressive behavior." While some researchers agree with this conclusion, others offer alternate explanations for the findings. More research is needed.

An Internet posting by Jacqui Cheng in 2009 reported work by British neuroscientist Susan Greenfield. Greenfield believes that the brains of children and teens have been infantilized as a result of the quick, attention-shifting aspects of Internet sites such as Facebook, as well as video game playing. She was reported as saying that today's youth have more trouble understanding each other and focusing in school, and that this may be a result of the widespread exposure of short clips of information in the online world that causes their brains to physically change. Rather than developing the ability to stay on task and focus for longer periods as they grow up, video game- and Internet-exposed youth are not progressing as they should. As noted in the article, Greenfield's conclusions are based on observation anecdote, and her understanding of brain development rather than hard research.

Such a clear finding would, of course, be the proverbial smoking gun. Can anyone demonstrate permanent brain rewiring or changes caused by Internet/video game exposure? And worse, are they related to poor learning or deficiencies in information processing?

The 1992 work of neuroscientist Richard Haier first looked at how frequent playing of the game *Tetris* actually changed the players' brains.

The so-called Tetris effect showed how video game play could make brains work more efficiently. This finding eventually led to the creation of brain-training games, intended to help people achieve certain skills and abilities.

Haier and three colleagues—Sherif Karama, Leonard Leyba, and Rex Jung—reported on a 2009 experiment with 26 girls, aged 12 to 15, assigned to play *Tetris*. This age group was chosen because their developing brains were more likely to reflect changes. Girls were employed because, having less experience with video games than boys, changes would reflect effects from the new experience of video game play.

After three months of regular play, Haier and his colleagues analyzed the brain changes in the game-playing group compared with a control group. They found that the *Tetris* players' brain function, measured by fMRIs, became more efficient in areas linked to critical thinking, reasoning, language, and information processing. They also looked to see if certain areas of the brain became thicker—proof of structural changes underlying the improved function. To their surprise, they found areas of the cortex did become thicker, but in areas of the brain linked to the planning of complex movements as well as the coordination of sensory information. These areas of structural change are *not* linked to the functional improvements in critical thinking and reasoning.

So what does all this mean? For this experiment, whatever changes that led to the better brain function were not related to changes in brain area size. We know the brain is quite complicated and that there are many pathways and circuits that control behavior. In the case of the Tetris effect, the behavioral changes are real, but our ability to explain them is not quite there yet. Haier and his group have plans for future research to try to find the explanation for what is happening.

What does all this research mean for the educated parent deciding on how much play and what kinds of games she/he may allow in the home? Read on.

In a 2010 report, Christopher Ferguson found that the level of depression in young people strongly predicted how aggressive and violent they may be or may become. Contrary to popular belief, and with some skepticism, he found exposure to violence in video games or on television to not be related to serious aggression in the U.S. Hispanic sample he studied.

Involving 300 10–14-year-old Hispanic subjects, Ferguson had two interview times established 12 months apart. He looked at the subjects' exposure to violence both in video games and on television as well as negative life events, including neighborhood problems, negative relationships with adults, antisocial personality, family attachment, and delinquent peers. In addition to those variables, he also assessed the family interaction and communication styles, subjects' exposure to domestic violence, depressive symptoms, serious aggression, bullying, and delinquent behavior.

Results included the following: 75 percent of the participants played video games within the past month on computers, consoles, or other devices, and 40 percent played games with violent content. More boys than girls played violent games. At the one year follow-up, seven percent reported taking part in one or more criminally violent acts such as physical assaults on other students or using physical force to take an object or money from another person. Nineteen percent reported nonviolent crimes in the year, with shoplifting and thefts on school property the primary offenses.

More so than the exposure to violence variable, Ferguson found that depressive symptoms were a strong predictor for aggression and rule-breaking, and the depression effect was greater for those who had preexisting antisocial personality traits. Additionally, neither exposure to violence from video games or television at time 1 predicted aggressive behavior or rule-breaking at time 2.

Ferguson argues that current levels of depression may be a better variable of interest in the prevention of serious aggression than violence exposure. Finding no evidence in support for a time-related association between video game/TV violence and subsequent aggression was a surprise. These data add some confusion to the debate over violent video games and violence in teens. Once again, these issues are complex and multileveled with few easy explanations or solutions.

WHAT PARENTS CAN DO TO PROTECT THEIR CHILDREN FROM OUTSIDE STRESSORS

So what can/should an educated parent do to protect his/her children? The advice, whether related to the Internet, video games, television content, or other sources of danger or stress would be the following:

- Monitor your child's activities and limit total tech-based time.
- Sit with your child and play some games together.
- Surf the 'Net and/or watch TV shows together.
- Know your child's friends and what they do together.
- Talk about appropriate/inappropriate activities.

- Consider adding a spyware system to track/report computer histories.
- Keep computers and TV sets in open family areas.
- Make "surprise" visits to see what's up.

No surprises here—this is list of common sense parenting behaviors. Technology is not going anywhere. It is up to parents to guide their children through the best ways to use and benefit from it, and to shield them from its dangers.

EIGHT

Why Fathers Matter

Sometimes the poorest man leaves his children the richest inheritance.

~Ruth E. Renkel

A father carries pictures where his money used to be.

~Author Unknown

The guys who fear becoming fathers don't understand that fathering is not something perfect men do, but something that perfects the man.

The end product of child raising is not the child but the parent.

~Frank Pittman

In this chapter we will discuss the role of fathers in child development. The chapter title could as easily have been "How Fathers Matter," as we will look to many different studies and reports which document the importance and ways in which fathers impact child development. We will begin with a brief historical account of how fathers' roles have changed over the past 100 or so years. We will discuss some research on fathers as caregivers. We will turn our attention specifically to fathers of divorced families and the ways in which a father can stay involved and engaged in his children's lives. We will then consider who the 21st-century father is—how his responsibilities are defined and what impact his actions have. Finally, we will review research on how fathers impact child outcomes.

FATHERHOOD—DEFINITIONS, ROLES, AND HISTORY

Let's begin with a look back at the research on the importance of fathers. To really appreciate where we are today, you have to see where we have been. In the 1980s, research on fathering hit full bloom. The first reports of increased involvement of fathers, and increases in time spent on child care, began to creep into the contemporary literature and news. These "new fathers" were described as caring and nurturant and emotionally sensitive to children. These initial reports also touted the newly discovered relationships between fathers' involvement and greater intellectual and emotional development in their children. A movement toward embracing androgyny, allowing men to explore their feminine side, also came about.

In Michael Lamb's 2000 review, these nurturant fathers were men actively involved in the daily care of their children. True parenting behavior, as of the '80s, was considered a central component of the definition of a good father. This definition of fathering emerged in part in the 1970s as a response to society's support for feminism. This nurturant role was not a replacement but an added-on duty. Men were still breadwinners and sex role models in family life.

As the roles of fathers changed in society, the research approaches evolved as well. In the first half of the 1900s, Lamb notes, Freudian perspectives dominated the scientific literature. For Freudians, a father's role was to be not only a good provider, but also a psychological rock within the family. This was especially true as Freud's theory emphasized identification processes as key for both boys' and girls' healthy development.

According to Freud, boys learn how to be men by incorporating their fathers' beliefs, attitudes, values, and sexual orientations, all by age six years or so. In a process termed *identification,* a boy resolves his internal psychic struggles to form a unique personality by coming to see his father as *the* role model. In this psychodynamic view, a father's masculinity is a key ingredient in developing a healthy son. If the father was absent, or a mother dominated in a family, that scenario would lead to a possible homosexual outcome in the son. (At the time, homosexuality was considered a disorder or personality abnormality to be avoided.) So, in this view, to be sure a son develops a healthy, normal personality and sexual orientation, a strong father is needed.

Girls' relationships with fathers are also important in this psychodynamic model. Similar internal, unconscious psychic forces that shape boys' personality development also occur in girls. For girls, the proper, healthy outcome is identification with their mothers' femininity after a process involving an attraction to their fathers and the strength and power they represent (the so-called penis envy phenomenon). Much was written about such Freudian concepts, most of which is now viewed with historic interest as little of his work is scientifically verifiable.

Research in the 1960s led to an interesting conclusion about the role of fathers in gender typing. This research found that a boy's masculinity depends upon a strong father role model, while a girl's femininity is less tied to parental example. Boys with weak fathers and powerful mothers are much more likely to exhibit feminine behaviors. Fathers who are dominant and who set limits and enforce structure are more likely to produce masculine sons.

The next areas of research to emerge studied the topics of father absence effects and maternal deprivation. Paralleling WWII and major losses of family intactness, research demonstrated the need and importance of attachment, considering only the role of mothers. The father absence literature repeatedly showed that boys were worse off for life if separated from their fathers.

In fact, both the early maternal deprivation and father absence studies were methodologically flawed. Put simply, the results of most of this work were overstated and inaccurate. Later research was an improvement, but researchers soon concluded that their approaches were too simplistic to yield truly meaningful results. However, these efforts helped lay the groundwork for the next wave of research.

More recently, Tami M. Videon explored the influence of father involvement on teens' psychological well-being. Using data from the AddHealth database, she tested a sample of 7th–12th graders living in intact homes. Using a multivariate analysis, she found further proof that "the father-adolescent relationship has an independent impact on adolescents' psychological well-being beyond the mother-adolescent relationship." The effects were equally strong by parent and child gender.

Videon's research view of parent-teen relations over time indicated that adolescents have more unstable relations with fathers than with mothers. Changes in teen satisfaction with the father-adolescent relationship significantly influenced fluctuations in sons' and daughters' psychological well-being. In fact, she found that this effect persists even after control-ling for changes in mother-adolescent relationships. Videon summarized, "these findings underscore fathers' unique direct contribution to their children's psychological well-being."

What does it mean when we say *fathering*? Is there a job description? Is fathering truly different from mothering? How does one learn to be a father? Does it matter to a child if there is a father in his/her life, and what if there isn't? Let's see what the research literature says.

To begin, *fathering* is the term given to describe *the special and specific traits and behaviors that men bring to the child rearing experience.* In 2006, Mark T. Morman and Kory Floyd looked at the question of what makes a good father. In the first study, fathers of at least one child responded to an open-ended question regarding what makes a good father. In the second study, fathers and adolescent or young adult sons responded to the same question. The results fell into 20 types of responses. Here are the top 10:

1. Role Model—"A good father is a role model in every way to his son."
2. Control—"It means setting limits and boundaries for their lives."
3. Love—"A good father loves his son as much as he can."
4. Provider—"Being a good father means to care for your kids."
5. Sacrifice—"Being a good father has meant self-sacrifice for the betterment of my children."
6. Availability—"I will always be there to help if needed."
7. Forgiveness—"A good father may not always agree with his son's ac-tions but must always be willing to forgive him."
8. Listener—"I want to be open and listen when he needs to talk."
9. Father as teacher (general)—"A good father teaches his son from what he has learned."
10. Father as teacher (specific)—"A good father loves God and teaches his son to do the same."

Morman and Floyd found that fathers and sons agreed on what makes a good father; both fathers and sons mentioned 3 of the top 5 characteris-tics and 9 of the top 10 items mentioned as essential for good fathering. Their research helps us to better understand what good fathering is and allows researchers to develop a consistent and stable list of factors central to the concept. This should lead to establishing a possible model of good fathering.

SOME CONTEMPORARY PERSPECTIVES ON FATHERING

Mark O'Connell, a Massachusetts psychologist and psychoanalyst, has written on fathers and fatherhood. In his 2005 book, *The Good Father,* he defines fatherhood as having three essential facets—authority, leadership, and responsibility. Of these, the bedrock paternal function is based on authority.

O'Connell's book—a recommended read for the educated parent—discusses where and how fatherhood has evolved in the 21st century. Modern notions of fathers, he says, are linked with a range of qualities such as kindness, love and loving, discipline, strength, violence, and absence. He worries about the impact of so many families left fatherless, whether through true physical absence or psychological distancing and remoteness.

O'Connell shares his struggles, as a child whose father died, in defining his own fatherhood. He begins with paternal authority—what it is and how it is gained. He laments that, for many men, their authority is seemingly "fluid and negotiable." When authority is not established, there is a breakdown. Part of this breakdown occurs as a result of men trying to be authoritarian or just not knowing what true authority is or should be. This, O'Connell says, is linked to an issue of authenticity versus disingenuousness. He argues that good fathers are authentic and true to themselves.

Some men are confused by messages they get from the culture linking fathers and their masculinity. O'Connell argues that one modern notion of masculinity and fathering is based upon a "passive man" theory. In such a theory, "soft" men are to be in touch with their feminine side and to be empathic, caring, and nurturing. On the other side are "real men" who are macho, self-sufficient, competitive, in charge, and "proud of it." O'Connell claims that while both paradigms hold some truth, they are also exaggerated polar ends of a spectrum. He says, "Fatherhood and authority are based upon core elements of men's masculinity—the very elements devalued by the sensitive man movement and caricatured by the real man movement." Ultimately, a good father needs to be secure in his version of masculinity in order to raise his children.

On the issue of a father's authority, O'Connell says that it is based upon "anger, power and aggression." Like it or not, aggression is a basis of authority as it is a function of being male. This is, hormonally, a fact of life. To a child or wife, a father's aggression can be scary. But when included as part of a father's authority, it involves harnessing and controlling this aggression for positive and constructive purposes. This controlled aggression becomes the power behind the father's authority. It is there to be used when needed.

To illustrate this point, O'Connell relates a story about Jorge Rivas (pp. 75–76). It is about Rivas's management style with employees, but it is a perfect analogy for fathering. In the story, O'Connell relates that Rivas used a very democratic, nonhierarchical style with his employees. While it would appear that he may or could be challenged or disobeyed, he knew he always had the ultimate response—firing an employee. He rarely resorted to this extreme end, but all of his workers knew that he could and would if needed.

Like Rivas, fathers always need to know and communicate that they have an authority based upon power and aggression. As O'Connell writes, "Jorge was willing to act decisively, firmly; even, when needed, punitively. He was willing to be aggressive." And so it must be for a father with his children.

The theme of paternal authority is a cornerstone of the parental role. O'Connell states that a good father must have the capacity to own and use his power and aggression, and to have a willingness to assume a position of parental responsibility. This role includes that of providing safety and protection for his children, as well as discipline.

Toward this end, O'Connell offers guidelines and advice on spanking. Like Diana Baumrind, O'Connell believes that spanking should be part of a collection or range of discipline strategies. On pages 146–147 of *The Good Father,* he asks a number of key questions for a father to consider should he wish to spank. (Fathers can choose to never spank if they have other effective means to discipline.) These include concerns about spanking daughters, or spanking children who are already aggressive. They also include issues related to the purpose of the spanking—is it retaliatory or sadistic? And how does the child interpret the spanking experience? He then defines controlled spanking and what behavioral guidelines need apply.

Finally, O'Connell tackles the issue of the good father's role in the developing sexuality of his children. In his 10th chapter, he writes about his views on "how parents can raise children whose sexuality will be responsible, meaningful and personal." This is accomplished by recounting stories and lessons from several young adults with whom he met and worked in therapy relationships.

O'Connell's message about a father's roles and sexuality is more difficult to summarize, but I will try. He argues first that parents need to teach children "to respect the independent personhood of others" and themselves. By this he means that children must be allowed to safely grow in a place where they are protected from sexual abuse or assault. Parents must observe and respect the natural boundaries that allow for a child to develop in a healthy way.

On the issue of a safe space to grow, he also argues that parents need to "have their [children's] privacy recognized and respected." As a child grows up, needs for privacy increase. At the same time, parents need to be careful about their own privacy—adult matters are not for children or teens. Parents have to be aware of their own sexuality and feelings as well as their children's. A father's hugs can become uncomfortable when a daughter now has breast development—for the daughter and for the father. What was once harmless wrestling or roughhousing may now have a sexually charged facet when done with teens.

O'Connell recounts a story of a woman who recalled that after she reached puberty, her father never touched her physically. She interpreted his behavior as having to do with her in a negative way. Nothing untoward ever happened, but she was left to wonder "whether there was something dark in him, whether he just didn't trust himself." O'Connell writes that a father has to walk a fine line between overstimulation and abuse and "physical and erotic withdrawal." Fathers have to be honest and in control.

Jeremy Adam Smith has written on a modern, still evolving new family pattern involving fathers, the "stay-at-home dad." Using the term *reverse traditional families,* Smith's book is a blend of good journalistic research and real-world couples interviews, held together by his personal reflections and discoveries. I found it to be a good complement to the O'Connell work cited above.

Smith's book provides what he calls a "snapshot of male caregiving" in modern America. The book chronicles his own self-discovery about what it is to be father. He had to struggle in his first months of full-time care with adjusting his self-image. For fathers, there is an effect contrary to that of mothers. Fathers have to deal with feeling like losers for wanting to spend more time with their kids and less at work; mothers feel like losers when they experience the opposite.

Smith poignantly reports on his and his son's experience when he had to leave him at a preschool in order to start a new job. He talks about having to pretend to his son that leaving him was a good thing even though both knew otherwise at the moment. It is a feeling experienced by many parents after spending lots of uninterrupted time in home care.

Smith also points out a number of myths about stay-at-home dads and fathers' abilities to deliver quality child care. He argues that stay-at-home dads are subject to many stereotypes and half-truths. Among the myths he debunks with good research is that stay-at-home dads are a "luxury of educated elites." In fact, many families who choose this arrangement have financial issues to deal with. Another myth he encountered was that stay-at-home dads are "lazy men and inattentive fathers." In other words, if they could be at work, they would be. At the same time, Smith argues that when men are at home they become more attentive to their child's needs and more responsive. Other myths are related to stay-at-home dads being an economic decision, that "men are marginal to networks of care," and that men would not use parental leave or flexible hour schedules if they were "more widely offered."

In a later chapter, Smith debunks three more myths related to the research based on men as child care providers. He shows that men are indeed "biologically fit" to perform parental tasks, that fathers can be competent caregivers, and that children raised by stay-at-home dads are at lower risk for negative outcomes. His research was similar to that presented in *The Educated Parent,* with some additional data on how a present father makes a positive impact.

Smith's work is a good read, with stories from his friends in the San Francisco area, many in nontraditional couples and family arrangements. It is a true picture of modern-day fathering from a real-world stay-at-home dad who was walking the walk. His work shows how the parenting roles have evolved of late, and how time devoted to tasks has changed.

On the subject of how time spent in parenting duties has changed, sociologists Liana C. Sayer, Suzanne M. Bianchi, and John P. Robinson have reported "time diary data" which look at trends in mothers' and fathers' child care time from the mid-1960s to the late 1990s. Surprisingly, the results showed that both mothers and fathers reported spending greater amounts of time in child care activities in the late 1990s than in the family-oriented 1960s. Mothers spent less time in routine child care in the years 1965–1975, with an increase in 1975–98 that included a steady increase in time doing more developmental activities. By 1998, fathers reported more time spent in routine child care as well as in more "fun" activities. Fathers' time increased relative to mothers' time in all of the major child care activities. So no one can rightly say that fathers have not become involved and engaged.

The American Psychological Association has posted a literature review related to the changing roles of fathers. The APA says the so-called modern-day father is found in various roles and identities and in many shapes and forms: single or married; employed on a job or stay-at-home;

gay or straight; in adoptive or step-parent roles; and more involved in more caregiving roles to children with disabilities and challenges. As we have already reviewed, the body of psychological research on families "indicates that fathers' affection and increased family involvement help promote children's social and emotional development."

Allow me to present more of the APA's review with my commentary. The APA's online report covers two cultural trends and four different father type situations that now characterize modern fathers.

Economically, the father's place in the family has undergone a several-hundred-year evolution. For many years, fathers, as heads of households in patriarchal family structures, held the important roles of resources provider (food and money) and teachers of values—moral and religious. Fathers and sons (and to a much lesser extent, daughters) spent full days together, especially in agrarian cultures. Sons learned many lessons from their fathers, who showed them how to farm and raise animals and how to be a man. In whatever conversations ensued, fathers had a central role in raising their sons.

In the mid-1800s, when the Industrial Revolution came full bore, families left the country and moved to cities where fathers could work in factories. Fathers left their families each day to go to work and earn money. Children were either kept home to assist mothers or sent to schools. Father-children time was at a minimum compared to earlier years.

Over time, says the APA review, "fathers became distanced from the household and their families. Growing rates of abandonment and illegitimacy led to the development of welfare programs to assist widowed or unmarried women in supporting their children." In the 1960s, in the midst of these negative changes, women began to assert their independence. With women in the workplace and more autonomous, the need and importance of men/fathers was minimized—the woman could perform the man's roles in his absence.

This led to a new range of issues including higher divorce rates, more single parenting by choice, and the growth of assisted childrearing through daycare, schools, and other places. Fathers had choices to make—stay involved in a new way with their children or walk away.

As a result of these forces, fathers have played a more intentional role and have taken on tasks and responsibilities that had been turned over to mothers. Most of the psychological research on child development in the 20th century focused on mothers as the exclusive caregiver as that was simply the reality.

Only since the 1970s/80s has there been enough father involvement to conduct research on how fathers raise children and how fathers impact child development. The ongoing National Institute of Child Health and Human Development (NICHD) study, which looks at all facets of child care and caregivers, has more details about the new role of fathers. As cited in the APA report, the NICHD study "found that fathers tended to be more involved in caregiving when:

- they worked fewer hours than other fathers;
- they had positive psychological adjustment characteristics (e.g., high self-esteem, lower levels of depression and hostility, and coping well with the major tasks of adulthood);
- mothers worked more hours than other mothers;
- mothers reported greater marital intimacy; and
- when children were boys."

Much other research (as we review elsewhere in this chapter) has found a number of beneficial child outcomes when fathers are involved in their children's lives. All areas of development—social, emotional, cognitive (educational), physical, and behavioral—are positively shaped by fathers' presence and engagement.

In fact, the "status of the father's relationship with his child's mother serves an important influence on father involvement." Much research has shown that mothers serve as gatekeepers for access or denial of access to children. Because of physical separation and other mother-father relationship variables, "non-residential fathers are at high risk for becoming disconnected from their children over time." These are the children who are unwitting subjects in father absence research.

As we discussed in chapter 1 and elsewhere, the number of families of divorce has had a major impact on parenting. As most children have primary residency with their mothers, divorced fathers have a more difficult time getting access and involvement. Some states have required co-parenting for the protection of children. The Internet has more than a few sites run by divorced fathers who have tales of court fights and resistance from ex-wives to raising their children.

The father-of-divorce research shows that fathers can have significant influence on their children even without spending as much time as they would if living together. It is a version of the old quality-not-quantity-of-time argument. Again from the APA report, research is presented which found "key factors that contribute to healthy adjustment for children post-divorce." These include:

- "appropriate parenting (i.e., providing emotional support, monitoring children's activities, disciplining authoritatively, and maintaining age appropriate expectations),
- enough access to the non-residential parent,
- suitable custody arrangements, (joint legal custody often results in shared decision making, more father-child visits, regular child support payments, and more satisfied and better adjusted children)
- low parental conflict, and
- parents who are psychologically healthy."

Related to divorced fathers are the new roles of stepfathers. Stepfathering involves a fine balance in relationships—with your new spouse, your own ex-spouse, and your new spouse's children's biological father(s). And then there are the new relationships to build with the children. Complete books are available for the educated parent interested in the many facets of these family structures. I will say simply, there ain't too many Brady Bunch groups out there.

With the advent of the ongoing cultural shift in attitudes toward homosexuality in American society, gay fathers are on the rise. (Interestingly, TV has been a "softener" of attitudes, with shows like *Modern Family* portraying healthy, loving gay men in positive family scenarios.) Gay men become fathers in different ways—through adoption and related arrangements with women they know, or by raising biological children from previous marriages to women. The many stereotypes and negative attitudes regarding gay men as parents have no research support. Gay men as parents can be as capable of providing love and nurturing, and guidance and support—the basic parenting skills we have reviewed previously—as heterosexual couples.

As we discussed regarding the work of Jeremy Adam Smith, stay-at-home dads are a new breed of the modern father. Stay-at-home dads are a fraction of household structures, but represent a growing trend. These fathers get to play the role of the traditional mother—with more caregiving and day-to-day responsibilities than are typical in American families. Men choose to be stay-at-home dads for different reasons, but they are the same as women's: the other spouse can make more money; the father wants the privilege of child rearing; and the father does not want his child in daycare.

As the APA report states, "stay-at-home fathers are routinely confronted with stigma due to their flouting of the social norms surrounding masculine behavior." This was a theme of the Smith book we reviewed.

William Doherty and his team have given us four tasks completed by a responsible father. They are:

- providing financial support;
- providing care;
- providing emotional support; and
- establishing legal paternity.

This definition came from a federal government project I reviewed in *The Educated Parent*. It was part of a general policy shift by the Bush administration, seen as controversial by some since it was designed to promote marriage and two-parent families. James Levine and Edward Pitt have also more clearly defined responsible fathering. A responsible father does the following:

- He waits to make a baby until he is prepared emotionally and financially to support his child.
- He establishes his legal paternity if and when he does make a baby.
- He actively shares with the child's mother in the continuing emotional and physical care of their child, from pregnancy onward.
- He shares with the child's mother in the continuing financial support of their child, from pregnancy onward.

RESEARCH ON THE EFFECTS OF FATHER INFLUENCE

In a 2008 publication, Anna Sarkadi and a group of Swedish researchers reported on a systematic review of 24 longitudinal studies on the effects of father involvement on children's developmental outcomes. The studies are important because they reveal the impact of fathering for a long period of time and show the results of this involvement. The group defined *father involvement* as referring to "accessibility (cohabitation), engagement, responsibility and other complex measures of involvement." (Cohabitation was independent of marital status.)

Among their summary conclusions was that "there is certain evidence that *cohabitation* with the mother and her male partner is associated with less externalising behavioural problems." It was also found that, "Active and regular *engagement* with the child predicts a range of positive outcomes, although no specific form of engagement has been shown to yield better outcomes than another." Father engagement has an impact on child outcome through "reducing the frequency of behavioral problems in boys and psychological problems in young women, and enhancing cognitive development, while decreasing delinquency and economic disadvantage in low SES families."

From their work, Sarkadi and her colleagues believe "there is enough support to urge both professionals and policy makers to improve circumstances for involved fathering," as father presence leads to significant improvements for the children affected by their fathers' involvement.

Let us look into more details of some of the studies reviewed and the outcomes discovered. For example, a longitudinal study of 985 low birth weight and/or preterm infants was conducted by pediatrician Michael Yogman and his group. Their study revealed the importance of a father's presence in the home and involvement to cognitive performance at three years of age. This study counted both biological fathers and men acting as fathers. Yogman's group found that in 41 percent of the homes, fathers maintained a stable presence in the home and also engaged in play and other child care activities with their children. Children raised by these stable and highly involved fathers scored significantly higher on the Stanford-Binet Intelligence Test at three years old compared to three-year-olds from homes with less stable paternal presence and involvement.

In another study reviewed by the Sarkadi team, Marcia Carlson of Columbia University used data on biological fathers' relationships with their children from the 1979 National Longitudinal Survey of Youth. Analyzing data from this large-scale study (2,733 participants), Carlson assessed whether father involvement mediated the relationship between family structure (i.e., father absence) and four measures of adolescent behavior.

She examined father involvement based upon different family structures from birth to the teen years (aged 10–14). These included:

- biological parents married and/or cohabited for all years;
- biological parents married at birth, then divorced, with the mother alone since;
- biological parents married at birth, then divorced, with the mother remarried to a stepfather;
- the mother unmarried at birth who later married a stepfather; and
- the mother unmarried at birth and acting as a single parent for all years.

When parents had been married the entire time, teens had the best results on measures of externalizing behaviors, such as shoplifting, damaging of school property, getting drunk, or other school problems. Similarly, in intact families, teens exhibited significantly less delinquent behavior compared to families with the mother alone after a divorce or the mother alone and never married. In families where there were two parents, teens reported less negative feelings as measured by the Behavior Problem Checklist.

Carlson concluded, in a 2006 publication, that differences in father involvement accounted "for a sizeable fraction of the variance in outcomes by family structure." She also found that father involvement did not affect boys and girls differently, but teens' lives were more beneficial when the father lived with the adolescent.

Other reviewed studies looked at father involvement on educational achievement and attainment levels. Eirini Flouri and Ann Buchanan examined the effect of father engagement on children at 7 years of age as they related to educational outcomes at age 20. Their goals were "to explore the role of early father involvement in children's later educational attainment independently of the role of early mother involvement and other confounds, to investigate whether gender and family structure moderate the relationship between father's and mother's involvement and child's educational attainment, and to explore whether the impact of father's involvement depends on the level of mother's involvement."

They used data from a British longitudinal study that consisted of 17,000 participants. They had valid data on educational outcomes and parental involvement from 7,259 cases. The data included both biological fathers and father figures. Data collected when the children were seven years old included surveys by the mothers about whether the fathers read to their children, took the children on trips, were engaged in the children's education, and if the fathers had regular child care responsibilities.

Flouri and Buchanan found that father engagement at age 7 years had "a general, independent and significant effect on educational outcomes" at age 20 years. Specifically, father involvement and mother involvement with children at 7 years old independently predicted educational attainment at age 20 years. The association between parents' involvement and educational attainment was no different by child gender. Looking specifically at when the mother's child involvement was low rather than high was not affected by the father's involvement. It was also the case that an intact family structure did not weaken the association between fathers' or mothers' involvement and educational outcomes.

In a related 2006 study, Flouri also looked at parental interest in a child's education and child self-esteem levels at age 10 years as they relate to the child's level of educational attainment at 26 years of age. She also looked at a variable called locus of control at age 10 years. (*Locus of control* refers to whether a child believes that she/he is responsible for the outcomes of his/her efforts, or there is a more external influence or cause. It is generally the case that children with internal loci of control function at higher levels.) Flouri found that although mothers' and fathers' interest in their children's education was not linked to educational attainment via their impact on children's self-esteem or locus of control, it was a significant predictor of educational attainment, especially in daughters.

Does involvement by nonresident fathers affect a teen's tendency to remain in school? That is the research question asked by Chadwick L. Menning of Ball State University. He says that, in fact, level and type of involvement matters a great deal. Using data from the National Longitudinal Study of Adolescent Health, Menning has shown that nonresident fathers' involvement and increases in this involvement over time are associated with lower probabilities of school failure among adolescents.

It is also true that those who have no involvement with their nonresident fathers may experience lower odds of school failure than those who have low or moderate levels of involvement. Further analysis of the involvement measures into component parts suggests that increased variety of activities—especially the discussion of schoolwork, grades, or other things going on in school—is important (although not critical) to the observed effect.

Leah Y. Hughes and Robert J. Fetsch of Colorado State University have reported on a program designed to involve fathers early on in their children's emerging literacy skills. The program is called Fathers Reading Every Day (FRED). It is a four-week program, developed at Texas A&M University, designed to improve children's reading skills and academic performance through reading and father involvement and to strengthen the emotional bond between fathers and their children.

By report, the program is targeted to fathers (and father figures) of young children, and can be adapted for use with other male role models if the father is not present. Hughes and Fetsch evaluated the FRED program on four criteria, determining that it was research-based, empirically determined to be effective, and easily reproducible and set up for multiple community interventions.

Now let us review examples of research related to fathers and their offspring's sexual development. As early as 1972, research had shown that father absence had particularly negative effects on children, especially daughters. E. Mavis Hetherington showed that adolescent girls from early father-absent homes (parents divorced before the girls reached age five) tended to initiate more contact with, and seek more attention from, adult males than did girls from late father-absent homes (parents divorced after the girls reached age five). She also reported on other aspects regarding daughters' personalities and behaviors negatively impacted by loss of father contact.

More recently, Bruce Ellis and his group investigated the impact of father absence on early sexual activity and teenage pregnancy in longitudinal studies in the United States and New Zealand. The United States and New Zealand have the highest rates of teenage pregnancy among Western industrialized countries, with around half of these pregnancies culminating in a live birth. They measured community samples of girls who were followed prospectively from 5 years old to approximately age 18.

Ellis and his team found that more time experiencing father absence was strongly associated with an elevated risk for early sexual activity and adolescent pregnancy. This finding is consistent with so-called life-course adversity models of early sexual activity and teenage pregnancy. Such models suggest that a life history of family- and circumstance-based stress results in earlier onset of sexual activity and reproduction. But those studies have typically presumed that father absence was just one of a range of variables (such as divorce, poverty, conflict-filled family relationships, absence of parental monitoring and control) that promote early sexual activity and pregnancy in daughters.

Ellis's group demonstrated that father absence was *the* key variable associated with early sexual behavior and pregnancy. The group found that higher levels of father absence placed daughters at special risk for early sexual outcomes, even when controlling for all sorts of other variables that are seemingly important as well. In fact the team looked at 16 different variables including early sexual activity, teenage pregnancy, and six measures of psychosocial adjustment and educational achievement in each of the two samples.

So, does father absence place daughters at some special risk for early sexual activity and teenage pregnancy? Ellis's group found three converging lines of evidence which suggest that the answer is yes. First, in both sample groups, there was "a dose-response relationship" between when father absence began and early sexual outcomes. The early father-absent girls had the highest rates of both early sexual activity and adolescent pregnancy, followed by late father-absent girls, followed by father-present girls. The pregnancy rates "were 7 to 8 times higher among early father-absent girls, but only 2 to 3 times higher among late father-absent girls, than among father-present girls."

Second, in both samples, father absence was the primary path to early sexual activity and adolescent pregnancy. After controlling for all of the related variables, early father-absent girls were still about five times more likely in the U.S. sample and three times more likely in the New Zealand sample to experience an adolescent pregnancy than were father-present girls. The Ellis group believes that "these data suggest that father absence may affect daughters' sexual development through processes that operate independently of life-course adversity and go beyond mere continuation of early conduct problems."

Finally, in the U.S. sample, father absence was associated with early sexual activity and teenage pregnancy, but not to academic, behavioral, or mental health problems more generally. In the New Zealand sample, "there was still a pattern of at least trend associations between timing of father absence and the measures of adolescent adjustment, with early sexual activity and adolescent pregnancy occupying the upper end of this range of associations." The study concluded with these remarks:

> Considering the U.S. and New Zealand findings together, after controlling for measures of early conduct problems and life-course adversity, the effects of father absence on sex and pregnancy (a) were generally stronger than were the effects of father absence on other outcome variables and (b) clearly replicated across the two studies whereas other effects of father absence were more equivocal and replicated only in the sense of being in the same direction. In sum, after covariate adjustment, there was stronger and more consistent evidence of effects of father absence on early sexual activity and teenage pregnancy than on other behavioral or mental health problems or academic achievement.

The impact of the quality of relationships between fathers and daughters extends well into adulthood and married life. Eirini Flouri and Ann Buchanan explored the roles of father and mother involvement at age 7 and father-child and mother-child relations at age 16. They also examined the role of closeness to father and closeness to mother at age 16 as it was linked to the relationship quality with an adult partner at age 33. The father involvement measures at age 7 included the mother's report of whether the father read to his child, went on outings with the child, was interested in his child's education, and engaged in child care responsibilities. At 16 years old, the measures included self-report data by the child as to level of closeness to the father with a one to five rating in response to the question: "Do you get on well with your father?" At 33 years of age, the relationship quality with the adult partner was measured by a modified version of the Locke-Wallace Marital Adjustment Test.

Among the results: Findings of high father engagement levels at 7 had an independent and significant effect on having a good relationship with the father at 16. It was also found that having a good relationship with the father at age 16, in turn, had an independent and significant effect on good relationship quality with the adult partner at age 33, as did closeness to father with closeness to mother, early father involvement, fewer emotional and behavioral problems in adolescence, male gender, and academic motivation. Closeness to fathers at age 16 was more strongly related to the level of father involvement at age 7 for daughters than for sons, and to closeness to mothers for sons than for daughters. Marital adjustment levels at age 33 were related to good relationships with siblings, mother, and father at age 16 years, and less current psychological distress.

We turn now to a few more examples of recent research on the roles of fathers. William V. Fabricius and Linda J. Luecken of Arizona State University tested a biopsychosocial model of young adults' paternal relationships, the ongoing distress surrounding their parents' divorces, disruptions in time with parents, and how all of this impacted their later physical health. Fabricius and Luecken looked back five years to see what levels of conflict their subjects (college students) had experienced and also looked at how much time was spent with their fathers after the divorce.

For those 266 students whose parents divorced before they were aged 16, Fabricius and Luecken found support for their model. Specifically, they found the following:

- The more time children lived with their fathers after divorce, the better their current relationships were with their fathers, independent of levels of parental conflict.
- The more parental conflict they experienced, the worse their relationships were with their fathers and the more distress they currently felt about their parents' divorce, independent of time spent with their father.
- Poor father-child relationships and more distress, in turn, predicted poorer health status years later.
- There was no interaction between exposure to parent conflict and time with father.

For this last finding, it was shown that "more time with father was beneficial in both high- and low-conflict families, and more exposure to parent conflict was detrimental at both high and low levels of time with father."

Elizabeth Goncy and Manfred van Dulmen examined the relationship between various dimensions of parent-child involvement and three adolescent alcohol use outcomes. The parent-child variables were measures of shared communication, shared activity participation, and emotional closeness. The teen outcomes were level of alcohol use, alcohol-related problems, and risky behavior co-occurring with alcohol use. Participants, 7th–12th graders, were taken from the first wave of the National Longitudinal Study of Adolescent Health (AddHealth) data set, numbering 9,148.

All of the teens lived in two-parent residential homes, with 12 percent (1,100) also having a nonresidential biological father and 5 percent (523) having a nonresidential biological mother.

Eleven items measured parental involvement separately for both fathers and mothers. Six items measured teen alcohol use, 9 items measured alcohol-related problems, and 12 items measured co-occurring risky behaviors

Goncy and van Dulmen addressed previous shortcomings in the fathering research base by investigating both father and mother involvement in understanding teen alcohol-related outcomes. Two variables, shared communication with fathers and emotional closeness to fathers, but not the third, shared activity participation, had a unique impact on each of the three alcohol outcome measures. The father variables were predictive "above and beyond" the maternal involvement factors. This finding suggests that these father-related variables do make a difference.

Patricia M. Schacht, E. Mark Cummings, and Patrick T. Davies have examined the relationship between fathers' behavior within the family context and children's adjustment. Their research looked at variables such as fathers' depressive symptoms, marital conflict behaviors, fathers' caregiving, and the level of their children's emotional security. "The impact of fathers' behaviors on family factors and children's adjustment has been neglected in past research," they write. Their results indicated that father behaviors play an important role in children's adjustment over time. They also found that children's emotional security was an intervening variable between fathers' behaviors and children's adjustment.

Regarding child adjustment, fathers' alcohol use and depressive symptoms may start "a downward spiral of detrimental behaviors by fathers and negative reactions by children, eventually leading to externalizing and internalizing problems for children." Schacht and her team found that fathers' drinking problems were directly related to negative marital conflict behaviors. These "destructive marital conflict behaviors" were followed by a decrease in the men's positive parenting behaviors at the same time. This lack of positive parenting was then related to decreased levels of emotional security in children. The resulting emotional insecurity was significantly associated with the development of externalizing and internalizing problems in children. Externalizing behaviors are those related to acting out, like truancy and school problems and fighting. Internalizing behaviors are related to anxiety, fearfulness, and depression.

The study looked at 235 families with a six-year-old child; the families were followed longitudinally each year for three years. Specifically, fathers' depressive symptoms were thought to be directly related to children's internalizing problems. The data did not find this result. However, paternal depressive symptoms were directly associated with internalizing problems in children over time. These findings mirror the research on maternal depressive symptoms.

Support was found for the notion that due to mounting problems from alcohol use and marital conflict, "fathers may withdraw their warmth and affection from their children and engage in less positive parenting, contributing to adjustment problems for children over time." This was the first study to look at how decreases in positive parenting impact children; most other studies have focused on the increased negative parenting behaviors' effects.

A child's state of emotional security predicted whether the child would experience externalizing or internalizing problem behaviors. The team writes, "It seems that how secure a child feels about his or her family can change the impact that the father has on this child." These study results are in line with what is known about children's states of emotional security and their reactions to family conflict as intervening variables between family processes and children's adjustment.

Are there useful, clinical implications for these study results? The authors believe that "the emphasis on fathers' positive parenting, the significance of multiple fathers' behaviors in the context of family for children's emotional security, and the demonstration of multiple pathways for the influence of fathers' behaviors on child development each provide possible avenues for advances in conceptualizing clinical treatment approaches for fathers, children and families." Translated, this means that insights about how children and families are impacted by the variables looked at should be helpful in therapies that work to restore healthy family functioning. For example, clinicians should be careful to look for children's emotional security levels and to work toward giving children in therapy an outlet for their worries and concerns regarding parental conflict or father depression.

And so I believe I have more than made my point that active, involved, and engaged fathers do matter in the lives of their children. Fathers can play many different roles and be active from different positions in a family (biological father, adoptive father, stepfather), but all make their impact.

POSTDIVORCE FATHERING ISSUES

How can fathers remain connected to their children after a divorce? Many studies show that connections between fathers and children are tied to fathers who feel good about their ability to be a father. Even among divorced fathers, one sees a relationship between connections and involvement levels. One study has shown that fathers with joint custody (where visitation is a constant) pay full child support at 90 percent compliance rates. By comparison, 79 percent of fathers with visitation rights pay child support and only 44 percent pay if they are without visitation privileges.

The postdivorce fathering research base has two typical findings: (1) children are better off from the involvement, caring, and economic support they receive from fathers; and (2) a father's presence is important across different aspects of child development.

A survey of postdivorce effects on children provides a variety of outcomes. Work by Mavis Hetherington and her group and Judith Wallerstein and her group has generally concluded that fathers are important to a child's postdivorce adjustment status. Paternal contact in most research studies has been found to play an important role in reducing child behavioral problems, improving child self-esteem, and other positive outcomes. However, research findings also suggest that father absence was not associated with negative outcomes.

Inge Bretherton and her team investigated 71 sets of mothers and preschool-aged children, all described as well-functioning. Their research focused on questions related to how mothers and children perceive postdivorce co-parenting by fathers, as well as attitudinal measures. Among their findings:

- Mothers held fathers in low esteem for two or more years postdivorce.
- Mothers were able to separate their negativity from their children's more positive views.
- Many mothers reported improved parenting and child relations postdivorce (somewhat relieved to have the father out of the way).

- In a measure using child-generated stories, many reported family reunification.
- Mothers prefer father absence; children want more accessibility and contact.

Given other data indicating that both mothers and fathers have negative views of each other postdivorce, the goal of co-parenting seems harder to achieve. The Bretherton team acknowledged this and argued that postdivorce parenting education needs to address and correct these perceptions.

What does the research say about the factors associated with future levels of father involvement in the postdivorce family? The emotional stability of the father *and* the mother, and how both parents see how important they are, matter. The sex of the children is another variable—men are more likely to stay involved and return regularly for sons. Other variables include the father's economic well-being as well as the amount of encouragement and support he receives from others (extended family and friends) to continue his fathering role. Finally, how good the co-parenting relationship is matters as well. Parents who can work cooperatively and with little or much less fighting and conflict are the pairs where continued father involvement is most possible and likely.

The relationship that fathers have with their co-parent (the mother) is directly related to father involvement levels. A father's role and his feelings of how he sees himself are highly influenced by the support and encouragement received from the mothers of their children. Fathers are clearly more committed to staying around and helping when they are valued and supported by their co-parents, especially after divorce. This is similar to Bretherton's findings.

Nonresident fathers' attitudes are affected by many different things. These include the resulting family status of the father (being single, remarried, and/or having stepchildren). In general, a remarried father has less involvement with his children from the first union as a result of the time he now invests in the new marital relationship. In some cases however, remarrying a woman who cares about fathers will help add to the level of involvement with the man's children. So again, the marital support variable is important when looking at father involvement.

Other nonresident father variables include the characteristics/qualities of the ex-spouse/ex-co-parent. Resident mothers are the gatekeepers to child access, with much control over the when and where of child contact. Remarriage by the resident mother may also lessen a father's access, as the family situation becomes more complex and more likely to lead to conflict. Women gain even more control over their children's lives when they are not living with the fathers, especially in the case of children under six years of age. Some fathers give up rather than fight for their parental rights in these circumstances.

A nonresident father's social status and education level are also variables to consider. More educated fathers have more positive father attitudes in general, and probably played a more significant predivorce role in their children's lives. They may see themselves positively in the role of father, have established a father identity, and continue to participate in their children's lives even after divorce. Hetherington has reported that fathers who see their lives becoming more complicated or who are experiencing pain at the loss of their families may then stay away and limit their involvement in their children's lives as a result. Support and other mental health resources for these fathers are needed in order for them to reconnect.

Gordon E. Finley and Seth J. Schwartz, from south Florida, investigated the relationship between levels of father involvement and current psychosocial adjustment among 1,989 college students. Participants were 69 percent female, 31 percent male, averaging 20.6 years of age. They were from intact or divorced families and considered their biological fathers as the primary father figures in their lives. The survey data were retrospective, meaning that they were from reported recollections. Psychosocial adjustment outcomes included subjective well-being, a traditionally used outcome of divorce, and reported desires for more or less father involvement in their lives.

The results indicated that reported father involvement was related to subjective well-being for children from intact families, but was related to *desired* father involvement in children from divorced families. Among those from divorced families, young women were more likely than young men to desire more expressive father involvement than they received.

Finley and Schwartz state that "the most striking finding in the present results is that the types of outcomes to which father involvement is linked in the long-term appear to be strongly determined by whether the family remains intact or undergoes divorce." In intact families, father involvement was positively related to subjective well-being (items related to self-esteem, life satisfaction, and future expectations) in young adulthood. There was no such relationship for divorced families. In those divorced families, the absence of father involvement was related to greater long-term desires for father involvement. Emotional longing and missed opportunities with fathers are outcomes in divorced families. This variable is considered a marker of divorce-related distress in adult children.

It appears that divorce leaves many children with unmet desires for paternal involvement that remain important for many years after the divorce is finalized. Adult children of divorce were more likely than those from intact families to desire more father involvement than they had received and less likely to desire less involvement than they had received.

Important frequent father functions such as discipline, monitoring schoolwork, and provision of protection are aspects of father presence that adult children of divorce miss when living apart from their fathers. A father's actual presence is needed for these obligations. Significantly more women than men wanted more father involvement than they had received. Finley and Schwartz suggest that missed fathering opportunities, especially for emotional aspects of fathering, are more prominent in females. Of note, there were no gender differences in the relationship of father involvement to the subjective well-being measures.

So there you have it—the case for the importance of fathers is made. It is up to each family to ensure that children have the advantages of father involvement and engagement, and it is up to every father to take his father responsibilities—all of them—seriously.

NINE

How Daycare Affects Your Child

The most important thing she'd learned over the years was that there was no way to be a perfect mother and a million ways to be a good one.

~Jill Churchill

In bringing up children, spend on them half as much money and twice as much time.

~Author Unknown

You have a lifetime to work, but children are only young once.

~Polish Proverb

Placing a child in a daycare is one of the most important decisions a parent can make. For this chapter, *daycare* means caregiving for a child by people other than a parent in the child's home, the caregiver's home, or a daycare center. This care is provided during daytime hours, usually because parents are unavailable due to outside work.

There are many issues to consider in reaching a decision on whether to place a child in daycare. These include:

- whether it is best for a parent to stay home until the child reaches a certain age or developmental level, or continue on in an outside-of-home career;

- whether a child is better off cared for at home with someone who comes to him/her or whether a child is better off taken to another place with many other children; and

- whether a full- or part-time daycare placement is best for a child even if there are parents or other family at home or otherwise available to care for the child.

Why is this decision such an issue? Because many people are concerned about how children do when not raised by their parents at home. Is the concern justified? In this chapter we will review the research—positive and negative—on how daycare affects children. You can decide what the risks and benefits of placing your child in daycare really are. And this chapter will explain what you can do to make the best situation possible for you and your child(ren) if you choose to use a daycare option.

We will look at the different research results in this field in an effort to help you to make the best choice possible in your family situation, starting with what we know works well for children. I will present some of the latest findings from a long-term, nationwide study on the effects of daycare participation—the National Institute of Child Health and Human Development (NICHD) Child Care Study. One study looks at effects on the young infant (15 months and younger) and a second looks at results after tracking children for 15 years.

In addition, we will expand the topic of daycare to include other parenting duties that may be done outside of the family. There has been concern raised about parents outsourcing key adult duties to others—to schools and other organizations where children spend many hours.

DAYCARE DONE RIGHT

I like to use the phrase "daycare done right" to describe child care for younger children that will provide the healthiest daily routines in a safe place with good opportunities for adult-child interactions. Using this definition, there are some things that educated parents should consider in determining where they might place their daughter/son.

Most psychologists would agree that the following variables make for a high-quality daycare experience. This, in turn, should lessen any negative effects or problems that could arise. These conditions are:

- proper attention levels given for each child;
- age-related and ability-related activities (appropriate developmental opportunity) and encouragement to interact with adults;
- proper safety and health precautions;
- regular family communication and interaction; and
- trained and professional stable caregiver staffs.

Let us look at each of these in order.

Infants especially need lots of ongoing attention. They are always looking for new things to see and hear and touch and need adults to provide them with activities and play at their level (proper stimulation). *A small caregiver-to-infant ratio is a must.* Although each state provides guidelines and mandatory ratio requirements, few are as tough (or costly) as the ratio recommended by the research. For infants, a ratio of two dependable, trained adults for every five infants is the ideal. For toddlers, the number can be doubled to one adult per five preschoolers. Having this amount of adult attention ensures that children's needs are met and that chances for quality interactions can take place regularly over the course of a day. Spreading adult attention too thin does not allow for the one-on-one time that infants need.

Giving a child opportunities to actively explore his/her environment and to have enriching experiences in doing so is also important. This means that a child needs to be stimulated in all ways at a level suited to where they are in their growth and development—in motor skills, thinking skills, language skills, and social interactions. Infants especially need toys that help them to look at the world in ways that provide the right stimulation for their developing muscle coordination. Chances to develop language are also key, with the best environment exposing children to interactive conversation, songs and sing-a-longs, and age-appropriate games. Toddlers require the same developmental opportunities, with the level of supervision needed to ensure safe exploration and activity.

Health and safety routines are also regulated by states. An ideal daycare placement practices hygienic measures such as frequent hand washing by staff, accident prevention and child proofing, and providing a safe, protected area for play and physical explorations. Food preparation and general housecleaning must be done by the book. Climbing apparatuses should be child safety approved, and they should be clean and on a soft surface that can provide a good landing spot. Meeting nutritional needs is just as important. Snack times with healthy alternatives and proper hydration through the day are essential.

Regular family communication and interaction are also important. Reports to the parents about the child's behavior and progress are important so that parents are aware of developmental changes (e.g., toilet training status) or problems that might emerge. For example, biting behavior may begin, and the caregivers need to deal with such negative behavior as a team—parents and the daycare staff must work together to stem this behavior.

It is also important that parents feel welcome at the center at all times. A parent who knows she/he can drop in at any time can be fairly sure that all is well. Having the option to come by and see what is happening can be very reassuring, and it is more reassuring to actually stop by periodically. During field trips or other special activities, encouragement of and participation by parents is also a good way to bridge the home-daycare gap.

Finally, a well-trained and prepared daycare staff is equally important for an ideal daycare. Staff stability is another issue. If a daycare has rapid staff turnover, this can be confusing for infants and young children who need the security of knowing and expecting the same faces each day. Expecting a staff of college-trained caregivers at $7 per hour is unrealistic, but the more such staff is educated in developmental and educational practices, the better the child outcome. Many states require ongoing continued education for caregivers. These in-service trainings often cover items such as health and safety, attention levels, and developmental skills training as listed above.

Daycare settings employing high school students or very young staff may offer a mixed situation. In exchange for their youth, enthusiasm, energy, and willingness to learn, you lose experience and stability as these young people often move on to other jobs or are otherwise forced to leave due to competing activities. All things being equal, an older, more experienced and patient staff is better for a child.

Some daycare placements offer profit sharing to valued staffers who remain on the job in a year-to-year, reliable and dependable schedule. If these staffers are responsive and sensitive to children, and experienced, they alone can satisfy the four conditions just reviewed. Of course, the more quality delivered, the higher the expenses—and the weekly fees. In urban settings, good daycare placements can easily run to $200 per child per week—that works out to $10,000 per year.

So what can you do to find the best daycare setting? Many caring and nurturing people work in the daycare industry. They work hard to provide the necessary supervision for the many children whose families require this help. Before placing your child, personally check out the potential setting. Look around for yourself. Are the children and the rooms relatively clean? Are the children interacting and showing positive emotions?

Inspect the kitchen or food preparation area. Check for child proofing of electrical outlets or other potentially hazardous situations. What toys are available? Are they in good shape? Are there enough to go around? What outside activities are provided for? Is there room to run and jump and climb in a safe way, either outdoors or indoors? The educated parent can make up a checklist of criteria to look for.

Ask about the staff training and how long the staff has worked in the daycare. Ask about the most recent training or continuing education received. If you can get as many positive answers to all of these inquiries as possible, your child will be in a better position. If a daycare fails on many of the above points, look around for another place.

Basically, you want to be sure the daycare isn't dangerous or potentially harmful. First and foremost, you want to look for adequate supervision and safety. This is accomplished in part by the staff to children ratio. Other health matters such as proper food preparation can be examined by checking for a posted inspection certificate or through a phone call to the local government health agency responsible for daycare supervision and oversight.

Of equal importance to me is the level of stimulation in the environment. A good outdoor or open indoor space for physical activity and a wide variety of age-appropriate toys are a must. The NICHD study has found that even mediocre daycare was not found to cause harmful effects in most children. The same study reported that the observed attachment problems were more likely the result of mother-child issues than daycare experiences. Steady, stable care in a less than ideal place was better for children than an assortment of different providers that parents had to assemble on a week-to-week basis.

Diane Adams has reported on the mazes that parents must run in order to find proper daycare. She reports the mazes are cost, regulations, and quality. Cost is often a first if not primary consideration for any family. Governmental and private sector approaches to aid working parents have been tried, tinkered with, and teased. The unfortunate truth is that every family must budget an acceptable cost and then go from there. Tax credits and deductions only go so far.

As for regulations, the parent maze is related to amounts of training for workers, child to caregiver ratios and age limit restrictions. Constant tinkering and revisions to these rules have created confusion in many states. For parents, the issue is in learning what the rules are so one can choose a daycare that is functioning legally and safely.

The final maze of quality goes back to earlier comments about stimulation levels, safety, and nutrition. Here a parent must ask many questions, get referrals from friends, monitor their child's responses, and be involved where possible.

The last word on all of these issues has been produced by three big players in the field of child development. The American Academy of Pediatrics, American Public Health Association, and National Resource Center for Health and Safety in Child Care and Early Education have combined resources to produce an online source of information related to providing safe and healthy child care. Their report, which can be downloaded, covers the gamut from child-staff ratios to health and hygiene standards to accommodating special needs children. They even include information on brain development research and practical applications for activities, proper sleep positions for nap times, and nutritional guidance for meals and snacks.

This document is worth the educated parents' time for a careful read in order to see the level of detail and content coverage. It leaves the reader with a healthy respect for what must be planned and provided in order to deliver a safe, quality daycare experience.

THE DEBATE ABOUT DAYCARE

In *The Educated Parent,* I devoted a few pages to criticisms of daycare authored by Karl Zinsmeister. The interested reader can read his provocative comments there or more fully in his original writings. In this edition, I wish to present some of the work of Mary Eberstadt, a research fellow at the Hoover Institution and contributing editor to *Policy Review* who works from her home. In 2004, she wrote *Home-Alone America: The Hidden Toll of Day Care, Behavioral Drugs, and Other Parent Substitutes.* I will present a summary of some of her main points, from a more conservative political perspective. I refer the interested reader to her book for more details. Hers is a philosophical argument that questions whether daycare placements and having too many nonfamily members raising children has led to serious negative consequences. You, as an educated parent, will need to decide what is best for your family situation and children.

To start, Eberstadt makes clear her concern about the cumulative effects on families from deciding to place children in daycare and not stay home to raise their children. Her book outlines more than just daycare issues, but a range of problems she believes are tied to our *separatist* culture, which she defines as a way of life in which parents now live separate lives from their children. Specific examples of this include the fact that there are few parents available for volunteer work in kindergarten and elementary school classrooms, limiting teachers' options; and child behavioral issues having seemingly exploded in the past several decades.

Eberstadt's premise in writing her book, in her words—is this: She hopes parents consider the consequences of "more and more children" spending "considerably less time in the company of their parents or other relatives" while "numerous measures of their well-being have gone into ... decline." She believes that there is a causal connection between this daycare generation of children and teens and the number of problems those children live with. The book cover blurb is even more succinct—"It might be the most taboo question in America: What do today's unprecedented numbers of absent parents *really* mean for children?" I will try to do justice in several paragraphs to summarizing a 200-plus-page argument that is both well-written and well thought out.

There is a cumulative effect on children as a result of being raised away from and apart from daily frequent contact with their parents. Looking at daycare effect studies, Eberstadt argues that many people look to the summary results and are fine with the overall data showing that "most kids turn out fine anyway." She argues that for some, the case "is closed" once you see that most children seemingly have no long-term negative effects from daycare involvement. However, Eberstadt argues that the daily immediate effects of daycare—like being sick or missing your parent—lead to a lot of unhappiness. She argues that children and their personal stories are lost in the larger social conversation where daycare is advocated for "personal and social goals." These would be goals related to allowing women to feel good about contributing at work or following a career and raising a child who is successful.

Eberstadt then covers specific "unhappiness" issues where it seems that a parent's freedom (to work or do whatever) outweighs the needs or good of the children:

- *Illness rates.* The rates for childhood illness are higher for young children in daycare, especially painful and annoying ailments like ear infections and respiratory infections. More sick children are in daycare than should be because parents feel they cannot miss work. Some parents resort to dosing children with Tylenol so they are dropped off without a daycare-attendance-barring fever. These children later have their fevers return or spike during the day. To make it all worse, Eberstadt decries the response of daycare advocates that getting sick is good for young children so that they will be less sick when they are in school later. She asks how many parents would expose their children to repeated sickness on purpose, no matter the later "benefits."

- *Aggression.* Many early studies on daycare effects, including the large data samples from the National Institute of Child and Human Development (NICHD), showed that children became more aggressive and developed social-behavioral problems. Again, Eberstadt denounces the advocates who then say that these behaviors are actually good; these children are showing "independence" or are "cheeky" as a result of daycare exposure.

- *"Furious" children.* Eberstadt argues that there is an epidemic of teen violence related to "home alone" children. These children are in hours of daycare followed by being after-school latchkey children and/or raised in single-parent homes with lesser amounts of adult interaction and contact. She likens such children to being feral, raising themselves. She believes that links exist between these children and problem behaviors such as suicide rates, increased school violence, increased delinquency and crime, and poorer school performance.

- *Obesity rates.* Eberstadt sees the higher rates of childhood obesity as also related to lack of adult time. She states that America has many fit parents and fat children. Childhood and teen obesity rates are linked to many problems and specifically later serious adult health issues. Why are children fat? As a group fewer are breastfed, they spend too many hours babysat by TV and TV-related activities, and they are often indoors instead of out playing and running. To top it all off, children are also given treats as a way for parents to ease the guilt caused by their absence.

- *Diagnosed mental illness rates.* One in five children meets the criteria for a diagnosable mental, emotional, or behavioral disorder, cites Eberstadt. She can further point to rates of childhood anxiety and depression, as well as ADHD and more serious early childhood disorders such as autism spectrum disorders and other pervasive developmental disorders. These are then countered by a generation prescribed large quantities of medications. There are side effect and abuse issues that go along with these developments.

- *Miscellaneous culture-related issues.* These would include the effects on developing children and teens exposed to music and music videos with questionable content, the glorification of many celebrity bad boys and girls, and a range of bad behaviors brought into the house via TV.

The problem is made worse without adult monitoring and chances to discuss these behaviors and. This is compounded further by other data Eberstadt cites regarding teen sexual behaviors and attitudes, STIs, and pregnancy rates. Finally, a number of teenaged children are now sent to boarding schools. This is another example of separation of children from family.

So what can/should an educated parent do with this kind of information? Knowing the arguments both for and against daycare, and how you spend your adult time, gives you the information to make the best decision for your children. As I have mentioned previously, the question of daycare placement is often not an option; it is more about where and for how long than whether. But does it have to be this way? And when daycare placement is not a choice but a need, how can we minimize any negative effects or unwanted outcomes and maximize positive results from the daycare experience?

ATTACHMENT SUPPORTS AT HOME

What can you do as a parent to promote healthy attachment so that any potential negative daycare effects will be minimized? Recall the work of Marianne DeWolff and Mariuns van Ijzendoorn reported in chapter 3 in the attachment section. To review, they found six key parenting variables associated with optimal attachment bonds. They are:

Sensitivity—the prompt response of the parent to the child's signals/needs;

Positive attitude—expressions of positive emotion and affection toward the child;

Synchrony—the structuring of reciprocal interactions with the child, matching parental behavior to the child's mood and activity level;

Mutuality—the coordination of mother and infant to the same activity or event;

Support—watching for the child's signals to provide emotional support for the child's activities and behavior; and

Stimulation—the active direction of behaviors and stimuli to the infant.

Let's revisit these with some added information on what you can do to make these criteria a reality for your child. Sensitivity is the same as responsivity in this context. Making and taking the time to become aware of your infant's and child's needs is a start. Is she/he a hearty breakfast eater or are mid-morning snacks best after a light first meal? Can you tell when a good mood is going south due to your child being overstimulated or tired out? If you cannot do this at first, you will soon learn with more interaction time.

Talking to your child and nurturant touching (hugs and kisses and back rubs) are additional important concrete signs of your love and affection. Children need to be praised and acknowledged, sometimes for something special they have tried or accomplished, sometimes for just being there. Your positive attention and interactions will bring positive responses in return and increase your emotional bondedness. This can solidify a secure attachment.

Matching your parental behavior to your child's mood and activity level are also important in establishing attached behavior patterns. Is your child more active when first awakened or after awhile? When is the best time for physical play or a visit to a park? When is the best time for a quiet activity like reading a book or singing together? Try to figure out your child's daily rhythms when you spend time with him/her. See if you can get a report about activity level from the daycare provider for the times you are not together. Most children get into somewhat predictable cycles of activity levels, moods, hungry times, and quiet times. Try to match your interactions with your child's cycles.

Coordination of mother and infant to the same activity or event is also important for your infant's well-being and connectedness to you. Playing a sing-song game like patty cake or the itsy bitsy spider song are reassuring to your child, who now has your total interest and attention. You can also eat a meal together, alternately taking bites or drinking a beverage.

Providing emotional support for your child's activities and behavior is similar to some of the above behaviors. Watching your child's efforts will lead you to know when to step in and help with a frustrating situation and when to stand back and allow your child to learn to persevere and overcome problems. And praising success or a good effort are parental behaviors which go well beyond infancy and attachment establishment.

Proper stimulation helps your child grow into the next level of developmental ability. Making sure your child has age-appropriate toys and activities keeps him/her interested. A child's natural curiosity and desire to explore will be aided with the right supply of materials and opportunities for activities that match your child's internal drives to learn about the world. You don't have to spend thousands of dollars to provide the right materials. Many parenting websites and magazines have more detailed explicit information about proper stimulation. Equally important is the need to not overstimulate your child. Such a child is actually quite stressed out and overwhelmed since she/he cannot sort out everything that she/he is experiencing. The end result can be that a child will shut down and avoid you.

HEALTH ISSUES

In a February 2002 study, the health aspect of daycare attendance was taken up. The Archives of Pediatrics & Adolescent Medicine reported that two-year-old children in daycare have twice as many colds as 2-year-old stay-at-home children. But looking long-term, when these children were in elementary school (ages 6–11), the daycare children had ⅓ fewer colds than their stay-at-home counterparts. By adolescence, the difference disappeared. The research group concluded that the daycare exposure to germs was actually good in the long run by helping to develop immune system responses. So having more colds and coughs early on made for better defenses by the grade school years.

Sylvana Côté and a group of researchers out of Canada provided an update in 2010. This study reviewed health outcomes of more than 1,200 children, comparing those raised at home to groups at small or large group child care facilities. They looked at children with early (defined as prior to 2½ years old) or later placements (3½ to 4½ years of age). They measured mothers' reports of children's respiratory tract, ear, and gastrointestinal tract infections during the early preschool, late preschool, and early elementary school (5–8 years old) periods. Compared with children cared for at home, those who started large group daycare facilities in the early preschool period had higher rates of respiratory tract infections and ear infections while there, but lower rates of respiratory tract infections and ear infections during their elementary school time.

Writing about these results, health.com writer Denise Mann interviewed the lead author. "Children have infections at the time they initiate large-group activities, whether they do it earlier or later," said Dr. Côté, who further argued that "earlier is better to have infections because then kids do not miss school at a crucial time—when learning to read and write."

Of note, group child care did not affect risk for stomach bugs one way or another during the study period, and the researchers "found a protection against later infections only when they looked at kids who went to the larger child-care centers, not those cared for in small facilities, such as those in a home setting with three to eight kids."

Children raised at home, but who went into a larger daycare setting after age 2½ had more colds and ear infections, but they also had just as many infections as kids cared for at home when they started elementary school. How does this work? The larger daycare facilities may allow exposure to many different viruses, boosting their immune systems to fight these same infections later on.

Mann also reported such exposure can allow toddlers to build up their immunity early. "Those who attended large day-care centers after age 2½ did not receive the same protection against illness during their elementary school years as their counterparts who started group day care at younger ages," she wrote. Mann also quoted a pediatrician who argued that "the enhanced ability to fight off infections can be added to the list of benefits of group day care."

A BRIEF REVIEW OF RESEARCH ON DAYCARE EFFECTS

Much has been written in child development research on the topic of the effects of daycare participation by children. I will present three recent studies as examples of what is done as well as the types of findings that have been obtained. A deeper look at this research can be found in *The Educated Parent*.

In 2010, Rachel Lucas-Thompson, Wendy Goldberg, and Jo Ann Prause published results from a meta-analysis of 69 studies, looking specifically for effects of maternal employment on a child's achievement levels and behavior problems. These are two areas which have raised red flags in a number of early studies on daycare effects. They looked at studies published between 1960 and 2010, making this a fairly comprehensive analysis.

Their overarching conclusion was that, overall, children whose mothers return to work early in their lives (before age three years) are no more likely to have significant academic or behavioral problems than those raised by stay-at-home mothers. The key word is *significant,* as some small effects were noted when the researchers looked into subgroups of subjects.

So-called sample-level moderator analyses found early maternal employment was most beneficial when families were challenged by single parenthood or welfare status. Maternal employment when children were between two and four years old was associated with higher achievement. This might be due to the fact that employment lifted some of the mothers' stressors associated with poverty when they had more available money. Further, one could argue that in single-parent families, an employed mother might be a better role model for her children, resulting in benefits that might outweigh potential negative outcomes from being separated.

Negative effects were also found. Maternal employment for middle-class and two-parent families and for very early employment (during the child's first year) was associated with slightly worse performance on formal tests of achievement and showed a slight increase in behavior problems. So it may also be the case that in families where there is no pressing economic need for the mother to work, the extra income might not outweigh the advantages of a full-time mother.

Finally, Lucas-Thomas's group believes that the small effect size and mostly statistically "non-significant results for main effects of early maternal employment should allay concerns about mothers working when children are young." Regarding the negative findings, the group calls for more generous maternal leave policies as a possible solution.

Henry Tran and Marsha Weinraub, using data from the NICHD Study of Early Child Care, examined the effects of several variables during the first 15 months of life. These included: quality, stability, and multiplicity on infants' attachment security, cognitive development, language comprehension, and language production. Seven questions were addressed in their study. I present them with their "answers."

1. How frequent are arrangement changes over the first 15 months, and what types of arrangement changes are these? Most infants experience "relatively stable care" between 6–15 months with 61 percent of babies in the same arrangement at all four data points of the study. Of these, 32 percent of families were using family daycare.

2. How frequent is the use of multiple arrangements at any time during the first 15 months, and what types of multiple arrangements are used? Thirty-nine percent of those infants in nonmaternal care had at least one arrangement change. Most common was a switch from one placement to another similar type. Forty-six percent of infants were provided for in multiple, simultaneous placements for at least one month.

3. Do quality, stability, and multiplicity predict attachment security, cognitive development, language comprehension, and language production at 15 months? For one, quality of care was "significantly related to cognitive and language performance." The relationship between stability and outcomes was described as "complicated." Without including too much detail to lose the reader, they concluded that "unstable care may hinder positive growth" in cognitive and language development.

4. Do different types of arrangement changes or multiple child care differentially affect children's development? The study found that more use of multiple caregivers (fathers and grandparents) was "significantly related to higher language performance." When there was a mix of providers there was a poorer outcome. The final conclusion was that there was a benefit if multiple arrangements were of high quality, and the outcome was poorer if these different arrangements were of low or moderate quality.

5. In line with the protective factors model, does high-quality or increasing quality of care protect against the risks of unstable care and multiple arrangement usage? In short, the research suggests this is the case—higher quality care in general outweighs the multiplicity of child care arrangements.

6. Does the combination of low quality, decreasing, or constant quality of care and unstable care or multiple arrangement usage function to increase the risk of poorer child outcomes? It was reported that there was a "consistent pattern related to greater use of multiple arrangements and low quality care." Further, infants with the poorest care and most placements had the worst language outcomes. Moderate care quality and multiple arrangements also led to poor levels of performance on language measures.

7. Building on a previous NICHD data that examined patterns of interactions involving maternal sensitivity in predicting attachment security, does low maternal sensitivity in combination with low child care quality, unstable child care, or multiple child care increase the risk of insecure infant-mother attachment security? The research indicated that there was no adverse effect of child care on attachment quality. Rather, the quality of the mother-child attachment security is related to the mother's responsivity and caregiving patterns.

Deborah Lowe Vandell, Jay Belsky, Margaret Burchinal, Laurence Steinberg, and Nathan Vandergrift reported on the latest long-term findings from the NICHD Early Childhood Study. (This study has followed over 1,000 children randomly selected on their day of birth from ten U.S. hospitals in Arkansas, California, Kansas, Massachusetts, North Carolina, Pennsylvania, Virginia, Washington, and Wisconsin.) Research teams have checked in periodically with the families over time, measuring both their family situation variables and the child care provided. When the kids entered school, the teams tracked their progress, got teacher reports on their social behavior, and continued to monitor the quality of their parenting (in addition to whether the kids were in afterschool care programs).

Of interest for this discussion are issues related to the quality of daycare received and the way parenting quality was taken into account. One clear result so far: both high-quality child care centers and good parenting skills are associated with better results for kids. What seems to be needed now are policy changes to support ways to make both of those things even better.

Child behavior and academic problems among children who received low-quality care in their first 4½ years of life stayed steady through their 15th birthday. This trend suggests the potential for lifelong difficulties. The differences between teens who received low- and high-quality care when they were very young were relatively small. How could such small differences last over time?

Child development experts say the findings show the serious need for governments at all levels, and others, to improve access to better quality child care. Child care was measured by collecting data on whether child care was done by parents, other relatives, nannies, babysitters, or daycare centers in or outside a home. They also measured the number of hours of which kind of care each child received.

Research team members believed that the negative effects of lower quality care would disappear as the influence of other factors negated the early childhood experiences. The current data show that teenagers who had received higher quality child care earlier were better off. They were less likely to display problem externalizing behaviors (arguing, being mean, and fighting). Those who spent more hours in any type of child care were more likely to engage in impulsive and risky behaviors. At the same time, those who received moderately high- or high-quality care scored higher on tests gauging cognitive and academic achievement.

To measure parenting, every two years, age-appropriate tasks were assigned to the mother-child pairs. These included parent-child interaction samples such as working on Etch-a-Sketch mazes, trip planning, and making a bungee-jump device for an egg. These activities were videotaped and coded by trained observers for effective parenting skills.

Did time spent in daycare affect school performance? We can talk about the correlations only, because causal links were not assessed. So what was correlated? There was a small, but significant finding between quality of care received in a child care center and vocabulary scores, and this correlation remained significant through the fifth grade.

There was also a significant correlation between number of hours spent in child care and externalizing behaviors such as misbehaving in school or hitting others, but this decreases with age. Externalizing was significantly correlated with the amount of child care provided by daycare centers, and this correlation continued through to the sixth grade.

Independent of daycare time or type, the factor that most strongly predicted both academic success and good social skills throughout the study period was the quality of parenting. If the mother-child interactions (in those assignments described earlier) revealed good parenting skills, then the child was more likely to have good reading, math, and vocabulary scores and have healthier social skills.

Even this finding was correlational. So it could be that parents get along and work better with kids who score higher on academic and social skills measures.

For this book, we would want to assume the correlations of the NICHD study really reflect causation, which they in fact might. If so, here are the results to date from the longest running, best designed and measured study on daycare effects—better parenting makes for better kids, and daycare involvement makes for marginally smarter, but also somewhat less well-behaved kids. And the quality of daycare matters and can have long-lasting effects.

How do such data inform our decision about whether or not to put kids in daycare? Not much for the individual case. So many other variables come into play for any individual child in a family. Read on.

SOME CONCLUSIONS

So what can be concluded by reviewing the above? The educated parent should feel free to further explore the reference material and to sort through the limited data I have presented. Again, within the framework of your family values and needs and your abilities as a parent, you can make an informed decision on what is best.

In teaching my child psychology class, I always required my students to read popular commentary as well as the more pure psychology research related to daycare issues. I have at times set up a pro- and anti-debate for class discussion. I then had as an exam question the following: "A mother asks your opinion about placing her young child in daycare. What would you tell her? Reply, citing the research, and give her a decision one way or the other." In the real world, they and I cannot tell you what to do. Instead, I offer the following from my perspective to help you make your decisions.

Issues to Consider Before Placing Your Child In Daycare

What you do at home with your child, for whatever amount of time you have, can affect whether or not daycare will help or hurt your child. If you make time to have quality interactions that promote secure attachment behavior, your child will be better off. This secure attachment foundation will allow your child to function better in daycare if needed. As long as the daycare is at least of good quality, few negative effects should emerge.

If your parent-child interactions at home are few and of an under-sensitive or nonresponsive quality, your child will likely form an insecure attachment with you. This can be made into a more negative outcome if the child is then placed in a poorer quality daycare setting. At the least, an insecurely attached child will have a more difficult time in daycare than a securely attached one. However, it is also possible that an insecurely attached child can benefit from a "corrective" attachment experience in a high-quality daycare setting.

Your attitude toward the daycare placement/work outside the home issue will affect the outcome of the daycare versus no daycare place-ment decision. Parents who stay at home but are resentful of their loss of employment do no favors for their children. Similarly, a situation with a miserable, conflicted parent who hates to go to work and feels perpetu-ally guilty every time the child is dropped off will not lead to a positive outcome for the child. Full agreement by both parents who then support each other and the child makes for the best decision, whether it is staying at home or placement in a daycare.

Quality of daycare is a very important criterion. The better the quality of daycare, the more positive effects demonstrated by the child. Social competency and other healthy child outcomes are clearly associated with daycare staffers who are well-trained and who are in smaller caregiver to child ratios. Quality daycare experiences can, for some, enhance a child's development in the physical, cognitive, and emotional spheres.

The amount of time spent in a daycare placement has been shown to negatively correlate with maternal sensitivity toward the child and the child's level of affection toward his/her mother. Working mothers have more insecure attachment relationships with their children, but this can be due to non-daycare caused reasons. If your child is in daycare because you don't want to be with him/her, a negative outcome is more likely. But this will not be due to the daycare exposure.

Parents who are unsure of their parenting or otherwise feel unsupported are more likely to have children with problems. Getting some parenting training or other sources of support should be a priority. When a mother and father are agreed in their reasons and decisions in where children will be raised, the children will be better off.

The decision to have children in daycare should be reviewed annually. Do the family benefits of a two-career/two-income situation with daycare help outweigh some of the needs your children have? It may be that one parent can alter a schedule so that daycare time can be minimized. It may also be the decision that financial sacrifices while the children are under five are worth the trade for at-home care with a parent who wants that experience. Only you as parents can decide.

Afterword: Some Conclusions and Final Thoughts on Parenting Today

Live so that when your children think of fairness and integrity, they think of you.

~H. Jackson Brown

Your children will become what you are; so be what you want them to be.

~David Bly

A baby will make love stronger, days shorter, nights longer, bankroll smaller, home happier, clothes shabbier, the past forgotten, and the future worth living for.

~Anonymous

Writing this book has proved to be a most enjoyable, personally rewarding, and thought-provoking task. Initial research had begun in 2008, but the project was delayed and not restarted until late 2010. Over those years, I had numerous thoughts about what I might include or not include in this edition.

I decided early on that I wanted this edition to be more Internet-based, both in where I found some of the content, as well as in being sure to include follow-up resources and the initial sources. In this way, the educated parent can follow up and read directly about what has been presented.

Along the way, I also began to observe parents more closely and paid extra attention to news articles and media reports related to parenting. What I have found is equal parts encouraging and discouraging.

In my observations, I have seen many families working hard to do the right thing for their children. Some of their hardship is due to families living in isolation from extended family social supports. This has been made more difficult by the economic stresses and the financial fiasco brought on by a group of greedy people who impacted all of us. Parents are making the best of a bad situation.

I am also encouraged by the amount of time and content devoted to parenting education and information online. There are easily more than 250 websites and blogs with quality information for parents. These include online support groups for moms. The web pages I have looked at usually had some legitimate expert as a writer or reviewer/approver of the information before it was posted.

I have also seen some things that worry me and have me concerned about the future of families and children. Little things like seeing so many young children ignored by parents glued to their cell phones or texting away are more common. I worry about how those children will get their attention needs met.

I wonder where the celebrity culture obsession will lead us. What have the Gosselins and TLC wrought? Stories appear to emerge monthly. The spring 2011 hoax/story of the California woman who allegedly gave Botox treatments to her eight-year-old beauty pageant contestant was both believable and repulsive in the shadows of *Toddlers and Tiaras* on cable TV. This followed the 2009 story of the so-called balloon boy, whose family was trying to get a reality TV show by creating a false story of child endangerment and then lying.

Then came the Canadian couple who decided to raise their baby in a gender-free environment by not telling anyone whether the child is male or female. An intriguing idea, this looks more to me like another forbidden experiment. Certainly developmental researchers would love to test and retest this child, assuming the parents can pull off their plan. ("Forbidden experiment" is the name given to the story of a grossly abused girl called "Genie." She was raised in neglect and abuse, without proper language stimulation. When she was discovered, researchers tried to then use her situation to test competing hypotheses about language development. Look it up—you will be fascinated.)

How will the children from these families be affected and impacted by what their parents have chosen to do? A strong case can be made in each example that the parents have not acted in the best interest of the children involved. And what was their motivation? Fifteen minutes of fame? A YouTube video moment? Or were these just shots at exploiting a child for money?

In my concluding remarks, I will present my opinions about trends or movements I have either read about, seen, or believe to be unfolding. Some are research-based, others are anecdotal. I made a list and rated items positive or negative. I will begin with the negative trends only so that I can end this book with the positive ones. These are presented in an order of importance to me, meaning that those listed first are believed to have a greater impact on children. I am sure that not everyone will agree with the order I have chosen, and perhaps that will lead to a teachable moment for readers who can discuss the issues further.

I now present my list of negative trends in child rearing. Allow me a few more caveats. Some of these issues only affect a minority of families; others are more widespread. But the impact, regardless of the quantity, is what concerns me. The negative list will seem longer, but only because we have previously reviewed so many of the positive parent behaviors to this point.

I begin with the issue of the amount of quality time that parents spend with their children. Mary Eberstadt (chapter 9) writes in her book, *Home Alone America,* about the "separatist culture" in which many children are raised. By this, she refers to the large numbers of children who spend few waking hours with their parents in any given week. For teens, the problem is even worse as they are busied by school, work, and peer needs. Who then provides guidance and value formation? The culture and media?

These children are raised separated from the types and amounts of family contacts that used to be taken for granted. Those contacts—family dinners, monthly get-togethers, family holiday celebrations—transmitted family identities and values. Some of this has been made worse by the transient residential nature of American families who seem to all live many zip codes away from potentially supportive relatives like grandparents and aunts and uncles.

Given the nature of our culture and economy, this may be a problem without a solution.

This issue of lack of contact time between parents and children leads to another problem of great impact on children and teens—too little supervision, involvement, and engagement. This is another time-based issue. It seems that children and teens have more unmonitored time than is good for them. I am not calling for 24-hour surveillance or camera systems or attached/imbedded GPS monitor systems in children. What I am asking is this—do today's parents know where their children are, who they are with, and what they are doing? Too often the answer is no.

Part of the obligation of good parenting is control and guidance. This is an obligation that continues until adulthood—and sometimes beyond if your child requests it. As your child/teen grows up, their natural tendencies toward autonomy and independence will cause them to spend less time with you. That is normal and appropriate. The problem comes in when this freedom is unaccompanied by accountability.

Teens already too often live secret lives, as a 2009 *Chicago Magazine* story pointed out. A survey of nearly 300 teens revealed what 13–18-year-olds think about, how they spend their time, and what they do all day long. Among the most interesting data are those which compare what parents think and what their teens are saying is really going on. I will leave you with this quote from the online article:

> "We know the peak time of day for kids to experiment with sex and drugs is the hours between the end of school and when parents come home from work. That is a robust and replicated finding," says Laurence Steinberg, a Temple University psychologist. "And the place where kids are most likely to have their first experiments with sex and alcohol and drugs is within their own home."

You may argue that this is not a new problem. You are right, but it is a worsening one. And with social media and technology, a more out-of-control one. The need is for parents to stay engaged in their child/teen's life. How to do this varies, but it involves conversations and time spent together.

Another negative trend I see is not necessarily parent-controlled. It is what I call the "pathologizing" of children and teens. As covered in chapter 7, the numbers of medically diagnosed youth (whether it be ADHD, ASD, or bipolar disorder) are rising faster than makes sense. It seems that every child on any given block has a diagnosed problem. Having problems is not the issue; we all will and do as we grow. Having outside parties get involved—often with medications—is alarming.

Not to sound too old, but when I grew up, my friends and I overcame our challenges with the support of our friends and families. I am not downplaying the fact that some of my friends probably had true, undiagnosed problems that should have been identified and remediated. But in the absence of such professional involvement they grew up and seemingly adjusted in their lives.

The related issue here is the debate about diagnoses versus disorders. Having a disorder means that you have a problem that can be remedied (or "reordered") with your involvement and effort. Having a diagnosed disease means that the problem has you, and you are at the mercy of others to help you. It seems that too many families have surrendered their authority and responsibility to well-meaning professionals who send the wrong message.

I know I will be called out by some for these remarks but I stand by them. Parents and their children have to take back their role in helping themselves, not yield their lives to people with more education. Again I am not calling for ignoring problems or denying serious conditions; I am saying that those affected must be part of their own recovery process.

The next trend I address is one I call "entitlement disorder." This phrase has been used by many others; I have been using it since my wife and I first discovered the issue in the 1990s. An *entitlement disorder* refers to a child raised feeling they are entitled to almost anything they want just because they are breathing. The notion that one has to work to earn rewards or benefits has not been learned (or taught apparently).

The broken link between work and reward and the overemphasis on having it all are leading to a generation that has lost the importance of responsibility in their lives. Many families no longer require children to do chores. Google "data on kids and chores at home" and you will find that this is a problem big enough to lead to many websites with answers. The good news is that the chores-responsibility association is understood and the issues—what chores are doable at what age, how to compensate for work, and how to avoid arguing—are all seemingly resolvable if families will tackle the issue.

The problem as I see it is not just the materialistic consequence of children getting too much with no attached connection to earning rewards, but the attitude it inspires. This attitude spills over to school relationships and teacher-student relationships as well as to other adult-child interactions. And the problem seems enabled by the parenting received.

Before I am accused again of sounding like an old guy, allow me to borrow a famous quote: "The children now love luxury. They have bad manners, contempt for authority, they show disrespect to their elders. . . . They no longer rise when elders enter the room. They contradict their parents, chatter before company, gobble up dainties at the table, cross their legs, and are tyrants over their teachers."

This of course is the remark credited to either Plato or Socrates—either way it is about 24 centuries old. I am not saying that this current generation is the first to be disrespectful or less understanding of responsible behavior. I am saying that I am concerned about the ways the issue has manifested itself into the current entitlement-type demeanor of some. And this is a lost opportunity for the children—they are robbed of learning the sense of achievement and accomplishment that follows from earning something by your own work.

I move next to the importance of discipline and follow through. As we discussed in chapter 4 and elsewhere, tired and overextended parents have to find a way to energize themselves in order to stay consistent with rules and consequences. The outcome of not doing this control/guidance obligation is a nonfocused, nonself-controlled, directionless life for the child. I shall say no more here, but I have observed that parents need continuous support and encouragement for their work in this area.

For these parents, there is a true need to stress- and time-manage their lives. Not doing so leads to bad parenting choices, overlooking problem behaviors so as to not get into a battle or expend more energy arguing/fighting with their child. On a related note is the consequence at the marital system level. When parents are too tired to parent, they are too tired to be a good couple. As covered in chapter 4, a strong healthy couple's relationship sets the foundation for a home environment for healthy, adjusted children.

My final concerns about negative parent trends are the helicopter parent issue and premature structuring. Helicopter parents, as covered earlier, take away their child's chances to grow up and learn how to solve life problems. What they do is called "infantilizing" behavior—keeping a child in a dependent and overprotected state as if they were still helpless infants needing every safeguard and intervention an adult can muster. There was a great *Time* magazine article in November 2009 by Nancy Gibbs on this topic. (It is available online for your review.) What she wrote was delightful and beyond improvement by me; I encourage your reading it.

Premature structuring is about pushing kids into a focused activity too early in their development. It's what happens when you make a child take tennis lessons or gymnastics training because you have an Olympics gold medal waiting to be won in 10 years. I wrote about this in *The Educated Parent* in 2004. I recounted the story of a great teen women's tennis player who walked away from the game in her 20s after a small injury and nearly 15 years of daily playing and training. She was burned out in her prime. A related issue we now face is the rush to perfection and excellence brought on by parents who forget that an essential part of childhood is down time and spontaneity and unscheduled life. Too often we hear of children and teens pushed by parents who demand adult-level expertise from still developing young people.

We see it also in dubious efforts like baby reading plans or "Baby Einstein" programs or prenatal classical music interventions (the "Mozart effect"—look it up). There is a fine line between early literacy and brain development efforts and teaching sight reading to 18-month-olds. There is also a certain gullibility in parents who are shamed/coerced into believing that their two-year-old child's brain development requires hundreds of dollars of special media inputs.

This is why we need educated parents. Know the research base and basic child development information and you will know that everyday stimulation through normal interactions will get the same results. (Recall some of the chapter 5 research.)

And now on to the positive trends I have observed—the reasons I have hope for the future. I begin with parent education and outlets which dispense parenting information. Whether it is the many quality online sites, books like this, parenting magazines and TV shows, or local community-based programs, more parent training and child rearing help is available than ever. Some are sponsored by college-based extension service providers, others by YMCAs or community mental health agencies.

There is a movement called parent coaching. It goes by that name as a proprietary title, but other similar programs are called names like sound parent and other like titles. No matter the name, these are excellent parent training and education programs that deliver on the many recommendations and best practices we have reviewed in the preceding nine chapters. (As a disclaimer, I have not been trained or seen directly all their materials. However, as I understand these systems, they work with parents to match your values and strengths to techniques and systems that make sense for your family.)

As I stated in the first edition and in this book, one can never know enough about the challenges of parenting and the mysteries of raising a healthy, adjusted child. That so many people know and recognize this is encouraging to me. Having said that, there is still much work to be done and many underserved and needy parents not yet connected to these types of services. It is my hope that more families be made aware of these types of programs and better themselves as parents through whatever means works for them.

The next positive trend I wish to highlight is the continued movement and cultural shift toward more paternal involvement and engagement in child development. Covered in chapter 8, we all know the benefits of father involvement and the downsides related to father absence. I shall not restate the information here, other than to note that it will be important for more men to be made aware of this evidence.

Hopefully trends in the media though positive movie and TV portrayals, support from women and mothers, and most important, role modeling by today's generation of fathers will continue this movement. More specific training and education geared toward men might be a further development and next step to make this more widespread. Internet sources and those programs sponsored by the federal government will help, as will private initiatives like the National Center for Fathering (www.fathers.com) and All Pro Dads (www.allprodad.com).

The next positive trend in parenting that I see as important and meaningful is the desire of parents to provide enriching experiences and opportunities for their children. Again, this is not a new thing, but is being played out with more accessibility than ever. Parents must surely walk a fine line between enrichment and overscheduling and premature structuring, but that can be done if you know your child and pay attention to how they respond to activities.

The idea of providing the tools and chances for success and optimal development are obvious in their importance and need. I see family after family working toward this goal. This is a trend that also needs support and encouragement from others in the wider community. Affordable, accessible community programs for youth, that also allow parental involvement and engagement, are investments worth making.

Finally, the move toward wellness, and values/spirituality development in families is a welcome trend. As covered in chapter 2, the many benefits in providing children with a healthy foundation grounded in good habits and character bode well for a future society that will need such leaders and members.

Out of the turmoil and chaos that many sectors of American society now endure, the trend toward strengthened families seems to me to be a way toward raising children who will have the skills to find solutions. Better parenting from stronger families will lead to a new generation of citizens who will be prepared to make the hard choices and sacrifices that the future will require.

It is my hope that this book will help parents and families (and their children) in this regard.

Chapter References, Sources, and Resources

(Unless otherwise noted, all websites were active and accessible as of August 5, 2011.)

INTRODUCTION

Chua, A (2011) *Battle hymn of the tiger mother.* New York: Penguin Press HC.

Hulbert, A (2003) *Raising America: Experts, parents, and a century of advice about children.* New York: Knopf.

Murkoff, H (2000) "The real parenting expert is . . . you." *Newsweek,* 136, (17A), 21.

Rizzuto, RR (2011) "Why I left my children." Accessed online at: http://www.salon.com/life/feature/2011/02/28/leaving_my_children.

Sclafani, JD (2004) *The educated parent: Recent trends in raising children.* Westport, CT: Praeger.

CHAPTER 1

Ambert, A-M (2001) *The effect of children on parents* (2nd ed.). Binghamton, NY: The Haworth Press.

Davies, PT, Harold, GT, Goeke-Morey, MC and Cummings, EM (2002) "Child emotional security and interparental conflict." *Monographs of the Society for Research in Child Development.* New York: Wiley-Blackwell.

DeNoon, DJ (2011) "As kids' CT scans rise, so do radiation worries." Accessed online at: http://children.webmd.com/news/20110406/as-kids-ct-scans-rise-so-do-radiation-worries.

Donald Woods Winnicott biography (2011) Accessed online at: http://www. answers.com/topic/donald-winnicott#ixzz1JJtsLOmc.

Ebster, C, Wagner, U and Neumueller, D (2009) "Children's influences on in-store purchases." *Journal of Retailing and Consumer Services,* 16, 145–154.

Kids Count Data Center (2011) "Children in single-parent families (Number)— 2009." Accessed online at: http://datacenter.kidscount.org/data/acrossstates/ Rankings.aspx?loct=2&by=a&order=a&ind=106&dtm=429&tf=38.

Knafo, A and Galansky, N (2008) "The influence of children on their parents' values." *Social and Personality Psychology Compass,* 2: 1143–1161. doi: 10.1111/j.1751–9004.2008.00097.x.

Moorhead, J (2001) "Judgment days." Accessed online at: www.guardian.co.uk/ society/2001/jan/24/socialcare.familyandrelationships.

Sclafani, JD (2004) *The educated parent: Recent trends in raising children.* Westport, CT: Praeger.

Smyth, BM (2005) "Time to rethink *time?* The experience of time with children after divorce." *Family Matters,* 71, 4–10.

Strohschein, L (2007) "Challenging the presumption of diminished capacity to parent: Does divorce really change parenting practices?" *Family Relations,* 56, 358–368.

Additional Internet Resources

"Developmental norms for speech and language." Accessed online at: http://www. asha.org/slp/schools/prof-consult/norms.htm.

"General information on physical development and developmental norms." Accessed online at: http://www.parents.com/toddlers-preschoolers/development/ physical/.

CHAPTER 2

Belkin, L (2010) "Unhappy helicopter parents." Accessed online at: http://parenting. blogs.nytimes.com/2010/07/07/unhappy-helicopter-parents.

Bennetts, L (2007) *The feminine mistake: Are we giving up too much?* New York: Hyperion.

Bennetts, L (2007) "The feminine mistake." Accessed online at: http://www.huff ingtonpost.com/leslie-bennetts/the-feminine-mistake_b_44690.html.

Bernstein, BE (2011) "Separation anxiety and school refusal." Accessed online at: http://emedicine.medscape.com/article/916737-overview.

Borgman, D (2006) "Bridging the gap: From social science to congregations, researchers to practitioners." In E Roehlkepartain, P King, L Wagener and P Benson (Eds.), *The handbook of spiritual development in childhood and adolescence.* Thousand Oaks, CA: Sage.

Campos, T (2009) "Spirituality for children: How to talk to kids about spiritual values and religious tolerance." Accessed online at: http://www.suite101. com/content/spirituality-for-children-a174159#ixzz1MFIO3cgI.

Chickering, AW, Dalton, JC and Stamm, L (2006) *Encouraging authenticity and spirituality in higher education.* San Francisco: Jossey-Bass.

Chua, A (2011) *Battle hymn of the tiger mother.* New York: Penguin Press HC.

Coker, TR, Elliott, MN, Wallander, JL, Cuccaro, P, Grunbaum, J, Corona, R, Saunders, AE and Schuster, MA (2011) "Association of family stressful life-change events and health-related quality of life in fifth-grade children." Archives of *Pediatric and Adolescent Medicine,* 165(4), 354–359.

Coles, R (1998) *The moral intelligence of children: How to raise a moral child.* New York: Plume.

Doe, M (2004) *Nurturing your teenager's soul: A practical approach to raising a kind, honorable, compassionate teen.* New York: Perigee.

Doe, M and Walsh, M (1998) *10 principles of spiritual parenting: Nurturing your child's soul.* New York: Harper Paperbacks.

Faludi, S (2010) *"The feminine mistake* book review quotation." Accessed online at: www.everywomansvoice.com/?q=node/20.

Feldmeyer, D and Roehkepartain, EC (1995) *Parenting with a Purpose: A positive approach to raising confident, caring youth.* Minneapolis: Search Institute.

Fisak, B, Richard, D and Mann, A (2011) "The prevention of child and adolescent anxiety: A meta-analytic review." *Society for Prevention Research,* 12(3), 255–268.

Fisak, B and Grills-Taqueshel, AE (2007) "Parental modeling, reinforcement, and information transfer: Risk factors in the development of child anxiety?" *Clinical Child and Family Psychology Review,* 10/2007; 10(3):213–31. doi: 10.1007/s10567-007-0020-x.

Fowler, JW (1981). *Stages of faith: The psychology of human development and the quest for meaning.* San Francisco: Harper & Row

Friedman, C and Yorio, K (2009) *Happy at work, happy at home: The girl's guide to being a working mom.* New York: Broadway Books.

Greenberg, CL and Avigdor, BS (2009) *What happy working mothers know: How new findings in positive psychology can lead to a healthy and happy work/ life balance.* Hoboken, NJ: Wiley & Sons.

Jackson HealthCare (2009) "Physician study: Quantifying the cost of defensive medicine." Accessed online at: http://www.jacksonhealthcare.com/media-room/press-releases/jh-summary-release.aspx.

Mellor, JM and Freeborn, BA (2009) "Religious participation and risky health behaviors among adolescents." College of William and Mary, Department of Economics, Working Paper Number 86, July 2009. Accessed online at: http://web.wm.edu/economics/wp/cwm_wp86.pdf.

National Wellness Institute website. Accessed online at: http://www.nationalwell
ness.org/index.php?id_tier=2&id_c=25.

Obama, M (2010) "First Lady Michelle Obama launches Let's Move: America's
move to raise a healthier generation of kids." Accessed online at: http://www.
whitehouse.gov/the-press-office/first-lady-michelle-obama-launches-lets-
move-americas-move-raise-a-healthier-genera.

Peskowitz, M (2005) *The truth behind the mommy wars: Who decides what makes
a good mother?* Emeryville, CA: Seal Press.

Search Institute Center for Spiritual Development in Childhood and Adolescence
(2008) "With their own voices: A global exploration of how today's young
people experience and think about spiritual development." Accessed online
at: http://www.search-institute.org/system/files/with_their_own_voices_key_
findings.pdf.

Somers, P (2010) "The helicopter parent: Research toward a typology." Accessed
online at: http://www.faqs.org/periodicals/201007/2148808521.html.

Teasdale, W (1999) *The mystic heart.* Novato, CA: New World Library.

Tiemann, A (2009) *Mojo mom: Nurturing your self while raising a family.* New
York: Gotham Books.

Waite, LJ and Lehrer, EL (2003) "The benefits from marriage and religion in
the United States: A comparative analysis." *Population and Development
Review,* 29(2), 255–276.

CHAPTER 3

Ainsworth, MDS (1979) "Infant-mother attachment." *American Psychologist,* 34,
932–937.

Anderson, S and Whitaker, RC (2011) "Attachment security and obesity in US
preschool-aged children." *Archives of Pediatrics & Adolescent Medicine,*
165(3), 235–242.

Baumrind, D (1971) "Current patterns of parental authority." *Developmental
Psychology Monographs,* 4, (1, part 2).

Birnbaum, GE, Reis, HT, Mikulincer, M, Gillath, O and Orpaz, A (2006) "When sex
is more than just sex: Attachment orientations, sexual experience, and relationship quality." *Journal of Personality and Social Psychology,* 91, 929–943.

Bowlby, J (1969) "Attachment and loss, Vol. 1: Attachment." New York: Basic Books.

Buss, AH and Plomin, R (1986) The EAS approach to temperament. In R Plomin
and J Dunn, (Eds.), *The study of temperament: Changes, continuities and
challenges.* Hillsdale, NJ: Lawrence Erlbaum.

Carlo, G, Mestre, MV, Samper, P, Tur, A and Armenta, BE (2011) "The longitudinal relations among dimensions of parenting styles, sympathy, prosocial
moral reasoning, and prosocial behaviors." *International Journal of Behavioral Development,* 35, 116–124.

Cody, T, Cole, M, Cole, M and Sweeney, W (2006) *Top 20 teens.* Top 20 Press.

Cooper, ML, Pioli, M, Levitt, A, Talley, A, Micheas, L and Collins, NL (2006) "Attachment styles, sex motives, and sexual behavior: Evidence for gender specific expressions of attachment dynamics." In M Mikulincer and GS Goodman (Eds.), *Dynamics of love: Attachment, caregiving, and sex.* New York: Guilford Press.

DeWolff, MS and van Ijzendoorn, MH (1997) "Sensitivity and attachment: A meta-analysis on parental antecedents of infant attachment." *Child Development,* 66, 571–591.

Kagan, J (1989) *Unstable Ideas: Temperament, cognition, and self.* Cambridge: Cambridge University Press.

Kagan, J and Snidman, N (1991) "Infant predictors of inhibited and uninhibited profiles." *Psychological Science,* 2, 40–44.

McElwain, NL, Booth-LaForce, C, Lansford, JE, Wu, X and Dyer, WJ (2008) "A process model of attachment-friend linkages: Hostile attribution biases, language ability, and mother-child affective mutuality as intervening mechanisms." *Child Development,* 79(6), 1891. doi: 10.1111/j.1467–8624. 2008.01232.x.

Sanson A and Rothbart, MK (1995) "Child temperament and parenting." In MH Bornstein (Ed.), *Handbook of parenting,* (4). Hillsdale, NJ: Earlbaum.

Schaffer, HR and Emerson, PE (1964) "The development of social attachments in infancy." *Monographs of the Society for Research in Child Development,* 29, (3, Serial#94).

Sclafani, JD (2004) *The Educated Parent: Recent trends in raising children.* Westport, CT: Praeger.

Sheeber, LB and McDevitt, SC (1998) "Temperament-focused parent training." In JM Briesmeister and CE Schaefer (Eds.), *Handbook of parent training: Parents as co-therapists for children's behavior problems.* (2nd ed.). New York: Wiley & Sons.

Sroufe, A (1996) *Emotional Development: The organization of emotional life in the early years.* New York: Cambridge University Press.

Thomas, A and Chess, S (1986) "The New York longitudinal study: From infancy to early adult life." In: R Plomin and J Dunn (Eds.), *The Study of Temperament: Changes, continuities, and challenges.* Hillsdale, NJ: Erlbaum.

Volbrecht, MM and Goldsmith, HH (2010) "Early temperamental and family predictors of shyness and anxiety." *Developmental Psychology,* 46(5), 192–205.

Weiss, LH and Schwarz, JC (1996) "The relationship between parenting types and older adolescents' personality, academic achievement, adjustment, and substance use." *Child Development,* 67(5), 2101–2114.

Wills, TA, Sandy, JM, Yaeger, A and Shinar O (2008) "Family risk factors and adolescent substance use: Moderation effects for temperament dimensions." In GA Marlatt and K Witkiewitz (Eds.) *Addictive behaviors: New readings on etiology, prevention, and treatment.* Washington, DC: American Psychological Association.

Internet Sources for Further Information

Attachment Theory: http://en.wikipedia.org/wiki/Attachment_theory. OR http://psychology.about.com/od/loveandattraction/a/attachment01.htm.

Parenting Style: http://en.wikipedia.org/wiki/Parenting_styles. OR http://www.athealth.com/Practitioner/ceduc/parentingstyles.html. OR http://www.devpsy.org/teaching/parent/baumrind_styles.html.

The Personality Project: http://personality-project.org.

Talk to Them website: http://www.talktothem.org.

Temperament: http://en.wikipedia.org/wiki/Temperament.

CHAPTER 4

Adler-Baeder, F, Shirer, K and Bradford, A (2007) "What's love got to do with it? The role of healthy couple relationships." *The Forum for Family and Consumer Issues,* 12(1). Accessed online at: http://ncsu.edu/ffci/publications/2007/v12-n1-2007-spring/adlerbaeder-shirer-bradford/fa-3-adler baede-shirer-bradford.php.

Amato, PR (2002) "Good enough marriages: Parental discord, divorce, and children's well-being." *Virginia Journal of Social Policy & the Law, 9,* 71–94.

Amato, PR and Booth, A (2001) "The legacy of parents' marital discord: Consequences for children's marital quality." *Journal of Personality & Social Psychology,* 81, 627–638.

American Academy of Pediatrics. Committee on School Health (August 2000). "Corporal punishment in schools." *Pediatrics,* 106 (2 Pt 1), 343. doi:10.1542/peds.106.2.343.

Booth, A and Amato, PR (2001) "Parental predivorce relations and offspring post-divorce well-being." *Journal of Marriage and the Family,* 63, 197–212.

Brown, SL (2004) "Family structure and child well-being: The significance of parental cohabitation." *Journal of Marriage and Family,* 66(2), 351–367.

Child Trends (2009) *Attitudes Towards Spanking.* Accessed online at: www.childtrendsdatabank.org/?q=node/187.

Dush, CK and Amato, PR (2005) "Consequences of relationship status and quality for subjective well-being." *Journal of Social and Personal Relationships,* 22: 607–627.

el-Sheikh, M, Cummings, EM, Kouros, CD, Elmore-Staton, L and Buckhalt, J (2008) "Marital psychological and physical aggression and children's mental and physical health: Direct, mediated, and moderated effects." *Journal of Consulting & Clinical Psychology,* 76(1), 138–148.

Gershoff, ET and Bitensky, SH (2007) "The case against corporal punishment of children: Converging evidence from social science research and international human rights law and implications for U.S. public policy." *Psychology, Public Policy, and Law,* 13(4), 231–272.

Gershoff, ET (1992) "Corporal punishment by parents and associated child behaviors and experiences: A meta-analytic and theoretical review." *Psychological Bulletin,* 128(4), 539–79.

Gibson, DG (1999) A monograph summary of the research related to the use and efficacy of the systematic training for effective parenting (STEP) program: 1976–1999. Accessed online at: www.steppublishers.com/files/Monograph.pdf.

Gordon, T (2000) *Parent effectiveness training: The proven program for raising responsible children.* (30th ed.) New York: Three Rivers Press.

Miller, MV (1998) "Spanking: To what extent is it still endorsed and who is most likely to endorse it?" Accessed online at: http://wps.ablongman.com/ab_henslin_essentials_6/28/7383/1890218.cw/index.html.

Mooney, S (1995) "Parent training: A review of Adlerian, parent effectiveness training, and behavioral research." *Family Journal-Counseling & Therapy for Couples & Families,* 3, 218–230.

Mulvaney, MK and Mebert, CJ (2007) "Parental corporal punishment predicts behavior problems in early childhood." *Journal of Family Psychology,* 21(3), 389–397. doi: 10.1037/0893–3200.21.3.389.

Stein, MT, and Perrin, EL (April 1998) "Guidance for effective discipline. American Academy of Pediatrics, Committee on Psychosocial Aspects of Child and Family Health." *Pediatrics,* 101 (4 Pt 1), 723–728.

Taylor, CA, Manganello, JA, Lee, SJ and Rice, JC (2010) "Mothers' spanking of 3-year-old children and subsequent risk of children's aggressive behavior." *Pediatrics,* 125(5), 1057–1065.

Taylor, CA, Lee, SJ, Guterman, NB and Rice, JC (2010) "Use of spanking for 3-year-old children and associated intimate partner aggression or violence." *Pediatrics,* 126(3), 415–424.

Trumbull, DA and Ravenel, SD (2001) "Spare the rod? New research challenges spanking critics." Accessed online at: http://users.rcn.com/mgfree/Spanking/spankResearch.html.

Zolotor, AJ, Theodore, AD, Runyan, DK, Chang, JJ and Laskey, AL (2011) "Corporal punishment and physical abuse: Population-based trends for three-to-11-year-old children in the United States." *Child Abuse Review,* 20: 57–66. doi: 10.1002/car.1128.

Zolotor AJ, Theodore AD, Chang JJ, Berkoff MC and Runyan DK (2008) "Speak softly—and forget the stick: Corporal punishment and child physical abuse." *American Journal of Preventive Medicine,* 35, 364–369. doi: 10.1016/j.amepre.2008.06.031.

Additional Resources

Project NoSpank—A resource for those concerned with the safety and well-being of children. Accessed online at: www.nospank.net.

CHAPTER 5

Association of American Publishers (2011) "Get caught reading." Accessed online at: http://www.getcaughtreading.org/readingtochildren.htm.

Bandura, A (1994) "Self-efficacy. In VS Ramachaudran (Ed.), *Encyclopedia of human behavior,* (4), 71–81. New York: Academic Press. (Reprinted in H Friedman [Ed.], *Encyclopedia of Mental Health.* San Diego: Academic Press, 1998).

Chang, H (2010) "Attendance counts: Advancing student success by reducing chronic absence. Accessed online at: http://www.attendancecounts.org/wordpress/wpcontent/uploads/2010/06/Attendance-Counts-August-17–2010-Revision1.pdf.

Christenson, SL and Peterson, C (2006) "Parenting for school success." Accessed online at: http://www3.extension.umn.edu/distribution/familydevelopment/00079.html.

Couwels, J (2011) "Florida lawmaker wants teachers to grade parents." Accessed online at: http://www.cnn.com/2011/US/01/26/florida.grading.parents/index.html.

Dyson, L (2010, January 1) "Unanticipated effects of children with learning disabilities on their families." *The Free Library.* Accessed online at: http://www.thefreelibrary.com/Unanticipated effects of children with learning disabilities on their . . .-a0222314082.

Jaynes, W (2005) "Parental involvement and student achievement: A meta-analysis." Accessed online at: http://www.hfrp.org/publications-resources/browse-our-publications/parental-involvement-and-student-achievement-a-meta-analysis.

Levine, J (2011) "Finnishing school." *Time,* April 11, 2011, Business, 7.

Michigan High School EduGuide (2008) "The top 5 factors for high school success." Accessed online at: http://michigan.gov/documents/mde/2008_HS_Eduguide_Final_252919_7.pdf.

Morrison, FJ, Bachman, HJ, and Connor, CM (2005) *Improving Literacy in America: Guidelines from Research.* New Haven, CT: Yale University Press.

San Diego County Office of Education (1997) "Parent involvement and student achievement." Accessed online at: http://www.sdcoe.net/lret2/family/pia.html.

Saunders, MK (2009) "Previously homeschooled college freshmen: Their first year experiences and persistence rates." *Journal of College Student Retention,* 11(1), 77–100.

Shyers, L (1992) "Comparison of social adjustment between home and traditionally schooled students." Unpublished doctoral dissertation. University of Florida College of Education.

Stortroen, E (2009) "Bill promoting parental involvement in education draws little flak in committee." Accessed online at: http://coloradostatesman.com/content/99973-bill-promoting-parental-involvement-education-draws-little-flak-committee.

U.S. Department of Education National Center for Education Statistics (2011) National Household Education Surveys Program (NHES). Accessed online at: http://nces.ed.gov/nhes.

Whitaker, T and Zoul, J (2008) *Four CORE factors for school success.* Larchmont, NY: Eye on Education.

Zeise, A (2011) "Number of homeschoolers in the USA." Accessed online at: http://homeschooling.gomilpitas.com/weblinks/numbers.htm.

Additional Internet Sources and Resources

Help Guide (for information and resources about learning and other disabilities). Accessed online at: http://www.helpguide.org.

National Center for Learning Disabilities. Accessed online at: http://www.ncld.org.

National Child Care Information and Technical Assistance Center. Accessed online at: http://nccic.acf.hhs.gov/poptopics/brain.html.

National Home Education Research Institute. Accessed online at: http://www.nheri.org/.

CHAPTER 6

American Academy of Pediatrics (2010) "Helping children handle stress." Accessed online at: http://www.healthychildren.org/English/healthy-living/emotional-wellness/pages/Helping-Children-Handle-Stress.aspx.

Anxiety Disorders Association of America (2011) "Childhood anxiety disorders." Accessed online at: http://www.adaa.org/living-with-anxiety/children/childhood-anxiety-disorders.

Bernstein, GA (2010) "Advances in child and adolescent anxiety disorder research." Accessed online at: http://aacap.org/cs/root/developmentor/advances_in_child_and_adolescent_anxiety_disorder_research.

Burke, AE and Silverman, WK (1987) "The prescriptive treatment of school refusal." *Clinical Psychology Review,* 7(4), 353–362.

Craske, M (2008) "New insights into teenagers and anxiety disorders." Cited in University of California, Los Angeles (2008, September 17). *ScienceDaily.* Accessed online at: http://www.sciencedaily.com/releases/2008/09/080915165832.htm.

Dadds, M, Spence, SH and Holland, DE (1997) "Prevention and early intervention for anxiety disorders: A controlled trial." *Journal of Consulting and Clinical Psychology,* 65, 627-635.

Dailey, K (2010) "Report shows teen girls are drinking more than boys, for different reasons." *Newsweek,* June 29, 2010. Accessed online at: http://www.newsweek.com/2010/06/29/study-shows-teen-girls-are-drinking-more-for-different-reasons-than-boys.html.

Egger, HL, Costello, EJ and Angold, A (2003) "School refusal and psychiatric disorders: A community study." *Journal of the American Academy of Child and Adolescent Psychiatry,* 42(7), 797–807.

Faraone, SV, Biederman, J, Wozniak, J, Mundy, E, Mennin, D and O'Donnell, D (1997) "Is comorbidity with ADHD a marker for juvenile-onset mania?" *Journal of the American Academy of Child & Adolescent Psychiatry,* 36(8), 1046–55.

Gámez-Guadix, M, Straus, MA, Carrobles, JA, Muñoz-Rivas, MJ and Almendros, C (2010) "Corporal punishment and long-term behavior problems: The moderating role of positive parenting and psychological aggression." *Psicothema,* 22(4), 529–536.

Grohol, JM (2007) "The story behind the rise in bipolar diagnoses." Accessed online at: http://psychcentral.com/bio.htm.

Hannesdottir, DK and Ollendick, TH (2007) "The role of emotion regulation in the treatment of child anxiety disorders." *Clinical Child and Family Psychology Review.* 10/2007; 10(3): 275–93. doi: 10.1007/s10567-007-0024-6.

Johnson, CP and Myers, SM (2007) "Identification and evaluation of children with autism spectrum disorders." *Pediatrics,* 120(5), 1183–1215.

Kim, YS, Leventhal, BL, Koh, YJ, Fombonne, E, Laska, E, Lim, EC, Cheon, KA, Kim, SJ, Kim, YK, Lee, HK, Song, DH and Grinker, RR. (2011) "Prevalence of autism spectrum disorders in a total population sample." *American Journal of Psychiatry.* Accessed online at: http://www.nimh.nih.gov/science-news/2011/many-school-aged-children-with-asd-in-south-korea-go-undiagnosed.shtml?WT.mc_id=rss.

Kirby, D (2009) "Autism rate now at one percent of all US children?" Accessed online at: http://www.huffingtonpost.com/david-kirby/autism-rate-now-at-one-pe_b_256141.html.

Lazarus, RS and Folkman, S (1984) *Stress, Appraisal, and Coping.* New York: Springer.

McShane, G, Walter, G and Rey, JM (2001) "Characteristics of adolescents with school refusal." *Australian and New Zealand Journal of Psychiatry,* 35(6), 822–826.

Middlebrooks, JS and Audage, NC (2008) "The effects of childhood stress on health across the lifespan." Atlanta (GA): Centers for Disease Control and Prevention, National Center for Injury Prevention and Control. Accessed online at: http://www.cdc.gov/ncipc/pub-res/pdf/Childhood_Stress.pdf.

Moreno, C, Laje, G, Blanco, C, Jiang, H, Schmidt, AB and Olfson, M (2007) "National trends in the outpatient diagnosis and treatment of bipolar disorder in youth." Archives of *General Psychiatry,* 64(9), 1032–1039.

National Institutes of Mental Health (2011) "Any anxiety disorder among children." Accessed online at: http://www.nimh.nih.gov/statistics/1ANYANX_child.shtml.

Olfson, M, Crystal, S, Gerhard, T, Huang, CS and Carlson, GA (2009) "Mental health treatment received by youths in the year before and after a new diagnosis of bipolar disorder." *Psychiatric Services,* 60(8), 1098–1106.

Pierce, K, Carter, C, Weinfeld, M, Desmond, J, Hazin, R, Bjork, R and Galla-gher, N (2011) "Detecting, studying, and treating autism early: The one-year well-baby check-up approach." *The Journal of Pediatrics*. 10.1016/j. jpeds.2011.02.036.

University of California, Los Angeles (2008, September 17) "New insights into teenagers and anxiety disorders." *ScienceDaily*. Accessed online at: http://www.sciencedaily.com/releases/2008/09/080915165832.htm.

Wall Street Journal Health Journal (2010) L.A. confidential: Seeking reasons for autism's rise. Accessed online at: http://online.wsj.com/article/SB1000142 405274870342290457503935 1632663996.html.

Werner, EE and Smith, RS (1992). *Overcoming the odds: High-risk children from birth to adulthood*. New York: Cornell University Press.

Youngstrom, EA, Birmaher, B and Findling, RL (2008) "Pediatric bipolar disor-der: Validity, phenomenology, and recommendations for diagnosis." *Bipo-lar Disorders*, 10: 194–214. doi: 10.1111/j.1399–5618.2007.00563.x.

Recommended Online Resources For Further Information

Anxiety Disorders Resource Center from the American Academy of Child & Adolescent Psychiatry. Accessed online at: www.aacap.org/cs/AnxietyDis orders.ResourceCenter.

Bright Tots, a website created to educate and spread awareness on different child-hood disorders, particularly autism. Accessed online at: www.brighttots.com.

National Survey of Children's Health, a website with national survey data open to your inquiries. Accessed online at: http://www.nschdata.org/Content/Default.aspx.

CHAPTER 7

American Academy of Pediatrics Clinical Report (2008) "How TV affects your child." Accessed online at: http://kidshealth.org/parent/positive/family/tv_affects_child.html.

American Academy of Pediatrics Clinical Report (2011) "The impact of social media use on children, adolescents and families." *Pediatrics*, 127(4), 800–804. doi: 10.1542/peds.2011-0054.

American Academy of Child & Adolescent Psychiatry (2011) "Children and TV vio-lence." Accessed online at: http://www.aacap.org/cs/root/facts_for_families/children_and_tv_violence.

American Academy of Child & Adolescent Psychiatry (2008) "The influence of music and music videos." Accessed online at: http: //www.aacap.org/cs/root/facts_for_families/the_influence_of_music_and_music_videos.

Anderson, CA, Gentile, DA and Buckley, KE (2007) *Violent video game effects on children and adolescents: Theory, research and public policy*. Oxford University Press.

Anderson, CA, Sakamoto, A, Gentile, DA, Ihori, N, Shibuya, A, Yukawa, S, Naito, M and Kobayashi, K (2009) "Longitudinal effects of violent video games on aggression in Japan and the United States." *Pediatrics,* 122(5) November 2008, pp. e1067-e1072. doi: 10.1542/peds.2008-1425.

Boy Scout Trail (2011) "Cub scouts video games academics pin and belt loop." Accessed online at: www.boyscouttrail.com/cub-scouts/acadsports/video-games.asp.

Bushman, BJ and Gibson, B (2010) "Violent video games cause an increase in aggression long after the game has been turned off." *Social Psychological and Personality Science.* doi: 10.1177/1948550610379506.

Carpenter, S. (2001) "Sleep deprivation might be undermining teen health." Accessed online at: http://www.apa.org/monitor/oct01/sleepteen.aspx.

Cheng, J (2009) "Neuroscientist: Internet, video games rewiring kids' brains." Accessed online at: http://arstechnica.com/web/news/2009/02/neuroscientist-internet-video-games-rewiring-kids-brains.ars.

Cullen, J, Sokol, NA, Slawek, D, Allen, JA, Vallone, D and Healton, C (2011) "Depictions of tobacco use in 2007 broadcast television programming popular among US youth." Archives of *Pediatrics & Adolescent Medicine,* 165(2), 147–151.

Ferguson, CJ (2010). "Video games and youth violence: A prospective analysis in adolescents." *Journal of Youth and Adolescence,* 40(4), 377–391.

Fleming, MJ, Greentree, S, Cocotti, D, Elias, KA and Morrison, S (2006) "Safety in cyberspace: Adolescents' safety and exposure online." *Youth & Society,* 38, 135–154.

Gentile, DA (2004) "The effects of video games on children: What parents need to know." *Pediatrics for Parents.* Accessed online at: http://findarticles.com/p/articles/mi_m0816/is_6_21/ai_n9772319/?tag=content;col1.

Gentile, D (2009) "Video games affect the brain—For better and worse." Accessed online at: http://www.dana.org/news/cerebrum/detail.aspx?id=22800.

Gentile, DA, Anderson, CA, Yukawa, S, Ihori, N, Saleem, M, Ming, LK, Shibuya, A, Liau, AK, Khoo, A, Bushman, BJ, Huesmann, LR and Sakamoto, A (2009) "The effects of prosocial video games on prosocial behaviors: International evidence from correlational, longitudinal, and experimental studies." *Personality and Social Psychology Bulletin,* June 35(6), 752–763.

Haier, RJ, Karama, S, Leyba, L and Jung, RE (2009) "MRI assessment of cortical thickness and functional activity changes in adolescent girls following three months of practice on a visual-spatial task." *BMC Research Notes,* 2, 174.

Kaiser Family Foundation (2006) "New study shows how kids' media use helps parents cope." Accessed online at: http://www.kff.org/entmedia/entmedia052406nr.cfm.

Kohn, A (2006) "The truth about homework." Accessed online at: http://www.alfiekohn.org/teaching/edweek/homework.htm.

Phillips, H (2005) "Violent video games alter brain's response to violence." Accessed online at: http://www.newscientist.com/article/dn8449-violent-video-games-alter-brains-response-to violence.html.

Schrock, A and Boyd, D (2008) Enhancing child safety & online technologies: Research advisory board literature review. Appendix C: Online threats to youth: Solicitation, harassment, and problematic content. Accessed online at: http://cyber.law.harvard.edu/research/isttf.

Scott, E (2008) "Social causes of school anxiety: School anxiety can have several social causes." Accessed online at: http://stress.about.com/od/studentstress/a/school_anxiety.htm.

Tomopoulos, S, Dreyer, BP, Berkule, S, Fierman, AH, Brockmeyer, C and Mendelsohn, AL (2010) "Infant media exposure and toddler development." Archives of *Pediatrics & Adolescent Medicine,* 164(12), 1105–1111.

University of Michigan (2009, June 18). "Some video games can make children kinder and more likely to help." *ScienceDaily.* Accessed online at: http://www.sciencedaily.com/releases/2009/06/090617171819.htm.

Internet Sources for Further Information

American Academy of Child & Adolescent Psychiatry Resources for Families. Accessed online at: http://www.aacap.org/cs/forFamilies.

American Academy of Pediatrics Kid's Health for Parents Site. Accessed online at: http://kidshealth.org/parent.

The Entertainment Software Ratings Board (ESRB). Accessed online at: www.esrb.org.

CHAPTER 8

American Psychological Association (2011) "The changing role of the modern day father." Accessed online at: http://www.apa.org/pi/families/resources/changing-father.aspx.

Baumrind, D (2005) "Patterns of parental authority and adolescent autonomy." *New Directions for Child and Adolescent Development,* 2005, 61–69. doi: 10.1002/cd.128.

Bretherton, I, Page, T, Golby, B and Walsh, R (1998) "Fathers in post-divorce families seen through the eyes of mothers and children." Accessed online at: parenthood.library.wisc.edu/Bretherton/Bretherton.html.

Bronte-Tinkew, J, Burkhauser, M, Metz, A (2008) "Elements of promising practice in teen fatherhood programs: Evidence-based and evidence-informed research findings on what works." National Responsible Fatherhood Clearinghouse. Accessed online at: www.fatherhood.gov.

Carlson, MJ (2006) "Family structure, father involvement, and adolescent behavioral outcomes." *Journal of Marriage and Family,* 68(1), 137–154.

Doherty, WJ, Kouneski, EF and Erickson, MF (1996) "Responsible fathering: An overview and conceptual framework." Washington, DC: US Department of Health and Human Services. Accessed online at: fatherhood.hhs.gov/con cept.htm.

Ellis, BJ, Bates, JE, Dodge, KA, Fergusson, DM, Horwood, LJ, Pettit, GS and Woodward, L (2003) "Does father absence place daughters at special risk for early sexual activity and teenage pregnancy?" *Child Development,* 74(3), 801–821.

Fabricius, WV and Luecken, LJ (2007) "Post-divorce living arrangements, parent conflict, and long-term physical health correlates for children of divorce." *Journal of Family Psychology,* 21(2), 195–205.

Finley, GE and Schwartz, SJ (2007) "Father involvement and young adult outcomes: The differential contributions of divorce and gender." *Family Court Review,* 45(4), 573–587.

Flouri, E and Buchanan, A (2002) "What predicts good relationships with parents in adolescence and partners in adult life: Findings from the 1958 British birth cohort." *Journal of Family Psychology,* 16, 186–198.

Flouri, E and Buchanan, A (2004) "Early fathers' and mother's involvement and child's later educational outcomes." *British Journal of Educational Psychology,* 74, 141–153

Flouri, E (2006) "Parental interest in children's education, children's self-esteem and locus of control, and later educational attainment: Twenty-six year follow-up of the 1970 British birth cohort. *British Journal of Educational Psychology,* 76(1), 41–55.

Goncy, EA and van Dulmen, MHM (2010) "Fathers do make a difference: Parental involvement and adolescent alcohol use." *The Free Library.* Accessed online at: http://www.thefreelibrary.com/Fathers do make a difference: parental involvement and adolescent . . . .-a0224989867.

Hetherington, EM and Kelly, J (2001) *For better or for worse: Divorce reconsidered.* New York: Norton.

Hughes, LY and Fetsch, RJ (2007) "Review of *Fathers reading every day (FRED): Leader's guide." Journal of Extension,* 45(2). Accessed online at: http://joe. org/joe/2007april/tt4.php.

Lamb, ME (2000) "The history of research on father involvement: An overview." In: HE Peters, GW Peterson, SK Steinmetz and RD Day (Eds.), *Fatherhood: Research, interventions and policies.* Binghamton, NY: Haworth Press.

Levine, JA and Pitt, EW (1995) *New expectations: Community strategies for responsible fatherhood.* New York: Families & Work Institute.

Marsiglio, W (1995) "Fatherhood scholarship: An overview and agenda for the future." In: W Marsiglio (Ed.), *Fatherhood: Contemporary theory, research, and social policy.* Thousand Oaks, CA: Sage.

Menning, CL (2006) "Nonresident fathering and school failure." *Journal of Family Issues,* 27(10), 1356–1382.

Morman, MT and Floyd, K (2006) "Good fathering: Father and son perceptions of what it means to be a good father." *Fathering: A Journal of Theory, Research, and Practice about Men as Fathers,* 4(2) Spring 2006, 113–136.

O'Connell, M (2005) *The good father: On men, masculinity, and life in the family.* New York: Scribner.

Sarkadi, A, Kristiansson, R, Oberklaid, F and Bremberg, S (2008) "Fathers' involvement and children's developmental outcomes: A systematic review of longitudinal studies." *Acta Paediatrica,* 97, 153–158. doi: 10.1111/j.1651–2227.2007.00572.x.

Sayer, LC, Bianchi, SM and Robinson, JP (2004) "Are parents investing less in children? Trends in mothers' and fathers' time with children." *American Journal of Sociology,* 110(1), 1–43.

Schacht, PM, Cummings, EM and Davies, PT (2009) "Fathering in family context and child adjustment: A longitudinal analysis." *Journal of Family Psychology,* 23(6), 790–797.

Smith, JA (2009) *The Daddy Shift: How stay-at-home dads, breadwinning moms, and shared parenting are transforming the American family.* Boston: Beacon Press.

Videon, TM (2005). "Parent-child relations and children's psychological well-being: Do dads matter?" *Journal of Family Issues,* 26(1), 55–78.

Wallerstein, JS and Blakeslee, S (1990) *Second chances: Men, women and children a decade after divorce.* London: Grant McIntyre.

Yogman, M, Kindlon, D, and Earls, F (1995) "Father involvement and cognitive/behavioral outcomes of pre-term infants." *Journal of the American Academy of Child and Adolescent Psychiatry,* 343, 58–66.

Additional Resources and Information

All Pro Dad. This is a fatherhood program of Family First, a national nonprofit organization based in Tampa, Florida and launched in 1997 by Mark Merrill and Tony Dungy. Accessed online at: www.allprodad.com.

Father Involvement Research Alliance. A Canadian alliance of individuals, organizations, and institutions dedicated to the development and sharing of knowledge focusing on father involvement. Accessed online at: http://www.fira.ca.

National Center for Fathering. A nonprofit scientific and education organization providing practical, research-based training and resources that equip men in virtually every fathering situation to be involved fathers. Accessed online at: www.fathers.com.

National Responsible Fatherhood Clearinghouse. The NRFC promotes and supports responsible fatherhood in an effort to advance the fatherhood movement, and support fathers and families. Accessed online at: www.fatherhood.gov.

Research on Children of Divorce. Accessed online at: http://2homekids.org/ RESEARCH%20BIBLOGRAPHY%20-Divorce%20&%20Custody%20_ July%202008_1.pdf.

CHAPTER 9

Adams, D (1998) "The parent maze: Searching for childcare in the United States." Accessed online at: http://parenthood.library.wisc.edu/Adams/Adams.html.

Belsky, J, Vandell, D, Burchinal, M, Clarke-Stewart, K, McCartney, K and Owen, M (2007) "Are there long-term effects of early child care?" *Child Development,* 78(2), 681–701. doi: 10.1111/j.1467–8624.2007.01021.x.

Côté, SM, Petitclerc, A, Raynault, M, Xu, Q, Falissard, F, Boivin, M and Tremblay, RE (2010) "Short-and long-term risk of infections as a function of group child care attendance: An 8-year population-based study." Archives of *Pediatrics & Adolescent Medicine,* 164(12), 1132–1137.

DeWolff, MS and van Ijzendoorn, MH (1997) "Sensitivity and attachment: A meta-analysis on parental antecedents of infant attachment." *Child Development,* 66, 571–591.

Eberstadt, M (2004) *Home-Alone America: The hidden toll of day care, behavioral drugs, and other parent substitutes.* New York: Sentinel.

Lucas-Thompson, RG, Goldberg, WA and Prause, J (2010) "Maternal work early in the lives of children and its distal associations with achievement and behavior problems: A meta-analysis." *Psychological Bulletin,* 136(6), 915–942.

Mann, D (2010) "Day care babies: More infections now, fewer later." Accessed online at: http://www.cnn.com/2010/HEALTH/12/06/daycare.kids/index.html.

Tran, H and Weinraub, M (2006) "Child care effects in context: Quality, stability, and multiplicity in nonmaternal child care arrangements during the first 15 months of life." *Developmental Psychology,* 42(3), 566–582.

Vandell, DL, Belsky, J, Burchinal, M, Steinberg, L, Vandergrift, N in NICHD Early Child Care Research Network (2010) "Do effects of early child care extend to age 15 years? Results from the NICHD Study of Early Child Care and Youth Development." Accessed online at: http://nieer.org/pdf/Effects_of_Early_Child_Care_Extend_to_Age_15.pdf.

Zinsmeister, K (1998) "The problem with day care." *The American Enterprise,* 9, 44–53.

Zinsmeister, K (1988) "Brave new world: How day care harms children." *Policy Review,* 44, 40–48.

Additional Sources and Resources

American Academy of Pediatrics, American Public Health Association, and National Resource Center for Health and Safety in Child Care and Early

Education (2002). *Caring for Our Children: National Health and Safety Performance Standards; Guidelines for Out-of-Home Child Care Programs* (2nd ed.). Elk Grove Village, IL: American Academy of Pediatrics and Washington, DC: American Public Health Association. Also available at http://nrckids.org.

Washington State Child Care Resource and Referral Network. An example of a state-provided resource for parents with helpful information. Accessed online at: http://www.childcarenet.org/families/your-search/.

AFTERWORD

Eberstadt, M (2004) *Home-Alone America: The hidden toll of day care, behavioral drugs, and other parent substitutes.* New York: Sentinel.

Gibbs, N (2009) "The growing backlash against overparenting." *Time.* Accessed online at: http://www.time.com/time/nation/article/0,8599,1940395,00.html.

Sclafani, JD (2004) *The educated parent: Recent trends in raising children.* Westport, CT: Praeger.

"The secret life of teens: A special report." *Chicago Magazine,* September, 2009. Accessed online at: http://www.chicagomag.com/Chicago-Magazine/September-2009/The-Secret-Life-of-Teens-A-Special-Report.

Index

About the Author

Dr. Joseph D. Sclafani, PhD, currently serves as a tenured professor of psychology, as well as interim associate provost and dean of academic services, at the University of Tampa. He now serves as the co-chair of the Leadership Resource Team, a group of faculty and staff coordinating many leadership development initiatives. Dr. Sclafani is the program coordinator for the minor in leadership studies. Earlier, he served as associate dean and later dean of the College of Liberal Arts & Sciences, and he is the former interim dean of the College of Social Sciences, Mathematics & Education, as well as former director of the Baccalaureate Experience.

Dr. Sclafani earned his doctorate at the University of South Florida in 1984 after completing a year-long internship in pediatric psychology at the Oregon Health Sciences University in Portland. He has maintained his psychology licensure in Florida since 1986.

After graduation, Dr. Sclafani worked full-time as a child and family therapist and parent trainer for three years before coming to the University of Tampa in 1987. He completed postdoctoral training at the Philadelphia Child Guidance Clinic in 1986. Dr. Sclafani opened a private practice in 1986, the Brandon Center for Family Therapy, where he worked for 10 years with families, stepfamilies, and children of divorce, as well as serving as a child custody evaluator. He later was trained as a Florida Supreme Court certification-eligible family mediator. In 1992, he returned to teach at UT full-time.

His first book on parenting, *The Educated Parent,* was published in 2004. In the summer of 2010, Dr. Sclafani, along with his wife, Linda, a social worker, completed a book on remarriage issues and saw it published.

Dr. Sclafani continues his research on the subject of spirituality and the search for meaning in college student populations. He is a member of the Resource Team for Faith, Values, and Spirituality at UT.

In the community, Dr. Sclafani and his wife provide marriage enrichment workshops for remarried couples, as well as marriage preparation workshops for newlyweds-to-be for the Diocese of St. Petersburg.